Shaena,

It was so lovely meeting you! I'm really excited for you to read this ☺

Rachelle

CHRYSALIS

A Dark and Delicious Diary of Emergence

RACHELLE CHARTRAND

BALBOA.
PRESS
A DIVISION OF HAY HOUSE

Balboa Press books may be ordered through booksellers or by contacting:

Balboa Press
A Division of Hay House
1663 Liberty Drive
Bloomington, IN 47403
www.balboapress.com
1 (877) 407-4847

Because of the dynamic nature of the Internet, any web addresses or links contained in this book may have changed since publication and may no longer be valid. The views expressed in this work are solely those of the author and do not necessarily reflect the views of the publisher, and the publisher hereby disclaims any responsibility for them.

The author of this book does not dispense medical advice or prescribe the use of any technique as a form of treatment for physical, emotional, or medical problems without the advice of a physician, either directly or indirectly. The intent of the author is only to offer information of a general nature to help you in your quest for emotional and spiritual well-being. In the event you use any of the information in this book for yourself, which is your constitutional right, the author and the publisher assume no responsibility for your actions.

Any people depicted in stock imagery provided by Thinkstock are models, and such images are being used for illustrative purposes only.
Certain stock imagery © Thinkstock.

Printed in the United States of America.

ISBN: 978-1-4525-2006-3 (sc)
ISBN: 978-1-4525-2008-7 (hc)
ISBN: 978-1-4525-2007-0 (e)

Library of Congress Control Number: 2014914340

Balboa Press rev. date: 09/09/2014

For my Little Girl - I appreciate you.

The important thing is this: to be able at any moment to sacrifice what we are for what we could become.

~ Charles Du Bos

Acknowledgements

To Mom and Dad - thank you for loving me unconditionally even when I had no idea what that meant.

To Tracy and Celina - thank you for teaching me the strength of a triangle.

To my family - thank you for accepting me even when I thought I was unacceptable.

To my friends - thank you for seeing me the way my Higher Self wanted me to see me.

To Celina, Jennifer, Erik and Christine - thank you for listening to my numerous rantings and revelations throughout the year and not thinking I was crazy... or at least not caring. I'm glad I let you in my chrysalis.

To my three soul mates whose paths I crossed this year - thank you for being telescopes into my subconscious and showing me what a wholly dark and delicious place it is to be. To the five I haven't met yet - thank you for the new depths you will bring me to.

Finally, to the boys, guys and men of my past - thank you for the role you played in my journey to discovering my true self-worth. I hope you appreciate the role I played in yours. We are healed.

Contents

A Pretty Little Prologue

I got my first diary on my thirteenth birthday. It was beige and padded and had a pretty little brass lock you could pick with a bobby pin. I wrote in it for four months, but then got bored.

<u>December 23, 1985</u>
Dear Diary,

If I don't have a boyfriend by New Year's Eve, I'm going to kill myself. I swear to God. It was my birthday wish tonight, so it has to come true.

If my wish doesn't come true, my promise to God will.

I can't go back to school without a boyfriend. I really want Tony to ask me out, but Minh is cool, too. I know Minh likes me, so that's cool, because then at least I will have a boyfriend. Tony asked me about my birthday yesterday. He is so cute. I really like him. Minh walked by and flirted with me and Tony smiled. I really want him to ask me to go around.

<u>December 28, 1985</u>

Minh phoned and asked me out. I knew it would happen. He wasn't going to. I think he just called to talk, but we talked for like an hour and I told him I liked him and he asked if I wanted to go out! I still really love Tony, but this is good because when he finds out he will be jealous and at least I will have someone until he asks me.

January 10, 1986

I don't think Minh and I are going out anymore. That's okay though because we really are just friends. His breath tastes like gum. It's fresh but weird.

Hieu asked me to come over tomorrow. I'm supposed to take Celina to her swimming lessons at Bonnie Doon and he lives just a block away, so I can go say hi.

January 11, 1986

I hate my dad. On the way home from the pool he saw I had a hickey on my neck. He yelled at me about what they do with girls like me, but I don't care. I went to see Hieu and he gave it to me. I'm not going to be called a flirt or a tease or frigid anymore. Tony will see it and be jealous and then he will ask me out.

If he doesn't ask me out by Valentine's Day, I am going to kill myself.

February 15, 1986

I hate my mom. Sheryl had a Valentine's Day party and I wasn't allowed to go. I cried and cried and cried, but she didn't care because they were going to a party of their own. I kept crying and crying and spitting and gagging until I felt weak. I weighed myself and I lost 2 lbs. Just by crying. Cool.

February 16, 1986

I tried last night. I put the grey belt around my neck and pulled really tight. My mom and dad and Auntie Lily and Uncle Sam were upstairs, but they couldn't hear me crying. I tried to pull it so tight, but then just got weak. I could feel my face bulging and I almost passed out.

March 7, 1986

I took a bottle of aspirin yesterday. Well, half a bottle. We had teachers' in-service and the boys had a basketball practice, so I went to watch. I thought I was going to puke the whole time. I felt really sick, but never passed out. Tim was flirting with me majorly, but I felt so dizzy and thought I was going to throw up. He's really cute. His sister hates me, though. She would be so mad if he asked me out.

March 10, 1986

I told Laura what Fred did to me. She said I was just saying it for attention. She's going to be sorry when I am really dead. I know she likes him. She always likes older guys. I'm never telling anyone again.

John said my hips look a meter wide. I am all hips and no boobs. Why can't I take my hips and put them on my boobs?

March 26, 1986

I saw Andrew on the bus today. He is so hot. I was shy, though, because my eyes were all blotchy. I threw up my oatmeal before leaving for school. My friend's aunt always throws up and she doesn't have any hips.

A Hypocrite's Oath

I have a confession to make. Well, I have lots of confessions to make, but that's a whole different book. I'm not much of a writer. I failed every essay I wrote in high school, even received a big fat *zero* on one. I'm an aspiring screenwriter, yes, but one of the reasons I like screenwriting (besides being an excuse to be alone), is that I don't have to worry about proper sentence structure or florid prose. I can just transcribe the conversations going on in my head... and there are a lot of them. I also love watching movies, which I also get to do alone.

The only other writing I do is in my journal. I do post the occasional witty comment on Facebook, but usually second-guess myself and delete it immediately.

So, why am I writing a book? I have no fucking clue. *Just kidding.* A week ago, I had the genius idea I should write one about the threshold age of thirty-nine. Babies born in 1972 turn forty this year. Most of the women

3

in my life are dreading it, but I can't wait. Bring it on! After the past two years I've had, I am so fucking ready for a new chapter, a new decade.

Ideas are energy (I love physics) and messages from the Universe (I'm quite spiritual but not at all religious - just so you know). For some reason, this idea came to me and I'm claiming it! The problem is, I turn 39 tomorrow and don't in the least feel like a woman. I still wear pigtails. I think being an alcoholic off and on for 25 years (ten of which were also spent binging and purging), impeded the maturation process. In many ways, I'm still fourteen. Throw in years of soul-numbing delinquency, promiscuity, and two failed marriages, and well, yeah, I have some growing up to do.

I am woman, hear me *roar! Rrrr-meeeowww*. He-he-he. Kittens are way cuter than, um, cougars.

My oath: I will be 100% honest as I chronicle my way through this year. For better or worse, we are in this together. For the first time in my life, I will keep my vow. 'Til death do us part.

Whoa, I hope I don't die this year. That would be weird.

I have no idea how much of my backstory to give, what locations to describe or what characters to introduce, but I figure we can just figure it out as we go. Deal?

Okay, here we go...

December 22, 2011

I bought a new journal just for this year. It is purple - the highest frequency on the visible light spectrum. Purple is the color of the crown chakra, which represents our connection with spirituality, which is where I feel the idea for this book came from, and wisdom, which is why I want to write this book - to share the wisdom I've gained. In feng shui purple is the color of wealth and abundance. Two things I want to attract more of into my life.

On the back pages, I've started a list of all the different 'woman' topics I want to reflect upon. It's a diverse list - in the 'C' category alone I have career, collagen, cervical cancer, (female) circumcision and my least favorite 'C' word - cunt.

I also wrote my horoscope quote for the year: *Honor the New Emerging Person*.

I'm in Beaumont for Christmas. Beaumont is the small town south of Edmonton that my family moved to the summer before Grade 10. My older sister, Tracy, still lives here with her husband, Martin, and their rad kids, Dylan, 13, Alex, 11, and Erin, 7. Tracy also has a son, Lee, 19, from her first marriage. Lee is my godson, although I'm not much of a Catholic role model.

Celina is my younger sister by 4.5 years, but we often forget who is older. She is married to René, and they have two beautiful daughters, Sara, 7, and Sadie, 4. They live in Camrose, a bigger small town about forty minutes from Beaumont.

My parents retired a couple years ago and now live at the cabin for nine months of the year and then go somewhere south from January to March. Since they no longer have a place in Beaumont, and I'm a single spinster now, when I come to visit from Vancouver the three of us split our time between Tracy's and Celina's. We are a package deal.

I've decided to meet with Carlos in Edmonton if he wants to. I'm not going to go out of my way, but I'm not going to avoid him, either. I see it as an opportunity to stand in my power, no making excuses, no downplaying my successes, no ego. An opportunity for closure - the perfect prologue to the year I become a woman.

I would also love to see the puppies. I miss those little shits.

Chapter 39

December 23, 2011

It's my birthday. Thirty-nine years old. *Whoa.*

I just had the most crazy-ass yoga session. Mid-Sun Salutation, as I was rising up from forward bend, my arms floating to the sky, I had an image that I was a butterfly. No biggie. A lot of yoga poses mimic animals - Down Dog, Cobra, etc., but each time I rose, the image became stronger and stronger and clearer and clearer. It became more than an image. It was a... *vision*.

A little voice whispered, "On my fortieth birthday I'm going to turn into a butterfly."

Now, I would laugh except it was so visceral I think it might come true. I have never experienced something so surreal. I have definitely felt like a caterpillar the past couple years, just nibbling on leaves (I eat a lot of salad) and avoiding getting stepped on.

Hmmmm.... On my fortieth birthday I am gonna turn into a butterfly. *Cool.*

I'm at the Starbucks in Beaumont (I can't believe there is a Starbucks in Beaumont). My main focus right now is to create a strong vision of what I want this year to be. I have lots of writing goals - finish *Making of a Faith Healer*, start *Happiless* the feature, and get *FLOW* optioned, but this is also the year I will meet my soul mate. Whoever he is, wherever he is. I'm ready, my love!

I have some fear of the power of what is unfolding, but I am the strongest, bravest person I know. I will not crumble to fear. I am no longer a coward.

December 24, 2011

I had a really chill birthday. Jen and I met for a couple drinks at Boston Pizza (I can't believe there is a Boston Pizza in Beaumont). I paid the bill. I never do that, but it felt really good to spend spontaneously on my soul sister. We also both apologized for the other night.

We were at Nicole's drinking and got into a heated discussion. Whenever I come to town, the three of us 'old roomies' get together for drinks at least once. Our conversations are always deep, we like to think we are solving the world's problems, but this one got very tense. We were talking about 'victims' and how I don't believe there is such a thing once you are an adult, especially when it comes to relationships. There are always signs and you always have a choice. Victim mentality pisses me off. They were both really upset with me.

Jen also mocked the spiritual online courses I've been taking. I was hurt. They said I was just being defensive. Of course I was, I was being attacked. What's it to them anyways? I don't feel like I can communicate or connect with people in Beaumont anymore. I have had such different life experiences and am in a way different place. To be honest, I don't feel like anyone is on the same spiritual level as me. I feel alone on this journey... maybe I am. I can't be worried about leaving people behind.

My divorce to Carlos became final that same day, though. Maybe I was being defensive.

Besides, I love Jen and Nicole. We have been friends for 23 years. I guess I just won't talk to them about spiritual stuff anymore. Or anti-depressants.

The rest of the night, I hung out with the family at Tracy's. I know I am lucky to have such a loving family, but I feel inauthentic around them. For most of my life, I've been the black sheep, but these past two years, the hardest of my life, my family has been there for me 100%. Loved and accepted me after Carlos and I broke up, supported me when the girls passed away. I feel guilty because I don't trust their acceptance or maybe I am scared of it. It's like I live behind a window of protection. I can see the love, but can't touch it.

Mom and Dad are at Christmas Eve Mass right now. I was worried they would be mad I didn't want to go with them, but they seemed okay with it. Instead, I did yoga in Tracy and Martin's front room, overlooking Four Seasons Park, and then went for a big walk through it for a little 'God and Rachelle' private time.

I cringed as I circled the lake, though. Flashes of debaucherous events came to mind. Fuck, we partied our asses off here. *Ugh.* I strolled over to the baseball diamonds. Slightly more positive, yet still beer-infused, memories... baseball tournaments, hall parties, falling for Matthew, walking the puppies with Carlos... It's always hard coming home to Beaumont.

Dear God, please let this be the year I leave it all behind.

December 27, 2011

Christmas is over! *Whew,* time to rest and rejuvenate. Time to just enjoy each other's company. I know Christmas is supposed to be about spending time with family, but for me it is exhausting and overwhelming and I usually withdraw to the sidelines. I just kind of drift around the perimeter energetically, like a fly on the wall that wants to be interested in what's going on, but isn't. The best part about being a functioning holiday alcoholic is being in a constant state of buzzing bliss. No one notices the numbness inside. Or at least, I don't notice if they notice.

Mom and Dad and I spent Christmas morning with Tracy's family and then we all went to Celina's for Christmas day. I ate way too much. If there is one thing René and I have in common is how we eat too much at supper and then complain the whole night. Our energy just plummets and it really pisses Celina off. Celina is basically Monica from *Friends*. Actually a better analogy is Celina and René are the real life Phil and Claire from *Modern Family*.

My mom and dad bought me a luggage set! They've been hinting for years, but I always hinted back I'd prefer cash. My mom didn't even ask this year and I'm glad she didn't. It's time to retire the hand-me-down oversized green suitcase they lent me when Carlos and I moved away 11 years ago. I think they may have received it as a wedding gift. This one is a white and black plaid pull-style with a matching carry-on. I'm gonna look so stylin'. Now I just need to travel to somewhere besides Alberta.

I also spent my birthday money on myself instead of just putting it in the bank. I bought a shiny new pair of white and pink runners and two new bras - the wires sticking out of my old ones are ripping up the side of my breasts. I had no idea what size I even was. I think the last time I was officially fitted was when I was 12 and my mom spread a training bra across my preteen nubs in the middle of Woolco. So mortifying.

<u>December 29, 2011</u>

Celina seems stressed. I'm sure it's just the season and the fact that René has worked the whole time, which never happens.

Whenever I come home to Alberta it makes me question whether or not I want kids. I'm really not sure. It has nothing to do with the children or the mothers here; it's the lifestyle. I think I'm too selfish. Maybe when I'm with my soul mate I'll feel differently, but I know for sure I would only do it if I had 100% support from him. I couldn't do it if he worked out of town unless I did, too. Taking turns I mean. I think it is hard on the relationship between the children and the mother if there is unequal responsibility for raising and disciplining.

I wish Celina and I would have more 'alone time'. We haven't laughed as much as we usually do. Even at my lowest points, Celina has always been able to make me laugh. I'm her 'pocket giggle'. I think she's tired. Tracy's tired. Jen's tired. It makes me very sad. I don't think I'm going to have children. Thank God for unanswered prayers!

Speaking of which... today would be Carlos and my 10th wedding anniversary. Instead our divorce became final 10 days ago. We were going to try to get together while I was in town so I could see the puppies, but it is probably best it didn't work out. Time to move on.

December 30, 2011

Edmonton International Airport: I'm on my way home! This was a better trip than the last couple, I didn't cry my way through it, so that was a bonus, but I'm still feeling disconnected. It's like I'm in my own little bubble floating around, appearing to be a part of the family, but with this invisible buffer.

Something's got to change. I can't live like this. I won't live like this. I guess there is one thing that has changed - I don't want to die anymore. Another bonus, I guess.

The biggest motivation is the kids. I love them so much and this block is killing me. I want to connect, but as soon as I start to go there, my heart reigns me back. I have to believe there is a cure for my sick heart. This is a massive leap from the past two years, when I had nothing, not even hope. Just fear.

Rock bottom came last summer while I was staying with my parents at the cabin for a month. Tracy's kids came out one week and Celina's came another. I was detached and focused on work the whole time. I had started an online mentorship on inkCanada with Karen Walton. It was an incredible opportunity, but quite demanding time-wise. It was a great excuse. I got to spend hours alone in my room with my laptop. I had to say no to Sara and Sadie a lot and it affected my relationship with them, especially Sadie. She called me on it, too. At the end of their week, Celina came to pick them up with my cousin, Janelle. Janelle looks a lot like Celina and they are very close.

Sadie asked if she could call Janelle 'Auntie' and it really bothered me. I thought I was being ridiculous, but then we were sitting around the table and Sadie was talking to Janelle. She glanced at me out of the corner of her eye and said, "*Auntie* Janelle".

I was quick to judge her insensitive (she's four), not realizing how her teasing might actually hurt someone... then it clicked. She knew exactly what she was doing. She was telling me, in no uncertain terms, "If you don't want to be my Auntie, fine, I'll find someone who does." She was trying to make me jealous and it worked. So, I went to my room and I cried.

I feel cloudy and nauseous, which is no surprise. I did pretty well with eating and exercising, but it's the drinking. It's always the drinking. Another reason to change - I don't want to be known as the bitter, drunk aunt who died a spinster.

We had a pre-New Year's party at René and Celina's and I bought a bunch of wine, which I mostly drank myself. The next day, we went for our annual walk around Mirror Lake and I honestly thought I was going to die. I puked in the public washroom. It's been a long time since I puked in a public washroom. I was going to lie about it, I didn't want my family to think I was *puking* puking, but when I looked in the mirror there was no denying it.

My eyes puffy and watery, I sighed, "Will you never change?"

Yes! This is the year I will change! I will not be forty years old and puking in public washrooms. Butterflies don't puke in public washrooms.

December 31, 2011/January 1, 2012

9:03 PM: Just rang in 2012 by myself (It's midnight EST). This is the first time I've spent New Year's Eve alone. I bought a mini-bottle of sparkling wine. I'm going to start a cleanse tomorrow, but I wanted to make a toast tonight.

Last year, at Celina and René's, surrounded by kissing couples, when the clock struck midnight, I whispered, "2010... Good riddance, you fucker."

2011 was the beginning of a new chapter. Most of it was spent in coffee shops and my basement suite, but that will change in 2012. I learned a lot, but now I'm ready to live and love.

Thank you, God. Thank you, Universe. Thank me. I am so proud of myself for pulling myself out of darkness. I am so strong.

Saying good-bye to an eye-opening year and toasting in a heart-opening one.

I am going to make 2012 the Best Year of My Life!

1:07 AM: The energy of the night won't let me sleep. Sam is having a party. Sometimes I forget who the senior citizen is. Maybe I should go join them...

My landlord, Sam

By the fall of 2009, Carlos had had enough of my distance and demanded I either leave or stay, but make a choice. So, one rainy November Saturday morn I drove from Squamish to Vancouver to look for a new home. Again. The second time I was moving out of the home I shared with my husband. My second desertion.

The basement suite I was going to look at was in Kitsilano - the land of beaches and yoga studios. The street was lined with huge trees and since it was the beginning of November, the lawns and sidewalks were carpeted with bright orange and yellow leaves. The house looked like a little cottage. As I got out of my car, a little man in his seventies popped out the front door with the energy of a 30 year-old.

He chatted away as he took me around back. I was in a dense fog. This was absolutely the last thing I wanted to be doing. The suite was half underground, just like me. It was small and clean and pink and warm, just like a heart.

I told the man I needed to think about it, so went for a drive.

Carlos and I lived in Kits before moving to Squamish. I drove by Grounds for Coffee. Grounds, as I like to call it, is my favorite place on Earth to write. There were days I would drive an hour from Squamish just to write there. They are famous for their cinnamon buns, but I love their Super Fruit muffins. It smells of cinnamon from a block away. Grounds is where I fell in love with writing.

I drove by Limelight Video, my favorite place to rent movies, and The Cove, my favorite place to drink beer, right to Jericho Beach, my favorite place to walk the puppies.

I need to be by the ocean.

I called the man and said I would take it and offered to give him some references.

"Oh no, I got a good feeling about you."

Really? Weird. "Who should I make the damage deposit out to?"

"Sam Pender."

"Pardon me?"

"Sam Pender."

"Can you repeat that?"

He was probably regretting his decision now. How could he know his name was one consonant off from the name of one of the most influential, for good and bad, men in my life?

The first thing I did, before even unpacking a plate, was set up my fake Christmas tree. That night, lying in the dark on an air mattress staring at the blinking red lights, I started to cry.

How the fuck did I get here... again?

Holy shit, it's 2 AM. Go to bed, Sam!

4

Inspired Ideas

January 1, 2012

Happy New Year!!! I just dumped all my wine and mini-bottle of Henkell Trocken. I will not drink alone anymore!

I'm a bit stuck of what to do. How exactly does one go about creating the best year of their life? I cleaned my home and feng shui'd it for love and abundance. I wrote and did yoga, read a bit, but now what?

Later: I went for a long walk, starting at Jericho Beach extending all the way to the tip of Spanish Banks. I have walked the stretch a thousand times, but this time was different. Standing on the rocks at the western most point, I looked out to the ocean, the mountains, up to the crystal blue sky, the Universe and made a pact with the Source of all creative energy.

"Okay, God! I'm creating the Best Year of My Life, but I have absolutely no idea what that means or how to do it. Please help me. Please give me what I need to do this. Whatever guidance you provide, I promise to follow."

A whisper, "*Inspired Ideas.* Any idea coming from a place of love, abundance and expansion, you must follow."

"How the hell am I supposed ...? Never mind. I'm sorry. Deal."

7 PM: I want to celebrate the New Year with some drinks, but I won't. Partly because I don't want to; mostly because I dumped my booze and the liquor stores are closed.

I feel like I'm ending a relationship. A friendship. Right or wrong, healthy or not, beer and wine have been my friends, my BFF's these past couple of years, but it is time to say good-bye to a relationship that no longer serves me.

Like the day I left Carlos, walking through that door... dumping the alcohol is the same thing, but this time I'm never going back. There are no puppies to miss or financial connections to disentangle myself from. This is just another strong decision. I've quit drinking before, but that was out of fear of my weaknesses, this is out of strength.

Lots of emotions going on, which is natural when you are making tough choices... and massive deals with God!

I've been thinking about it and I have to talk to Celina. I feel like no one is happy in their relationships and in general, really. I'm worried. There must be a way I can help.

January 2, 2012

My first Inspired Idea! I called Celina last night and asked her to come visit me. She practically jumped at the chance and might come in 3 weeks. Ever since I was there at Christmas I've felt like Celina needed a break. I checked my Air Miles and I have enough. Perfect.

January 3, 2012

First day back at BrainBoost, the private education centre I teach at. I only had two sessions: Donovan and Elliot.

Donovan is a full-time student and I teach him math and science. He is 11, but ranges between Grade 1 for subtraction and university for film knowledge. I've never met a kid who loves movies more than me. He thinks it's super cool I'm a screenwriter. I think he's super cool.

Elliot is 13 and a multiplying genius, but needs a tutor to help with the processes and more abstract concepts. It's not that he is not capable, it's that at any one moment he has 3 or 4 simultaneous thoughts going on in his head and it is hard for him to stay focused on something he cares nothing about, i.e. homework.

Elliot, who refers to people according to their date of birth, is one of the most fascinating kids, no people, I have ever met. His most impressive trick: present him with any date in the past 3 or 4 years and he can tell you what day of the week it is. How? He remembers all his dreams, when he had them and what day of the week it was, so with a few seconds of mental calculation he can figure out any other date. Like I said... fascinating.

January 4, 2012

It's all set. Celina's coming to visit! She said no to the Air Miles. I insisted. We argued, as we do. My sister is one of the most generous people I know, but has major receiving issues.

"This is coming from a place of love and abundance and generosity. How can you deny me the joy of this experience?"

Guilt, even out of jest, always works in my family - Catholic upbringing, I guess. Still, I was thrilled and surprised when she replied, "Okay."

Now my cheapness is stealing my joy. Making spontaneous decisions around money is baggage I carry from both my marriages. This has nothing to do with those experiences and I won't let them ruin it. Instead, I will EFT through my money and abundance blocks.

I first learned about the Emotional Freedom Technique, tapping, six years ago. Carlos and I tried it a couple times and it worked, but I stopped for some reason. I guess I wasn't ready to be free from my emotions. Actually, any thought of freedom scared the shit out of me. This was at the same time the *The Secret* first came out and I became obsessed with the Law of Attraction. The anxiety and fear of what I was attracting into my life was one of the things that drove me into a state of despair... and to the psychiatrist.

EFT basically involves tapping on meridian points, like in acupuncture, to release energy blocks. You can EFT around almost anything: pain, prosperity, even procrastination, which is ironic as I often EFT as a form of procrastination.

Celina said I made her year. Just that was worth it. Yay, Inspired Ideas!

January 6, 2012

I am at The Cove writing and having a beer. It's okay. I was overanalyzing drinking. Thinking I needed to be perfect or something. What the heck is fun about that? I am healthy. It's all about balance. Creating the Best Year of My Life does not mean depriving myself.

Focus on the positives. I am so proud of myself for all the writing I did this week. I worked through all of Act I of *Making of a Faith Healer* and most of Act II; some really tough parts, too. I'm really excited about this script. It is going to be awesome and it is through me that it is being told.

Later: I'm watching *the fifth estate*. It is about a 20-year-old Sikh girl from Maple Ridge who was allegedly killed by her family for marrying a rickshaw driver from Punjab instead of the 60-year-old friend her uncle arranged for her to marry. Wow... I am so grateful I have had the freedom to have the marriages I wanted and, I guess, the freedom to fuck them up, too.

January 7, 2012

In the wealth corner of my humble abode sits a table. It's an old fashion kitchen table where the sides flap down, just like the one my Grandma and Papa had. Sam gave it to me along with a yellow and orange flowered puffy chair. The only other furniture in my place is a futon and my double bed. Oh yeah, and the oak hope chest I'm writing on right now that my parents gave me when I graduated university. I keep the puffy chair covered with a cream Afghan my mémère crocheted, the futon with a blue and burgundy one my Grandma made and the table with a white silk tablecloth my great aunt gave me - hahaha, what a love lair!

My place is so small the sides of the kitchen table have to stay down, and forget about chairs - I eat sitting at my hope chest, but the table makes the perfect Abundance Altar. Atop the table, on a lace doily (okay,

I really need to redecorate) sits the crisp one hundred dollar bill my mom and dad gave me for my birthday. Theoretically, I already spent the gift on bras and running shoes, but it sits as a symbol of wealth.

It sits there to remind me that, whoa... Inspired Idea! I need to circulate it. Give it to someone or some place that has inspired me. Donate to a charity? Not this time. Tithe to a church? Not a chance. No. I know exactly what I'm gonna do.

January 8, 2012
7 AM at Grounds: I bought a gift certificate for the staff at Grounds for Coffee. It's for the pub across the street, so they can go have a few rounds on me. The pub manager had to practically pry the $100 bill from my hand. Funny how attached we get to a piece of paper.

Grounds saved my life and that is no exaggeration. For the past two years, practically every Saturday and Sunday, I have come here to write. I arrive at 7 AM and stay until 11 AM. Not many places let you do that. If I did not have this early morning writing ritual, my weekend nights would've been spent in drunken despair... guaranteed.

I arrive at 7, so I can get my spot. It is prime real-estate. Grounds is not a huge coffee shop and my spot has the open view of the door, the street and the counter. Perfect for people watching. It is also nestled next to a shelving unit, so I feel sheltered at the same time. The staff is friendly and feisty and fabulous, and obviously patient. It smells of cinnamon buns, just like my Grandma's. Hmmm... I'm noticing a theme.

What should I write on the card? I'm nervous. Why am I nervous? They are going to be so surprised. I hope they feel my gratitude.

Later: I did it. I gave the card. On my way out, I glanced back to see the kafuffle I created. I am so proud of myself that I saw that $100 on my Abundance Altar and listened to the Universe to get it out there with a grateful heart, and not to my fear of being homeless, who was telling me I may need that hundred bucks for rent some day.

January 10, 2012
I haven't had sex in two years. Carlos and I officially separated December 1, 2009, but I had a couple 'relapses' while visiting the puppies. The last one was January 10, 2010. I've been clean ever since.

Don't get me wrong, there have been times I've regretted ending it (the sex, not the marriage), but if there is one thing I've learned, there is nothing more meaningful than meaningless sex.

Take it from someone who has had enough one-night stands to last a lifetime, each and every event spoke volumes about how I felt about myself. Take it from someone who in 25 years of sexual activity has never once made love. Easily 90% of my sexual experiences have involved some level of inebriation. I've never been comfortable being touched, so alcohol helped numb my senses and sensibilities. I was never present enough in the moment to make love.

I'm not saying I've never had sex with someone I loved. I loved both my husbands, but I never really believed they loved me. I have only recently come to understand the difference between self-confidence and self-worth. I had confidence in the bedroom, but no self-worth.

How can you make love if you don't feel worthy of it?

8:37 PM: Enough is enough. I am having one of those relapses around drinking like I had with Carlos - safe and easy in the moment, but only emptiness to follow.

It is not just about the drinking, it is also about eating unhealthy. It is fine to have a treat sometimes, deprivation is not the answer, but my body does not want nachos three nights in a row! I want to love my body. It has put up with so much. There should've been a mutiny long ago.

Pigging out is just another escape and I can feel with every spoonful of peanut butter I swallow I am just trying to fill a hole that will never be filled by a nut spread! This is not about weight (entirely). It is about cheating my body and my soul by taking senna after. Just because it is natural does not make it healthy. Sunday morning I had the worst cramps. Not to mention the fact I have the worst sleeps on the weekend and need to take melatonin or a sleeping pill to sleep.

I am a channel for all the love and abundance the Universe has to offer. I am a channel for the giving and receiving of all the love and abundance in this infinite Universe.

January 11, 2012

I am on a giving spree! This fall, I was part of an NFL Football Survivor Pool organized by Justin, my teacher-friend at BrainBoost. I LOVE football.

NFL football, that is. The only thing Americans do better than Canadians is football. Following football is my one guilty pleasure. I don't like any other sport. I don't watch TV or read celebrity magazines, and the lives of NFL players are way more entertaining than any reality show!

I have two favorite teams: the Colts and whoever is playing the Patriots. I fucking hate the Patriots. I don't use the f-word often, but it always seems to slip out when I talk about the Patriots. Cheater, cheater, pumpkin-fuckin'-eaters. I hate them almost as much as I love the Colts. Yes, I'm an Indianapolis fan, which means I have to hate the Patriots, but I would even if they weren't our arch-nemesis. The one thing Carlos and I could always agree on was how awesome Peyton Manning is... and how overrated Tom Brady is.

I used to be a Titans fan. The first NFL game I ever watched was 'Music City Miracle'. It was January 2000 and I was living with three guys in Edmonton. It was Wild Card Weekend. I was hung over to the gills after a night at the club, so curled up on the couch and watched the game with my roommate Cory and his awesome black lab puppy, Eddie.

There was controversy from the start because the Buffalo Bills' coach started the young buck quarterback instead of Doug Flutie, who had got them to the playoffs. Since Flutie was the biggest star in the CFL, hence the only player I knew, I was mad at the coach for not playing him. Therefore, I cheered for the opposing team, the Tennessee Titans.

The game was pretty good, from what I understood, but the ending was one of the most exciting moments in sports I have ever witnessed. 'Music City Miracle' actually has a sub-plot in my latest script, *Making of a Faith Healer*, which takes place in Memphis.

The Titans made it all the way to the Super Bowl that year and almost won, but came up 'One Yard Short', another infamous play. I was hooked. This was also the era of Eddie George and Steve McNair. I would still be a Titans fan except living on the West Coast the games were barely televised and after a year in Korea, where no games played, I decided to pick a new team I could actually watch. I chose the Colts because Carlos was a fan and I thought it would be nice to be on the same team for something.

Oh yeah, the pool... we had to choose a winning and losing team each week and you could only pick each team once... Does that make sense? I was one of the winners of the loser pool (story of my life). My portion of the pot wasn't huge, but I had another Inspired Idea.

Justin is an amazing teacher. I love eavesdropping on his sessions. His passion for the youth and teaching inspire me, so I gave him my winnings - a thank you for organizing and inviting me into the pool.

Inspired Ideas - I'm a likin' them!

I went to the *Arctic Air* premiere last night. TV premiers are definitely not the norm in Canada, but CBC pulled out all the stops. It was held at The Vogue Theatre and even had a red carpet. All the hoopla is due to the fact that the lead actor of the new series is Adam Beach, a wonderful Canadian aboriginal actor who has experienced success down south as well. Him coming home to do a Canadian TV show is huge. The pilot episode was actually really good.

Adam Beach is yummy. Super cute and charismatic, he radiates positivity. As soon as he took the stage I got goosebumps, like our lives are meant to intersect. Weird. I'm rarely attracted to anyone and am not easily star-struck. The whole time I worked at Blue Water Café (a fine-dining restaurant in Yaletown) the only star that struck me was Judi Dench. I served everyone from Hugh Jackman to The Jackass (now there's a story), but it was the elegant Dame Judi that made me almost drop a crab platter.

My Little Peach Cobbler

January 13, 2012

Celina is on her way!! I woke up at 5:17 AM because I am so pumped. When I was a kid I thought adults never got excited and here I am at 39 years old, giddy as a schoolgirl because My Little Peach

Cobbler is coming to visit! That was my nickname for her when she was a teenager because she had, and still does have, the most beautiful peaches and cream skin.

Her nickname for me: Apple Cobbler. At the time I had very chubby cheeks. Both sets.

Two weeks ago this trip wasn't even a thought. Sometimes worry is good, because it is your intuition telling you something is out of sync. I'm proud of myself that I listened to mine, so now I get to shower my little sister in love and not second-guess myself. The best part is I have no expectations of the weekend.

January 15, 2012

It is amazing after knowing someone for almost 35 years, what you can learn when it is just the two of you for 48 hours. I just had the most amazing two days with Celina. I can't believe this is the first time she has gone away without René or the girls since Sara was born.

On Friday night, we went out with my Youth Future friends Scott, Jocelyn, Mike and his rad girlfriend, Teresa. Mike and I work together at BrainBoost now as well, but I haven't seen Scott or Jocelyn since I left in August.

We barhopped on Broadway and drank quite a bit. At the last pub, as I was tipping my end of the table dumping beer all over Scott (who barely flinched, bless his soul), Celina and Teresa were deep in conversation at the other end. Mike's face read 'awkward' and later I found out why.

I must preface this by stating that Celina is one of the most private people when it comes to sex; Teresa is not. Teresa is going for her Masters in something to do with women studies, and was talking about her research around sexual experiences, oppression and suppression, and how she thinks it is best for women to have multiple sex partners before settling down with one. She was trying incessantly to engage Celina in the discussion. Apparently, My Little Peach Cobbler tried to change the subject numerous times, but Teresa, a very passionate woman, kept persisting.

Finally, Celina broke. "Fine you want my opinion, well here it is: The first, second, third sexual experiences before you are in love are awkward and uncomfortable, not really an enjoyable experience anyway.

So, people who judge and say, 'You've only ever been with one person?' can't really say how many people you should sleep with before you settle down and get married, because what is the magic number? Are you doing it more than once to compare? Nobody says you should go on a holiday with more than one person before getting married or do home renovations or have a baby.... these are all things that can be experienced with the one person you choose to marry, so why can't sex? Only ever being with one person is not a bad thing, but can actually be ideal. I think going through those first few embarrassing times with someone you love is a gift."

Wow.

Teresa was apparently struck by this response, as well. She asked Celina what advice she would give her daughters as to when they would know they were ready to have sex.

"I would tell them to wait until they are okay if the lights are on. That is a very hard thing to do and until you are with someone who makes you feel safe and loved, you shouldn't be involved in the 'sex' part of the relationship, because really what is more personal?"

I would love to take credit for passing all this wisdom down to my little sister, but alas, if you knew the stories of the first, second, third, or twentieth time I had sex you would call me... what is the opposite of wise? Oh yeah. You would call me a fool.

On Saturday, hung over like hell, we went for brunch at The Cove and then walked around Granville Island, which is known for its crafty shops, overpriced restaurants, obnoxious seagulls and Farmer's Market, which I usually avoid like the plague, but Celina wanted to check it out, so we did. It was actually really cool. I forgot how vibrant the colors of all the fresh produce are. It almost made me want to cook. Almost.

I also forgot how ridiculous my sister's snake phobia is. No, they don't have snakes at the market, but they do have longneck squash, which apparently, when you catch one out of the corner of your eye, resembles a striking snake.

Celina yelped. I laughed. I am a recovering ophidiophobe, so I do understand, but my sister takes the fear to a whole new level.

We spent Saturday night with Jerrid, Christina and Charlie at their condo in Yaletown.

Jerrid, Janelle and their sister, Cassie, are our double cousins. My mom's brother, my Uncle Sheldon, married my dad's sister, my Auntie Diane. Yeah. Take a moment with that one.

Needless to say, we all look a lot alike. Especially Janelle and Celina, who are practically twins. We are all a lot alike personality-wise, too. This is Elliot's favorite thing to analyze about my family - what each of us double-cousins have most in common with each other.

Even though Jerrid has lived in Vancouver for a few years, I only recently started hanging out with him and his family. I'd like to a lot more. They're cool peeps. Jerrid is the silliest smart person I know... or the smartest silly person. Why are all the cool guys either in my family or married to women in my family?

Sunday morning, I took Celina to Grounds for a coffee and muffin. We sat in my spot and for the first time since Carlos and I split, she asked me about 'dating'. Yikes.

My relationships are not a popular conversation in my family. My first divorce was very hard on them, especially Celina. Matthew was like a big brother to her and she was very angry when I left him. My second marriage was a challenge for everyone to accept, the divorce not as much. Still, I've been single for over two years, so her curiosity was understandable. Deep down, I know my family doesn't want me to be alone.

I told her about this guy I met, at Grounds actually, just over a year ago.

"I was sitting right in this seat when I first saw him."

The story surrounding the moment is quite surreal and when I told her she said it gave her chills. Apparently, she had a similar feeling when she first saw René perform *Staying Alive* as part of a lip sync performance in Grade 12. She had gone to the same school as him since Grade 5, but that was the first time she *saw* him.

My coffee shop crush has come to visit now and then, and we've had some great conversations. He's actually from Stony Plain. Leave it to me to live in Vancouver, one of the most international cities in Canada, and the only guy to peak my interest is a small town Alberta boy. He hasn't been around in a few months though.

Also for the first time, Celina and I discussed why I've been divorced twice.

The truth is, I actually think I made a good wife. Neither of my husbands wanted me to leave, although they both found it impossible to show me they wanted me to stay. The truth is the marriages failed before they began. I knew both times, ahead of time, they were doomed. My intuition told me to run, but I didn't listen. I pressured both of them to get engaged, but once I got what I 'wanted', panic set in. I ignored it. Pushed it deep within. This was easy because I was bulimic during both engagements. Whenever a doubt rose, I puked it out.

Celina told me when her and René got engaged, even though they had dated for seven years, two of which were long-distant while he was going to school in California, she had doubts. *How could she not?* Both her sisters were on their second marriages.

Every morning, from the day he proposed to their wedding day, she would look at herself in the mirror and in a very stern voice, declare, "You are not marrying him." And every morning, it felt like a knife in her heart. That's how she knew.

Both times I was engaged, I couldn't even look at myself in the mirror. Still can't.

Wow. Making the intention to live the Best Year of Your Life, and promising to say 'yes' to Inspired Ideas, really opens you up to conversations you never believed possible. Simple conversations that should have happened years ago.

Later: I need a spiritual mentor. I need a community of like-minded individuals. I have all these thoughts going through my head and although I love reading and learning, I need to talk about these things. I need some guidance.

6

I am Not Cleaning the Bathroom on a Friday Night

January 16, 2012

Last night, I was reading *The Best Year of Your Life* by Debbie Ford for some tips and there was a poem by Portia Nelson, 'Autobiography in Five Short Chapters' in it.

Walking a different street.... perfectly sums up my relationship with my weekends.

Then this morning, I got an email from Light Watkins. I don't know him, but was going to take a meditation class of his once, so I'm on his emailing list. I usually press delete before even reading them, but for some reason today I opened this one. It had the same poem!

Obviously, this is a sign and I know EXACTLY what it means: Healthy Weekend Choices! I am not drinking alone ever again and I am not pigging out. These are two things I do in isolation that wear on me in so many ways. I've known for a long time they have and now I'm ready to leave them in the past. There are hundreds of things I can do instead. No excuses. Only love. I am manifesting the most extraordinary life and I have no room for self-sabotage or abuse.

Self-worth comes from doing what is worthy.

I was feeling low self-confidence and trust in myself, which is 100% the effect and the cause. There are so many amazing things I can create. I am a courageous creative girl and this is going to be so easy. Take another street. Don't just do the same things without drinking. Find new things to do.

In order to become a butterfly, I need to be willing to let go of my caterpillar behavior.

Dr. Pez once suggested, "There's lots to do on a Friday night. Clean the bathroom."

I blurted, "I am *not* cleaning the bathroom on a Friday night."

"Why do you label it 'A Friday Night'? It's just another night. Cleaning the bathroom would symbolize clearing away all the dirt and grime, instead of polluting yourself more."

He was not your normal psychiatrist. I have yet to take him up on this suggestion.

January 17, 2012

I am vice-president of Women in Film and Television Vancouver (don't ask me how that happened) and we had an Executive Meeting last night. Mary, the president, asked if I was looking for a job. Her husband is looking for a production coordinator assistant. What a huge compliment to be considered and recommended. I'm going to email her today and thank her. This is not at all the kind of job I am looking for and it feels good to know that, but it really is an honor she thought of me. I'm also going to tell her what an amazing president she is.

I am experiencing some major resistance around meeting my soul mate. I'm not sure the cause of the resistance, but it is huge. Part of it is definitely caused by my caterpillar weekends, when I promised myself 2012 would be different.

How can I trust the Universe when I can't even trust myself?

No. It is my choice whether I use this as an excuse to beat myself up or as an opportunity to grow. I choose to grow. I don't see this weekend as something to fear as I sidestep the potholes, but as an opportunity to take a new, exciting, different street.

That is what I'm scared of: the unknown street. I will not take a dark, seedy street. No more back alleys. Been there, done that.

<u>January 18, 2012</u>
7 AM at Grounds: I'm writing today. It's been 1.5 weeks since I've done any work on my script. Whenever I don't write for a bit, I feel like something is missing. I feel off track.

<u>January 20, 2012</u>
7:12 AM: I woke up with the beautiful realization that my calling in life is to write this book. As I emerge into my full womanhood, I can inspire others to do the same. I'm also writing it because I have this burning desire to share all I've learned, and am learning, and can do this best if my audience is captive. *Just kidding.* Sort of.

I'm organizing this PW 4 TV Producers Workshop for WIFTV and one thing I've noticed is how quickly people get back to me. Successful people get back to you quickly. Even if it is to say they'll get back to you.

<u>January 21, 2012</u>
Christine and I met for a couple beers last night. You know how sometimes when you meet someone, you just know you will be friends? That's the way it was with Christine when we both joined the WIFTV board. I had a friend crush on her from the get go. It's taken almost two years, but we are starting to hang out. She is a business analyst at BC Film & Media and is one of the most beautiful women I know, inside and out. We also seem to be at similar places on our spiritual journey. Maybe it's because we are both '72 babies.

For the first time, I shared my vision for the Canadian film industry with someone and how my first screenplay, *FLOW*, would be the perfect springboard project. The Canadian *Magnolia*. I have a meeting today with Amber, a producer friend of mine, and I wanted to get Christine's feedback. She loved it. So exciting. I love how this is all unfolding.

Later: Amber and I just met for lunch. Last summer I wrote a short film, *Happiless*, and approached Ana Valine, a super talented, up-and-coming director, to team up to apply for the annual MPPIA Short Film Award that BC Film sponsors. Amber is producing Ana's first feature and so asked her if she wanted to come on board as producer. Even though Amber was also submitting a short she was directing, she said sure. They both loved the project, especially the main character. We worked the script intensely, which was an amazing process for me.

We were one of the five finalists that got to pitch at the Whistler International Film Festival this past December. We didn't win, but on my way back from Whistler, I had an epiphany. I kept hearing Ana's pitch replaying over in my head. She referred to the short as a female Odyssey. I also reflected on the jury's feedback, which basically highlighted the fact that the main character's arch was too big for 10 minutes.

Then it dawned on me, "Duh! *Happiless* is a feature!" This always happens to me. Any time I try to write a short, it becomes a feature.

Amber is the Director of Development at Foundation Features, a prominent Canadian production company based in Vancouver, so I submitted *FLOW* to her. We were meeting for lunch to discuss. She really liked the script, only had a couple notes, and is interested in my ideas regarding casting and director. Marketing it as "The Canadian *Magnolia*" seemed to peak her interest. The only problem is they have five features on their slate right now and the producer, Rob Merilees, isn't reading anything new for a few months. It's probably a good thing. If they decided to option it right now, it would just sit on a virtual shelf.

Over these next few months, until someone options my script, I want to create some momentum for myself as a writer, however that may look. It will help whoever when they are shopping around the script. Amber thought this script and the characters were definitely of the caliber to attract talent.

I submitted *FLOW* for the Script Reading Program at the Female Eye Film Festival in Toronto and I've decided to go whether I get accepted or not. Time to get this baby out there. I am excited to finish *Making of a Faith Healer* and then get started on *Happiless*.

I'm having a beer. I've realized I'm not an alcoholic. I'm a bored-a-holic. How can such a creative person not figure out something different to do on a weekend night? I've walked this street for 25 years, but can't seem to see another one. I wish the Universe had a GPS.

Emotional pain, whether it is sadness, depression, anxiety, fear, guilt - really where does one end and the other begin, is caused by being reckless with our emotional and/or mental and/or physical and/or spiritual health. In the same way that professional boxing, smoking and walking down steep hills in the winter drunk can cause physical pain, so can being reckless with our thoughts and hearts.

I had a bizarre little daydream while meditating today. I saw my Emotional, Mental, Physical and Spiritual parts as separate characters. At first, they were fighting for my attention, each presenting their case as to why they've been the most abused.

Then Spiritual exclaimed, "We are not parts of Rachelle. We *are* Rachelle. We are one."

They all laughed at the ridiculousness of the 39 year old battle, apologizing to each other for not playing nice and agreeing to care for each other.

Why am I so weird?

For some reason, I have this perpetual patch of greasy hair on the back of my head. I thought it was my shampoo, but now I think it is from meditating on my foam memory pillow. Maybe this is why you're supposed to sit upright when you meditate.

January 22, 2012

I had a great WIFTV Education Meeting with Siobhan and Barbara, the other two ladies on the committee. Barbara is a beautiful black actress originally from Quebec. When I say beautiful, I mean beautiful. She was Halle Berry's stand-in. Siobhan is a director who is re-entering the industry after taking time away to raise her two daughters. She is married to Alexandra Raffé, a successful Canadian film and television producer. Alex is moderating the producing workshop I am organizing.

Siobhan said Alex is impressed with the work I'm doing. That has got to be the hugest compliment, but it feels especially great because I'm not trying to impress anyone except myself. I'm proud of the work I'm doing with WIFTV.

January 23, 2012

Gung Hay Fat Choy!

Welcome, Water Dragon, and all the good luck, fortune and prosperity you bring. I've loved Chinese New Year's since living in Korea. I'm a Water Rat.

My horoscope: *Wow. The Water Dragon is so good for you. This could be one of your best years. There are probably only two ways you can mess it up: Sit it out and accomplish nothing memorable, or try to outdo the outlandish Dragon. Don't let this opportunity pass you by. Fly with the Dragon and make your dreams come true!*

Fly, baby, fly!

I am so grateful for my life, the simplest gifts like my clean white cotton socks.

A bottle collector once told me, "There ain't nothing like a clean pair of socks."

I'll never forget how the words beamed through his toothless smile. I thought it was the most profound thing I had ever heard. Of course, that was back when I was identifying with homeless people. Long story.

Later: I made a $250 donation to the Women in Film Festival tonight. I am sponsoring the Best Screenwriting Award and naming it after my mom. I can't wait to tell her. Never in a million years will she expect this. Why would she?

When the Sponsorship Chair mentioned I was doing this (I had emailed her privately asking if it would be okay) at the board meeting, some other ladies said they wanted to sponsor awards, too. This is another amazing thing about giving from the heart... it's contagious.

January 24, 2012

I fell asleep listening to my Love Subliminal Messages CD. I actually bought it about a year ago, but it always made me feel anxious when I listened to it. I guess I wasn't ready yet.

It is important to be conscious of keeping the balance between creating my life and living and appreciating my now. My now is absolutely how I created it. There are an infinite number of ways the Universe aligns itself to make our outsides match our insides, so I know by nurturing and expanding myself the possibilities are endless. I am in a major expansion stage and I don't ever want to outgrow someone again. I never want to hurt someone again.

My soul mate and I are on this amazing journey together. He just doesn't know it yet.

I Skyped with my mom and dad today and told my mom about the award. She was confused at first. It was quite funny. Once it sunk in, she was overwhelmed. It feels good to overwhelm my parents with happiness instead of grief.

Mary emailed me today, "Rachelle, you are an inspiration." Wow. Wasn't expecting that. I have to be careful that this giving rampage doesn't become an ego-filler.

January 25, 2012

I'm going through a little doubt about where my soul mate is. I'm trying not to force believing and just savor the waiting.

I had a dream of my coffee shop crush last night. I was parked on the street in front of his condo when he hopped in my car. It was immediately comfortable, with him and our bodies. We kissed. It was nice and natural. *Who is this guy?!*

He was limping. Maybe he broke his leg and that's why I haven't seen him!

I also had a weird dream of Carlos. He was giving me all these cards - birthday, anniversary, Mother's Day... really nice pop-out ones. Maybe it's time I change my perspective on our time together. I always said he was the sand in my oyster; maybe it's time to see our time together as the pearl.

Right. Maybe a *pearl necklace*.

January 27, 2012

I had another dream about Carlos last night. I was having a party in the trailer Matthew and I lived in on the farm. I was trying to talk to Jen on the phone, but it kept breaking up. She was upset because Celina's friend just ate $100 worth of sushi and lit the Beaumont pub on fire. Then she showed up at the party. We ordered tons of pizza and I ate way too much. I was hoarding it and even tried to save some she had thrown in the garbage. Somebody had poured salt all over it and I was trying desperately to brush it off.

Then it was just Carlos and I. I kept pressuring him for his new address and asking when he would be packed to move; criticizing him for being 35 and not having things figured out.

Fuck! Do you think I may have some letting go to do?

6:10 PM: What an interesting day. A perfect mix of personal and professional.

The professional: The workshop is good to go. Two packed days with 23 panelists and moderated by Alex Raffé, Head of Production at Thunderbird Films. Not bad. Not bad at all.

The personal: I picked up my divorce papers. It was official on December 19th, but to hold the papers makes it all real. I'm working on letting go of the negative perspective of it... and Carlos. No judgment. It isn't good, it isn't bad, it just is. I'm working on it.

What are some of the lessons I learned? Listen to my intuition, believe in myself, stand in my power and that I look (and feel) way better as a blonde.

January 29, 2012

What an amazing weekend! The workshop was a huge success. It blows me away how generous our industry is, at least in Vancouver. I met such incredible people from all stages of TV production. There are some really cool people in the industry. I've seen Michele, a development executive, speak a couple of times. She has this great energy about her. I think we could be friends.

Amanda Tapping is such a sweetheart. I did an episode of *Stargate SG-1* once. The episode's title was *Memento Mori* (Latin for 'remember you will die', which was fitting as it marked the end of my dismal acting career). I played a mother in a diner that was held up by some hoodlums. A few years later, Amanda hosted the Spotlight Awards Gala, which WIFTV puts on. It was my first year on the board and I was her trophy girl. Although Amanda wasn't even on set the day my scene filmed, she said she recognized me from a photo in the hair and make-up trailer. I love her.

Christine was there, too. She had a great idea that we should create a pitching show and ask Alex be the host. Hmmm.... interesting.

My head is spinning with ideas; features, TV-drama, multi-cam lesbian comedy, reality! I'm feeling a little torn all over the place. I'll give it a week or so to mull over.

Present it as a question. I think I know. Yes, I know it's a career, but why do I need to choose? Think Tina Fey - sketch, sitcom, features. Yes! Think Tina Fey!

I guess what it is, is that I'm not really interested in being a writer for hire. I know my voice. For me, it's not about having a career in TV, i.e. starting as a junior writer and working my way up. Diablo Colby, another great example... I know my voice.

It feels good to not be envious of someone else's career like I constantly was when I was acting. I did have a tinge of jealousy for an infinitesimal moment today - *why am I not on that stage?* But I am so clear on my creative voice and it will not waiver. I don't feel torn all over anymore. This moment of confusion only helps me clarify my goals.

It's not the medium that matters; it's the content.

This weekend introduced me to TV industry professionals in a positive light. Up to now I've mostly met people in the indie film world. TV peeps aren't so bad after all!

January 30, 2012

My physical world no longer matches what's going on inside of me, which is confusing because the physical world is suppose to be a mirror for my inner one.

Feeling kind of down today. I'm trying not to fight it, but I also don't want to wallow in it. Suffering is a sign, though. Not that I'm suffering. I think it's just the natural down after putting so much work into something and then it being over.

I didn't eat very healthy this weekend and I drank alone. Those things never help. The weird thing is, at least last night, it was completely emotional and being tired.

I wanted to puke, which was bizarre. I haven't thrown up in years and it is odd, or maybe not, that just as things are starting to go so well... No. I'm not going there. This is just that part of me that wants to self-destruct or pull myself down. I'm really trying to learn to love my body and I don't want to ever abuse it ever again. Eating crappy food is abuse as well, as is senna, even if it is a slap instead of a kick.

January 31, 2012

The first month of the Best Year of My Life has come to an end and it has been awesome! I'm still feeling a little down today, but I know it will pass.

Besides, what does time mean? It is something man-made that often causes regret and panic. This moment that I am in right now, with my coffee, my journal, my cozy home... truly everything is perfect.

It is only when I look at my conditions or circumstances in the external world that I get frustrated. The physical is an illusion. Images of what's inside of my mind. The more I clear the resistance and my perspective and my vision, the quicker my exterior will catch up.

I can feel the resistance; I'm just not sure where it is coming from.

I'm thinking way too much. Over-thinking has been an issue for me my whole life. My brain is like a Border Collie; if I don't give it something constructive to do it gets itself into mischief. I am overanalyzing my exterior world, which is just a rut I will pull myself out of.

The best way to get out of a rut is to get up out of the rut.

I really need to spend some time in nature. Come on sunshine!

The Biggest Devil is Me

February 1, 2012

I am really grateful for all this internal work I am doing and all the tools I am gathering. It helps me bounce back so much quicker. The hard days are as important as the great ones. *Duality, right?* I get to write all morning - my favorite thing to do, plus the sun is out and I am soooooo grateful for that.

8:30 AM: I realized why I've been bothered the last couple of days. It was considering writing for TV. It was my intuition screaming at me, "No! Don't get sidetracked again!"

Writing for TV is not my dream and, for me, it is not the path to it. I don't even watch TV, for crying out loud.

Thank you, Intuition, for smacking me up the side of the head.

Getting wrapped up in the "Why am I not on that stage?" is about age frustration. *That* is not my dream, so why would I be *there*? Just needed a little reminder where my passion and flow are. Know your purpose. Feel it. When you go off the path, your intuition will guide you back on - sometimes with a tickle, sometimes with a cattle prod.

Good morning, soul mate. I hope you are enjoying the sunshine today.

Later: Meditation vision - My soul mate and I are a molecule of water. He is hydrogen and I am oxygen - perfectly complete, vital elements on our own, but when joined together our potential is unlimited... and ambiguous. It is the ambiguous nature of water that allows it to support life on Earth.

Of course H_2O has two hydrogen atoms for each oxygen... Does this mean I'm supposed to have a threesome? No, it probably just means my soul mate is twice as big as me. He must weigh 230 lbs, no biggie.

February 2, 2012

A day of semi-sunshine and I feel 1000 times better! I swear I'm solar-powered.

I went to the beach yesterday on my break and it is so incredible how that place makes me feel so abundant. I wasn't going to go, but then I remembered the day before I told the Universe I really needed a sunny day, so I wanted to show my gratitude. I am so grateful my schedule lets me do that. When I'm on the right path I feel this incredible flow.

February 3, 2012

This is going to be an amazing weekend! I am going to the Light Watkins meditation seminar tonight. After reading his email with that poem, I checked his schedule and he was coming to Vancouver this weekend! The Universe gave me a sign and I am following it, if for no other reason than to shake up the rut of my Friday nights.

I have too much writing to do this weekend, so can't do the whole retreat. I am interested in learning more about Transcendental Meditation, though.

The weather today was miserable. Vancouver's relationship with the Sun is fascinating. People don't talk about the weather to break the ice; it is the way we bond.

Last night, one of my students and I were discussing how depressing the lack of sunshine is. We checked the Weather Network to see if there was an end in sight and there were pictures of 5 bright yellow orbs all in a row starting tomorrow. We actually hooted.

Only in Vancouver can cartoon Suns make you cheer.

<u>February 4, 2012</u>

I want to dye my hair pink. Just some streaks. I used to do it when I was 13 using beet juice. I thought it was pretty, but am probably too old to pull it off now. Maybe when I'm eighty. Then people will think I just made a mistake.

The meditation seminar last night was fascinating. I'm interested in learning more about it and giving it a shot, but this isn't the right weekend. It makes me want to start Vipassana meditation again. I haven't done it in years, though, and don't really remember how.

Light Watkins is yummy (probably a good reason not to take the course), but too thin. There is no way he weighs 230 lbs. Hahaha I just got that. He's too *light* for me. I'm so funny.

I had an amazing epiphany yesterday on my walk. Two, actually.

1. I am already a professional screenwriter. I have been paying myself from my savings, investing in myself and my business. Soon I'll send my scripts out and be paid to develop more.

2. People create to develop and expand, so in order for them to want to work with me I have to show them all that is possible. Sharing my vision for WIFTV and the Canadian film industry as a whole is the way and it is already working.

3. (Okay, I guess I had 3 epiphanies) I am super wealthy and living the dream. Yesterday was a stunning Vancouver day and I got to take full

advantage of it. Sitting on a bench at Locarno, overlooking the ocean, I thought, 'This is all mine.' Everything I dream wealth will bring me, I already have. I get to spend sunny days at the beach.

Behind me, up on a hill, sits my dream house. Not the biggest or most lavish of the homes that line Marine Drive. It is a bungalow that needs some exterior work; a fixer-upper, just like me. I imagine it has an Earthy feel inside and seems to match the layout of the home in my visualizations. There is a balcony that overlooks the ocean and shares the view I have when I sit on that bench. The obscene oil tanks floating in the bay annoy me, though. *How dare they obstruct my view?*

I strolled through my *new* neighborhood. The address of my dream home is 4666. Elliot just pointed out the other day that whenever I make up math questions on the spot they work out to equal 666. He teases me I am the devil. I so own that house.

I got approved for a MasterCard! They told me at the bank. I was in shock. I applied a couple weeks ago, but deep down I didn't think I would get one until Carlos paid off the old one... which will take a couple years, I'm sure.

In a daze, I wandered out of the bank, down the street and into a consignment store. Standing between the racks, I started to cry, over a credit card. This symbolizes so much for me: independence, a clean financial slate, a fresh start, freedom.

My credit rating has been up and down my whole adult life. When I was 18, I signed a one-year membership at a gym. I only went once, but for some reason they still expected me to pay. Anyone who has had a collection agency after them knows the anxiety and apprehension of answering the phone. I hated that feeling, but by the time I was 20, I had numerous agencies after me. It took a few years to get my credit clean, but I did it. I was even able to lease a car.

When I was 25, at the peak of my quarter-life crisis, right after I left Matthew, I leased a brand new 1998 black Cavalier convertible. It was a gift to myself for getting my permanent contract in my first year of teaching. I loved that car.

I started dating Carlos two years later, in April 2000, and by that fall my credit was trashed. I'm not blaming him (anymore), it was my choice to take on two cell phone contracts, support two people on a waitress' income and not pay my taxes. By the time my lease was up that spring I was no longer credit-worthy, so we had to borrow money from my parents to buy a cheap used car.

Like most couples, money was the number one source of conflict between Carlos and I, but for us it was a symptom of a deeper issue of co-dependency. It also proved how being in a relationship derails me.

5:00 PM: I am so grateful I live in Vancouver. I resonate with this city perfectly. I think every city has its own vibration, which is why you can feel at home in a city you're just visiting, but like a complete stranger in the place you were born and raised. That's how I feel in Edmonton - like I was born in the wrong place.

8:00 PM: So, I'm driving home reflecting on what a genius I am - all these Inspired Ideas and epiphanies and such. I acknowledged I probably shouldn't share this revelation with anyone, when it donned on me: since thoughts are just energy, we are all capable of receiving them. We are all geniuses. Of course we are!

Then I started thinking about how geniuses are often thought of as crazy or are outcasts or even savant. I started thinking about Elliot and some other autistic youth I've worked with, when another epiphany hit. Maybe it's not that there is a biological, intellectual or genetic reason they are geniuses. Maybe it's because they do not have the social restrictions that limit their expression or experience of this genius.

Why am I able to then? Well, therein lies the *AHA*!

For over 2 years now, I have been in a somewhat self-induced autistic state, segregated and isolated from the social norm for most of my days. Really I don't have anyone on a day-to-day basis to answer to and never really have to censor myself. I realized when Celina was here how much I actually talk to myself out loud at home.

Living in countries where English is not the first language is when I think this first started, then continued with the puppies in Squamish. Carlos and I didn't spend a lot of time together at the end of our marriage and he was out of town quite a bit. I hung out alone a lot with only the puppies to talk to.

When I was bulimic, I could never be alone. If I was alone for over an hour, guaranteed I'd be binging and purging. Maybe one of the reasons is I couldn't handle all the thoughts, the energy of them. Maybe I couldn't handle my genius.

Anyways, the point is we're all geniuses if we allow the energy and ideas to express themselves through us without judgment. Einstein, da Vinci, Michelangelo, Jesus, Buddha, Beethoven... Conduits - all just channels of this infinite intelligence.

February 5, 2012

Super Bowl Sunday! My favorite day of the year! Please let New England lose.

That statement is bathed in negative energy, but I don't care. I fuckin' hate the Patriots.

It is bad enough that the first Super Bowl to ever be played in Indianapolis is the same year Peyton Manning is out with a neck injury. The Colts came in dead last because of it, when they were destined to go all the way. I swear if Bill Belichick and Tom Brady win the Super Bowl in Lucas Oil Stadium... the thought of their gloating faces... I can't even think about it.

They are playing the NY Giants, which could be sweet if it is a repeat of 2008, when the Giants produced one of the greatest upsets in Super Bowl history beating the 'undefeated' cheater-cheater pumpkin eaters (re: Spygate) in a Hollywood style ending.

Eli, this is your chance to redeem yourself after causing me to lose the winner Survivor pool. Make your brother, and me, proud.

I have been lying to myself about drinking and driving. I only had two beers last night, but they were pints of draft of which I have no idea the alcohol content. Plus I drank them on an empty stomach. Bottom line: if I feel hungover today, I should not have driven last night.

8:00 PM: I have so much to write about tonight, I don't know how I can get it out fast enough. To make a long story short, I was tired and slightly hungover this morning. When I got up, I was going to shower and get ready, but said, "screw it", put in pigtails and went to Grounds. I usually get ready to go there, ever since that first time I saw my coffee shop crush.

The last time he came for a visit was Thanksgiving Sunday four months ago. It was in the middle of the Vancouver International Film

Festival and I had gone to the Anniversary Gala the night before. I was working on only 2 hours of sleep and he was on day 8 of the Wild Rose Cleanse. I looked like death worn over; he was glowing radiant health. I haven't seen him since. Why was the last time I saw him when I looked like absolute shit? Coincidence?

Anyways, at 10 AM, I checked inkCanada Vancouver because there was a meet-up today at 10:30. InkCanada, the online screenwriting community where I did that mentorship with Karen Walton, has a Vancouver group that meets one Sunday morning a month for coffee. In Toronto, they meet on a Friday night for drinks. That says it all about the cities' cultural differences.

I had no intention of attending, so I'm not sure why I checked, but it showed Michele from the PW4 Workshop had replied she was going. *Shit, I should go. I'd like to connect with her, but I'm wearing pigtails and I promised myself I wouldn't wear pigtails to professional events anymore.*

Then at approximately 10:22 AM, I see my coffee shop crush cross the street to 7-Eleven. I knew it was him, because he was wearing his grey sweats and camouflage Edmonton Oilers hat. He is also the only person I know, besides me, who wears flip-flops in February.

I panicked. *Should I go accidentally bump into him?* I gathered my stuff, so if he came out with a coffee I would go, even though I was wearing pigtails and shaking like a leaf (nervousness and hungover-ness). He came out with just a newspaper, so I thought maybe he would come to Grounds for a coffee. I waited... and waited, but he never came. I was so bummed and then found it impossible to focus. I can't believe I have feelings for this guy. He is the only person who makes me nervous, him and Judi Dench.

I will not create an illusion. I will not create an illusion. I will not create an illusion...

At about 11 AM, who walks in? Michele! She got the dates mixed up for inkCanada and went yesterday instead. In-FRICKEN-sane! She lives in the neighborhood.

I realized I've been wishy-washy around my feelings for my crush and so that has been what the Universe has brought me. No more sabotage. My doubts and fears are resistance. I'm spending this week EFT'ing all 'dating' resistance. It is so beautiful how I felt when I saw him. It's been so long. I've been searching to have these feelings for someone when I already do.

AND the Giants beat the Patriots! A glorious day indeed.

February 6, 2012

I woke up feeling groggy and down. It is crazy how much drinking and eating like crap affects me. It's even crazier it still surprises me.

I had a solo-celebration because the Giants beat the Patriots. I watched the game at a pub with Christine, her boyfriend, Craig, and their friends Tom and Tawnya, who I know from my acting days. I didn't drink, because I had to drive, but when I got home, the party began.

Insanity: doing the same thing over and over again and expecting different results.

- Albert Einstein

I dragged my ass out of bed and onto my yoga mat. I hate doing yoga feeling like crap, but I wanted my body to know that I love it and I am not going to abuse it anymore.

Does it believe me? How could it possibly?

This week is all about clearing resistance. The only reason I do not have my desires is because I am resisting them on an energetic level.

No problem can be solved from the same level of consciousness that created it.

- Albert Einstein

I need to raise my consciousness.

I want to start dating. I want to date my coffee shop crush. All my visualizations about my soul mate have his face. I assumed it was because he's the only guy I've been attracted to in years, but maybe there's more to him. Regardless, the picture is always in the future. The resistance arises when I think of it happening now.

I watched Debbie Ford's *Shadow Process* DVD. This idea of our shadows is quite fascinating. Not sure I totally get it, but basically the shadow is our dark side, the parts of ourselves we judge and even hate. When we shun theses parts they rebel and are the cause of self-sabotage. The things we judge in others are our shadows reflected back at us. We also have light-shadows, which are the masks we wear to cover our shadows.

What is my shadow? Hypocritically and mask-wise I would say it is my health. I have created this mask of a healthy person. I also judge people who don't take care of themselves, so I guess this is a shadow.

<u>February 7, 2012</u>
  Elliot: Today's your cousin's birthday.
  Me: Which cousin?
  Elliot: Your double-cousin, the one that looks like April 23rd.
  Me: You mean Janelle.
  Elliot: Who does July 11th look like?
  Me: Tracy looks like their mom, my Auntie Diane.
  Elliot: Who do you look like?
  Rachelle: All of them, but I'm most like my Uncle Sheldon. We're both arguers.
  Elliot: You don't argue.
  Rachelle: You didn't know me when I was young.
  Elliot: How are you alike now?
  Rachelle: We both love to laugh and drink beer. Can we do some math?

  Later: I started another resistance clearing process: the Sedona method. I can't believe the feelings that came up with the words 'dating' and 'relationship', especially when I say "NOW".

  It's like when it is in the future, I can handle it, but in the now, pure fear. Fears that I'm not ready, that I'm going to get off track or lose my independence - a whole bunch of shit from the past. I know I am ready.

  My intuition tells me my crush is possibly, as far as I know him and what I feel for him, the one. That's right, I think my coffee shop crush is my Soul Mate.

  I want to date him. Even just writing this though, anxiety is arising.

  The Sedona Method is pretty simple. Just a few questions you ask yourself when a negative emotion arises.

  Could I let go of this fear? *I am not this fear. It is just a tool I've used to protect myself while I healed. I could let this fear go. Yes, I could release it!*

  Would I let go of this fear? *Yes, I love myself. No matter what happens, I will love and care for myself. Yes I would let go of this fear to experience all that love has to offer!*

41

When? *Now! It's released. I am free. I'm free to go on a date!*

I am also still doing EFT with Brad Yates on YouTube. I did a couple rounds around dating resistance and it was very intense. Not sure why, but then I did one on being loved and the floodgates have burst open. I bawled through the first two round. This is an amazing gift.

My 3rd round was better, but it's going to take a few I'm sure.

February 10, 2012

I love my morning coffee. I love my life. It is awesome to feel this way, but being too attached can cause me to get stuck. I am open to all the love and abundance the Universe has to offer. I embrace change. I embrace expansion. Great things have always come to me when I looked fear in the face, thanked it, loved it and let it go. It is just coming from a place of misguided protection. My life is stress-free and it doesn't want me to get unhealthy, which has always happened when I was in a relationship.

Thank you, Fear, for trying to protect me, but I am strong and healthy and I love myself. I promise that no matter what anyone says or does to me, I will love and care for myself.

Later: The washroom to my basement suite is separate from the main suite. In between is where I store all my shit like boxes, luggage, etc. - a real eyesore. A few months ago I sewed together a giant bright yellow scarf to an indigo blue one, both of which I got in India. I hung the massive curtain in front of this area to hide the clutter. The yellow reminds me of sunshine, and the blue of the ocean. While I am, uh, going to the washroom, I often leave the door open so I can enjoy the 'view'.

Today, there was a Wolf spider hanging out in my sunshine.

I freaked. I usually try to trap a spider and set it free, but Wolf spiders are big and hairy and vicious - like wolves. The last time I saw one was a year ago. It was lurking in the corner of my suite, but by the time I got back with a shoe, it was gone. I obsessed for days; wearing hiking boots constantly and sleeping under the covers, tucked in like a mummy.

This time, I kept my eyes on the sucker the whole time. I grabbed a shoe and batted it. There is nothing behind the curtain up that high, so my shoe pushed through and the spider went flying. I'm a physics teacher, but for some reason commonsense goes out the window when I panic. I have no idea where it flew since by this time I was on the floor.

Now I'm freaking out because the door to my suite was open... *FUCK!*

Later: Christine and I are going to a party at Erik's and I really want to cancel. It's gross out and I just want to do my thing. It's a Friday night though, so I should go. Take another street.

I'm also obsessing about the Wolf spider. *Where the fuck could it be?*

Plus, I don't want to cancel on Christine or Erik. This is the first time I'm doing something social with Erik. Our friendship is finally extending beyond Grounds.

Have I mentioned Erik yet? About a year and a half ago, it was super busy at the coffee shop. I was deep in my writing, and my fog, so didn't really notice how busy until I heard a voice in my ear, "Hey there."

I looked up and here's this grinning guy leaning against the shelf next to me holding a tiny espresso mug. For a moment I thought I was in a bar. There were no open seats, so he chatted my ear off for 20 minutes. We've been friends ever since. He didn't give me a choice.

Erik comes to Grounds to read the business sections. I'm not sure what he does or where he got his money - real estate or oil or something else I don't approve of. He's pretty much retired from whatever it is. He's in his mid-forties, but I thought he was in his 30's. He is very youthful. He travels and skis and surfs and I live vicariously through him.

We have an interesting relationship because we like each other, but don't agree on much.

Erik is having a birthday party for his friend. I really don't want to go because he is trying to set me up with the guy even though I told him I'm not interested. Partly because the guy's a lawyer, partly because he's turning 50 (I know I'm being a hypocrite about age) and partly because Erik thinks I need a sugar daddy. Man, he pisses me off sometimes.

I want to see his house though. He's my first friend who owns a house in Vancouver.

Later: Turns out I killed that spider. It had flown onto my jacket, which was hanging nearby. I grabbed it on my way out and the little arachna-corpse fell to the ground. If I wouldn't have gone to the party, I wouldn't have found it and I would've obsessed all night.

Maybe taking a different street *can* lead me to freedom.

The party was fun. Christine and I didn't know anyone, but Erik was the perfect host. His house is cool, of course. He has a huge painting in his living room of Jeff Bridges from *The Big Lebowski*, as 'The Dude'. He's such a dude.

February 11, 2012

I had a dream of Oprah. I told her about my book and she said she couldn't wait to read it. She promised to include it in her book club. *Does she still have a book club?*

6:48 PM: I had quite the emotional afternoon. I got home after writing and tried to meditate. It made me tense because I was planning to visualize manifesting my soul mate. I realized this was just more resistance, so I EFT'd. I couldn't believe the emotions that came up. Resistance to love, being in love... I did four rounds, had some lunch, listened to a webinar on EFT, which talked about letting go. I had a little rest while listening and then fell into a light nap. Then I woke up and EFT'd some more, asking the question, "What am I really afraid of?"

The answer that keeps coming up is that, deep down, I don't believe I can be in a healthy relationship. I have never, in my whole life, been in a healthy romantic relationship. It is hard to admit that, having been married twice. I know that to be in a healthy relationship, you have to first be in a healthy relationship with yourself. I am trying. I really am.

I attract healthy, loving, respectful, relationships.

The truth is I'm scared of myself. I am scared I will get off track or lose my mind. That I will once again, be lying on a bathroom floor wanting to rip my face off through the tears. I'm scared I will go to that crazy place where I lose control. Where I lose myself. Where I give my power to someone else. Where the only way I can look at myself in the mirror is to tell myself how fucking stupid I am.

It is not men rejecting me I fear, it is what I will say and do to myself when they do. What I will make it mean about me and mostly, the self-abuse that will ensue.

I am scared I will reject myself after spending two years trying desperately to accept myself. Fear is the absence of love. I am not that reject on the bathroom floor. I love myself and I am kind to myself. I just realized why I have yellow above my eyes and dark circles underneath them... I have created this unsightliness so that I won't let people look into my eyes.

Later: Whitney Houston died today at the young age of 48.

She once said, "The biggest devil is me. I'm either my best friend or my worst enemy."

I want to be my best friend. That is what this is about. I love you Whitney.

The Greatest Love of ALLLL....

Heart Wall Come Crumblin', Crumblin'

February 12, 2012

I had a beautiful night last night. I never drank, had a long shower, a healthy meal, painted my nails, watched *Father of the Bride 2* and was my best friend.

Going to bed, I just wanted to be with my own loving thoughts. No meditation or CD's with subliminal messages. I've never done that before, falling asleep just loving myself. Breathing. *I love myself.* Beautiful. Each time I awoke, I thought, "I love you", and gently fell back asleep. I've been trying to control the physical world. Hoping, wanting, wishing. I let go of that. I let go and just loved myself. I loved myself to sleep.

8:00 PM: I went to see *The Artist* today. Amazing. At the end, I thought, "Oh, how sad someone's pride could hold them back from a great life and a great love." Then it hit me. I never thought my pride could ever hold me back, especially after years of having pride in having "no pride". But it has. Not wanting to look like a fool, not wanting to be seen as a twice-divorcée-cougar prowling for love again, has held me back.

This is the power of great story, of great film. During the closing credits, I sat there in the dark and just felt grateful to the filmmaker. I actually whispered, "Thank you."

February 14, 2012

Happy Valentine's Day!

Many people are lonely today because they are not with a partner. Dr. Pez always said, "There is a difference between loneliness and being alone." I'm starting to see the difference.

Don't get me wrong, I would love to have some physical contact with someone, but trust me, there is nothing lonelier or more inauthentic to your soul than having sex or being touched by someone you don't love. It's even worse when you don't particularly like them. Some of the loneliest times of my life were when I was in a relationship... and being touched.

February 16, 2012

One of my students cancelled all her sessions; well her mother did. She's only in grade four. I know it's because I've called the mom out on a couple of things, like her daughter being exhausted and not doing the homework, but to be honest, I'm relieved. The daughter and I had fun, but it was a struggle not to let my frustrations with her mom spill in.

I know, I know, I've never had a child, so what do I know? I know kids. I don't think parents adequately fathom their influence. This is actually *why* I'm not a parent. I think I take it so seriously I wouldn't do it unless I was 100% sure... and over all my own shit first.

February 18, 2012

I'm reading a book called *The Emotion Code* and my mind is officially being blown. I almost finished it in one sitting. The author, Dr. Bradley Nelson, was a chiropractor who realized most physical and emotional pain is caused by trapped emotions - negative emotions that have been suppressed. He devised a method by which we can identify these trapped emotions using muscle testing and then releasing them. I was introduced to muscle testing years ago when I read the book *Power vs. Force*. I still have that book on my shelf. I should read it again some time.

This resonates with me on such a profound level. I know I have trapped emotions, how could I not? Bulimia is all about suppressing emotions. I swear I didn't process one emotion for ten years. Whether I was anxious or excited, I binged and purged. Drinking copious amounts in my teens, self-medicating as an adult, I've been trapping emotions for decades!

It's not just for physical illness, but mental as well; anything that holds you back and keeps you vibrating at low energy levels.

There are 60 possible emotions ranging from guilt to shame to unworthy to fear to disgust... Yep, got 'em all. Dr. Nelson has organized them into a chart with two columns and six rows, so by asking questions about where the emotion is located in the chart you can narrow it down to five within seconds.

Once you identify which of the final five it is, you ask, "Is there anything else I need to know about this trapped emotion?" Then you continue asking questions, like when it was trapped or who was involved. Often it will bring you to the exact event when it was trapped. Then you run a magnet over your head along the main meridian three times while repeating, "I release this trapped emotion."

The muscle testing can be done a variety of ways. It follows the idea that positivity (truth, love) makes our body strong, and negativity (lies, hatred) makes it go weak, the same with things that are healthy for us or not.

You can do it with a partner where one of you holds your arm straight out while the other presses down lightly on the extended wrist. If the person lies or thinks negatively, the arm will go weak. I am learning to do it on myself using my pointer finger on my right hand. I extend it and when I tell the truth or think loving thoughts, it stays strong, when I lie or think negative thoughts, it goes weak. It's hard, though, because I don't trust myself. I believe it on an intellectual level, but of course have doubts in my ability to execute.

I'm overwhelmed with all the information that is flooding my life, but I'm going with it. I asked the Universe to provide me with whatever I needed in order to create the Best Year of My Life and it is throwing me everything it's got. It's up to me to sort through what resonates and what doesn't.

Imagine if I could not only unblock myself, but friends, family and others of trapped emotions that are holding them back and causing them pain!

Later: I'm watching a one-hour Whitney Houston special on *20/20*.

Never judge. Some people go through hell and make choices that if we look upon with love and compassion can warn us of our own path. The clips of her singing horribly, raspy and out-of-tune after years of self-abuse... so sad. She believed her voice was a God-given talent and I think that overwhelmed her. She didn't feel she earned it, so sabotaged it. Some people might ask how she could ruin such a miraculous gift, but that's what you do when you don't feel you deserve something. It's not a lack of gratitude; it's a lack of self-worth.

Some of God's greatest gifts are unanswered prayers. If my dreams of fame and fortune would've been granted when I was at the peak of my self-abuse and depths of unworthiness, well, let's just say I can see parts of myself in Whitney Houston's story.

5:00 PM: I just checked my email and had a message from the Female Eye Film Festival. My first thought was, "Oh well, I guess I didn't get in." This defeatist assumption surprised me. Turns out it was confusion on their part with the submission and they'll get back to me. I guess I still have a lot of success blocks to release after all.

February 19, 2012

Oh my God, I'm freaking out. I've been up since 5:30 AM, but feel light and free. I did the Emotion Code on myself asking if there were trapped emotions around me not being with my soul mate. It brought me back to the time Carlos called me a 'cunt'.

It was when we lived in Kelowna. We had only been married for about two months. Lying in bed snuggling and chatting, the conversation was amorous. That is until the subject of money came up. I made a comment about him as a filmmaker. I honestly can't remember what I said, but his eyes shot a dagger through my heart, "You can be such a cunt."

I was on the bathroom floor crying in two seconds flat. The anger, humiliation, and heartache of being called that word, by my new husband, were overwhelming. I hated him, yes, but more so myself for marrying someone who would hurt me like that on the turn of a dime.

I looked at myself in the mirror, "You are such a fucking loser."

For the past ten years, whenever I think about that morning, that moment, I go right back there and relive it like it was yesterday. Instantaneous rage and shame, but The Emotion Code process has changed all that.

Magnet in hand, facing the chart, I kept asking, "Do I have a trapped emotion around this event?" One by one, each emotion bubbled to the surface. I felt it. I actually re-felt the emotion, and released it. The bizarre thing is that now when I think about the event, there is no emotional charge to it anymore. I try to relive it, but there is nothing but details, like it is a scene from a movie. I still don't like that this happened, but I'm not crying.

The other powerful thing is my mind has opened up to a new perspective of the event. I don't remember what I said to trigger Carlos, but I'm sure he does. Maybe what I said was equally hurtful. Words are powerful, but the energy we give them is personal. Maybe I blocked out what I said because I wanted to hang on to my part of the story, onto being the victim.

I desperately wanted him to apologize, but he never did. He said he wasn't sorry, he meant it. Yet I just realized, he never, *ever*, called me a cunt again. In fact, two years later a friend lent me the book *Cunt: A Declaration of Independence*, which is all about women regaining the word (perhaps originating from the Hindu Goddess Kunti) as well as our power; Carlos agreed with the book. Maybe he called me a cunt that morning because he felt vulnerable. Maybe he hated that I had the power to hurt him and he counter-attacked.

The word still bothers me, maybe because I still fear my power.

The potential of The Emotion Code has taken over my thoughts. It proves what I have thought for a long time around the source of illness, especially mental illnesses. *Why is this not known?* Because there is no money in it. If people realized they could heal themselves it would be the end of Western medicine and pharmaceutical companies. Western doctors go to school to study medicine, not health. Pharmaceuticals mask the pain and rob people of discovering the cause. *Dis*-ease is the physical body's way of communicating there is something wrong mentally, emotionally and/or spiritually. Drugs silence the message, they may even get rid of the symptom, but the physical will just manifest it in another way until it is heard.

I have to teach people how to do this. I wonder if I could become certified... *No!* Getting distracted is just another way of self-sabotage. I know my passion and purpose.

I'm going to write it out just to show how obviously silly it is.

I don't want to be a writer anymore. I want to be an energy healer.

Ha. Ridiculous.

Later: Shame, shame go away, come back another day! No. Actually don't.

I just did the Emotion Code and 10 'shames' and a half dozen 'guilts' came up all around my DUI. I got it one week before my 18th birthday, which I am lucky for as I would've been an adult then and had a criminal record for life. Of course, I'm even more grateful I didn't hurt anyone. I wasn't just tipsy... I was plastered. Jen and another friend were in the car with me when I was pulled over on an overpass in Edmonton coming home from the bar, by our high school constable, no less. Bizarre. This was when Nicole, Jen and I all lived together the year after graduation, but had gone back for upgrading.

After the charges were laid, I took off from the police station before my parents arrived. They went to the coach home to find me, but only Nicole was there. I had already taken off to the next party, you see. Poor Nicole. It must've been such a joy living with me.

February 20, 2012

I have discovered I have a Heart Wall. Sometimes trapped emotions can accumulate and create a wall around your heart. Sometimes the wall can be paper thin, but often it can be inches, feet or miles thick. It can be made out of any kind of 'material' such as wood or plaster. I have a feeling mine is brick.

I'm releasing the emotions trapped in my Heart Wall and, holy shit, there is a lot of them! Mostly from when I was young, which surprises me because I assumed it was created because of my divorces. Maybe the reason for the divorces is because I got married with a Heart Wall.

Some of the events that trapped numerous emotions, mostly 'shame' and 'heartache', were not surprising. Especially, the first three times I had sex:

Time #1: Losing my virginity at 14 to my friend's older brother in the backseat of his friend's car, which was parked in a back alley. Wasted, I didn't remember a thing, so it was easy to deny the rumors that spread on Monday. Even though the friend had 'physical evidence' that some girl had lost her virginity there. "It wasn't me." was my mantra my whole Grade 10 year.

Time #2: New Year's Eve at 16 with a guy I really liked. It was his first time and, even though we were wasted, I was so flattered he wanted to share the experience with me. A couple days later, he came to my house to talk. My face beamed as I watched him walk up the front step carrying a huge bouquet of flowers. Turns out his girlfriend had found out (the flowers were for her) and he was wondering if I would mind denying it. "Of course not." I was used to it.

Time #3: A couple weeks later, I actually had a boyfriend. Only problem was he was the town slut and also good friends with Time #2. One night at a house party, after dating for two days, we were up in a bedroom. I told him I wanted to wait. He was hurt. *How could I have sex with Time #2, but not him, my actual boyfriend?* Wasted, I gave in. I cried the whole time. He asked me to stop, but I couldn't. Apparently, neither could he. He broke up with me the next day. I guess he just wanted some competition for the title of town slut.

<u>February 21, 2012</u>

I just had a very intense EC session. Dozens of emotions trapped in my Heart Wall from when I was 25. This was when I left Matthew, so I assumed they were about that, but they were 'shock' and 'grief'. I asked more questions and it turns out they were trapped when Noah, the son of dear family friends, died in a tragic accident all those years ago.

Noah was in college, in love, had his whole life ahead of him... the phone call, the emergency room, the funeral, the years to follow... So many people loved Noah. I can't be the only one with trapped emotions.

February 22, 2013

My Heart Wall is shrinking. When I started, it was three feet thick. I periodically check and it is decreasing inch by inch. It's made of linoleum. Such a bizarre material for a wall, but while I was meditating I was brought to the kitchen floor in our house in Argyll, a south side neighborhood of Edmonton. It was one of those cookie-cutter bungalows they built in the 60's. I think we moved there when I was about four and lived there up until moving to Beaumont at the end of Grade 9.

I was tracing the swirl pattern on the floor with my finger. I was crying, not sure why. I was a crybaby as a kid, but always found the floor comforting. *What is it with me and floors?*

One shocking thing that came up was 'sadness' around Carlos because I thought he cheated on me when I was in India. The question popped out of my mouth without thinking. I didn't even know I suspected this, or maybe I wouldn't let myself consider it consciously.

1:48 PM: I can't stop crying.

After hours and hours of Emotion Coding hundreds of emotions, I just removed the last one from my Heart Wall. I can't even remember what it was. I knew I was getting close because I could feel my heart pushing on my ribcage. I felt like the Grinch when all the Whos in Whoville began to sing - my heart was expanding... exponentially.

Covered in goosebumps, I was shaky and lightheaded, but was guided by some, I don't know... knowing. I just kept releasing until, all of a sudden, the linoleum split. Metaphorically and energetically, my chest *cracked* open and a surge of energy burst through.

Love radiated out.

My heart, which had been hiding in the dark for decades, became the light.

The only way I can describe it is like my heart was having an orgasm.

Holy shit. That was the most surreal, cathartic ten minutes of my life.

February 23, 2012

Happy birthday, Erin!

I can't believe it was 8 years ago that my first little niece was born. We were living in Korea at the time, so I didn't get to meet her for another seven months, which was weird because she already had this incredibly independent personality by then. I hope she never loses it.

Bizarre Daydreams

February 24, 2012

I've always been uncomfortable with my appearances. I think I look decent from afar, but am afraid if someone looks at me close-up, or for too long, they will see all my flaws and not think I'm attractive anymore. How could they?

I'm trying hard to let go of this. Love sees, love knows. We are so much more than the sum of our parts. I am so much more beautiful than the sum of my parts. Imperfection is beautiful. Our quirks and flaws and uniqueness are what make our beauty. I'm grateful to Carlos, Matthew and all those men who focused on my flaws. I know I was just projecting my own judgment on them. They were just pointing out what I already hated.

My looks have also been linked to achievement. When I first lost weight, I would wake up in the middle of the night in a panic at the thought of getting fat again. I went from 145 lbs to 115 lbs in three months and the attention I received was addictive. I wanted to keep losing weight, so I could keep getting attention. If I ever actually GAINED a pound, it would be a devastating failure.

Losing was winning; gaining was losing.

February 25, 2012

I need sleep. Deep, healthy, restful sleep.

6:30 PM: Incredibly emotionally draining day of releasing emotions. Shame, worthlessness, self-abuse - dozens of emotions around dozens of one-night stands.

Being tossed off a bed, naked, by a guy I was trying to seduce at a party when I was 17. It was dark in his room and I couldn't find where I had dropped my clothes, so I hid in the closet praying he would fall back asleep. *How could he though, with me blubbering?*

Very gently he spoke, "Rachelle. Please come out."

Mortified, I did. He tried to make me feel better, but I just got dressed, told him to fuck off and went upstairs to get wasted with the rest of the gang.

Then there was my prostitution proposition in Grade 12, when the guy I had liked for months invited me to go to Calgary with him... Just for the night, of course. We were in the basement of Malone's, the bar Jen and I had become the stars of, and he was cozying up to me in a dark corner. He had a girlfriend, but that never stopped me. I liked him first.

He seemed to reciprocate the feelings, whispering in my ear, "You're so hot."

I was smitten.

"Other guys find you hot, too. We could make a lot of money."

I considered it. I was actually flattered he thought I would make a good hooker; that men would pay their hard-earned dollar to be with me.

Just when I think I'm ready to start dating, I discover more layers of shit to release. I am starting to think all I am is trapped emotions. *What if I release them all and I disintegrate?*

I'm also a little concerned I am using this as just another form of escape. Sitting in my basement suite, EFT'ing and EC'ing my nights away.

No. I'm not hiding; I'm healing. These trapped emotions are holding me back and have wreaked havoc in my life.

I had another bizarre little daydream starring my four parts:

Spiritual blurted, "I need help! She's meant for great things. I have all these Inspired Ideas for her, but she can't hear me. Can I get some back-up here, Mental?"

Mental replied, "Don't look at me. I've been holding things together for 39 years, and trust me, it ain't been easy. It's Emotional who won't let go of the past."

Spiritual, "Yeah, Emotional. You're supposed to be *Energy in Motion.* Get moving."

Emotional, "Hey, I'd love to flow, but I'm stuck in Physical."

Physical, "I know! She's being suppressing you for so long, I don't know how to let go."

Emotion Code flies in, "Here I come to save the day!"

Okay, I *really* need some sleep.

February 26, 2012

I need a day of fun and frivolousness - writing, hiking, the Oscars and fun, fun, fun in between. I've been taking life, and this process, way too seriously. I need to care for myself and be gentle and compassionate. The pain and memories I've recalled would've triggered a bulimic binge a few years ago. I'm proud of myself for how courageous I am for working through all of this.

7:30 PM: I have been on a roller coaster of emotions this weekend. This clearing is kicking my ass. Reminds me of the Vipassana Retreat I went on years ago.

I never realized how much shit I have carried from my past relationships in the form of trapped emotions. It's exhausting because I'm reliving every horrible fight I had with each of my husbands. The gift is that once the emotion is released, I can think about those events and there are no negative feelings around them. I can't even imagine the harm they've wreaked on the subconscious level, let alone the cellular. I think I am preemptively curing myself of cancer.

I can't believe I just discovered the Emotion Code a week ago. What a week! It feels like open-heart surgery at times. I have literally released hundreds and hundreds of emotions. Revisited events I never even knew affected me until the moment of release. I have to help people learn about this. I am so grateful that I'm only 39 and I know one of my purposes is to help empower people to heal themselves of emotional pain. And deep down, on an energetic level, all pain is caused by emotional pain.

Up until now I have been playing lip service to loving myself; sugar-coating the reality in the form of positive affirmations. I knew I wanted to love myself. I knew I wanted to spread positivity, but it was all so much effort. I feel light now. This time is precious to me. I would not be able to do this work if I was working full-time or in a relationship.

February 27, 2012

I got drunk by myself last night. Had my own little Oscar party. I pigged out, too. I feel like crap today and since I'm already emotionally vulnerable, it is no wonder. I'm trying not to judge myself. I know this is my own form of self-sabotage. It's just so frustrating. Even though I know full well while I'm eating and drinking I am being self-destructive, I do it anyways.

I don't think I should drink for a while. No. I'm not going to drink while I'm doing this emotional cleansing and releasing. It's not fair to my body or mind or soul and to be honest, it's quite dangerous. I ate so much last night when I went to bed I felt sick. *Yeah, very dangerous.*

I have a choice: use this as an opportunity to beat myself up or look deeper and figure out what's really going on. In only a few weeks, I have released toxic emotions I trapped over decades, but still not learned how to properly process emotions. I don't want to do all this work releasing emotions only to be continuously trapping more. Drinking by myself and pigging out is just a way of numbing all I'm uncomfortable with. This old stuff is being brought up and let out, which is important, but I have to be brave and be present through the whole process.

While I was watching the Oscars, I started killing myself laughing. I'm sitting here in my basement suite when I should be there. It's ridiculous I'm not. I'm living an existence smaller than my spirit wants. I have visions and dreams for a reason and I'm going after them.

I read an article about Evan Goldberg and the hours he and Seth Rogen put in writing. This is it. I want to live my life's passion. I need to do this full-time. No more part-time writing. I got to get out of this slump. I am a writer. So write!

February 28, 2012

It's Mom and Dad's 42nd Anniversary. It blows my mind they have been married for 42 years when they barely knew each other. I'm ashamed to say that growing up I had complete disrespect for them and their marriage. I am dedicating today to them. I will live this day in complete awe of the commitment they have made to each other and gratitude for their success.

February 29, 2012

Leap Year! I'm so grateful that the Best Year of My Life has an extra day!

I want to slow this down. I'm a caterpillar emerging into a butterfly and I want to savor every moment - the gross and the glorious. That's how EC'ing feels, like I am shedding the caterpillar skin that has kept me stuck in a caterpillar existence.

Martha and Kayla

March 2, 2012

How can a certain date feel like it weighs a million tons?

Two years ago today, the girls passed away. It was a Tuesday. Bryce called us into the meeting room at 4 o'clock. Dave sat next to him with a blank look on his face. Martha and Kayla had been absent, but missing a day of school was usually no call for alarm with our youth.

Bryce began, "It seems, uh, Martha was out drinking last night."

My mind started to wander, thinking Martha must've gotten kicked out of her foster home. Her and I had connected over the past couple months, which was a shock to both of us. Just before Christmas, she had threatened to hit me if I didn't leave her alone. I had been trying to *encourage* her to get some science work done, which she read as nagging. I never actually felt in danger, she was just frustrated, but creating a 'safe, nurturing, respectful' community was what the Youth Futures program was based on. She was asked to take a day or two to reflect and told she couldn't start back until her and I had done a one-to-one.

I picked her up at her foster home the next morning and we went for coffee.

As we drove, she barely spoke except to ask when she would get to come back to school. Most of the youth wanted to be there. If there is one thing they taught me, it was how much education provides hope. When I was a teenager, graduating was a given, but for these youth, graduating was a dream. One that takes more commitment and sacrifice than we of privilege can ever imagine. A measure of how our youth were doing in their personal lives could often be calculated by looking at the attendance form.

Martha was an extremely bright girl and her confidence intimidated me, but that morning I mustered my own, "We have to talk about what happened."

She snickered, "It was just a joke."

"I know, but I deserve to feel safe when I come to work."

She stared at me for a moment and nodded, "Okay."

I would like to say we were close from that moment on, but ours was a relationship in progress. There were ups and downs, but I knew I had cracked in a bit when we were planning off-site small group programming one day and her and a newer student, Kayla, her best friend from the outside world, wanted to hang out with me.

We got manicures and ate lunch at Swiss Chalet.

Martha and Kayla both had the special: Open-faced roast chicken sandwiches.

"Soggy bread and gravy?" I teased, "That's something my dad would order."

They teased me how gullible I was for giving my keys to the *Swiss Chalet* 'Valet', pointing out the window at a blue Yaris just like mine driving by. They laughed hysterically.

On the way back to school, Martha leaned forward from the backseat so both Kayla and I could hear her, "I don't want to drink so much anymore."

Kayla sighed, "Me, too."

I shared my own struggles with teen drinking; actually some pretty personal stuff. They were surprised. The youth were usually shocked when they discovered I was not some sheltered, naïve, *Blondie from the 'Burbs.*

"Hardest part is finding things to do that don't involve drinking. I get it, it sounds so simple, but when Friday night comes, it seems like there are no other options."

They nodded. We brainstormed options. You teach what you most need to learn.

"Martha didn't make it."

I snapped out of my daydream. Bryce had tears in his eyes; Dave's were bright red.

"What?" Do you know what complete and utter disbelief feels like? Like your head is about to explode. Like you want to rewind existence. Rewind to the moment before to make sure you heard incorrectly. To rewind to a time where you could stop the events from unfolding at all.

Melissa, Scott, Mike, we were all in shock. I did what I did best. I cried and cried and cried. I didn't care one fuck I was at work and probably should have tried to act professional. I think on some level I thought if I kept crying someone would tell me it wasn't true.

Mike grabbed my hand and held it in his. I let him. I remember thinking, "I'm letting him hold my hand. This is the most tender moment I have ever shared with a male."

Martha had been drinking at a house party in Richmond and gone to bed alone. Hours later her friends couldn't wake her up and called the ambulance, but she was already gone.

I was pissed. We had just had a guest speaker come talk about this - not letting friends go to a room and pass out alone. *Was Kayla there?* Oh my God, Kayla. She's going to lose it.

How are we going to tell the youth? At the time there were only 13 youth in the program, now 11... this was going to be devastating. We came up with a support plan then I drove to the beach. I parked and sat in my car for about an hour. I looked out over the ocean and asked the question everyone asks when a young person dies, "Why?"

I asked one more, "Why Martha and not me?"

Don't be so selfish. This isn't about you. Your job is to be there for the youth. You have to be strong for Kayla and the other youth.

My cell rang. It was Bryce. He asked how I was doing. He asked if I was sitting down.

"Yeah, I'm in my car at the beach."

He whispered, "Kayla's gone, too."

The first thought that entered my mind was she killed herself. Her best friend had died and she couldn't handle it. Nope. Kayla had been found passed out on a street in Burnaby hours before Martha was found.

The next few days are a blur. The rumors surrounding the night ran rampant, in the school, in the media... on Facebook. Who they were with, what they had consumed, how Martha died in Richmond and Kayla in Burnaby... so much confusion.

I lost all boundaries with the youth, answering texts and phone calls at all hours.

I lost all boundaries with myself. Each night glued to the 'In Memory of Martha & Kayla' Facebook page... and a bottle of wine.

Both girls were aboriginal, so that Friday we invited an elder along with some other members from the community to do a healing circle. Having a large First Nations population in the program, this was not the first healing circle I had been to, but it was my first memorial one.

For many of the youth it was old hat.

I snuck away. No, I ran away. I ran down the street to the park. I barely made it before having what I think was a nervous breakdown. Bawling and shaking and convulsing, I literally wanted to crawl out of my life.

I called Dr. Pez. I had his number in my phone because I had tried to contact him a week earlier. It had been a few years since I stopped seeing him, but I didn't feel like I was handling the breakup with Carlos very well. I had left a message, but he never got back to me.

I left another message. He must have sensed the desperation because he called me right back and made an appointment for Monday morning.

The promise of that appointment got me through the longest weekend of my life.

I thought we would talk about the girls and how to deal with the tragedy, but he steered the conversation to me. I didn't want to talk about me. I wanted to talk about the girls.

"Nothing has happened to me."

Dr. Pez gave me a glance, "We are all connected."

I didn't want to be connected. After Carlos and I broke up, I hid in my writing and work. Now my work was gone. Working in a place that was supposed to be 'safe' was killing me.

Anyone who knows me knows my feelings about pharmaceuticals, so will understand that when he offered me anti-anxiety pills, I snapped, "I don't want drugs."

"The amount of stress your body is under can be dangerous."

I nodded. Another student had recently had a panic attack that caused her to pop blood vessels in her face.

"Take half a pill to sleep and a quarter if you know it is going to be an upsetting day."

With two funerals coming up, I accepted.

On my way out, he put his hand on my shoulder, "I'm sorry you're going through such a hard time, Rachelle."

A hard *time*. The compassion and wisdom in that statement breathed a sliver of hope.

Kayla's funeral was on Thursday. The church was packed. I felt like an intruder.

Her best friend should be here, but no, we'll be going to her funeral tomorrow.

I had taken a quarter of a pill in the morning and another at noon. By the evening, I thought it would be okay to have some wine. I woke up at 6 AM and puked my guts out. I crawled back to bed and woke up at noon when Melissa called to find out where I was. She was on her way to Martha's funeral and we were supposed to meet at the Skytrain. I told her I was sick, which was true. After I hung up, I dragged myself to the bathroom to dry heave some more, then passed out for another five hours. I probably should've told Melissa the truth or called a doctor.

I know what a drug overdose feels like, but I didn't want to overshadow the girls.

Bullshit. I was embarrassed. I missed Martha's funeral, and could've died, because I couldn't go one night without drinking.

March 3, 2012

I feel so negative today. If I'm honest, I have been feeling negative a lot lately. I feel like I could go into full-on self-destructive mode. I feel like I shouldn't be around people, but being alone is dangerous, because all I want to do is eat and drink. Like BINGE eat.

What is the opposite of self-destructive? *Self-love.* Okay that's the secret. Today is a day of self-love and love for every person I come into contact with.

March 4, 2012

I had a very healthy night last night. I stayed home and watched *Inside Man* and had Taco Salad. It was good. I did lots of clearing and started reading *The Law of Emergence.* It's an ebook written by this guy, Derek Rydall. He was on the same healing webinar series where I first heard Dr. Nelson talk about *The Emotion Code.* I have been listening to a lot of them lately. The Universe is throwing me many options and I am picking the ones that resonate with me the most.

I like the metaphors Derek uses: I am an acorn breaking out of its shell, a caterpillar from its cocoon. It's easy when I let it naturally happen. I love myself. I care for myself.

I released some major trapped emotions about Kayla and Martha. No wonder I have felt down these past couple of days. I did this time last year, too.

When they passed away, I promised I would tell their story. Two teen aboriginal girls dying of drug overdoses under shady circumstances - I couldn't let their deaths be another forgotten 'unfortunate event in a tragic history'.

The guy, a Caucasian male, whose house Martha and Kayla were partying at, and where Martha died, was a convicted sex offender who targeted teen aboriginal girls. After the girls' death, a woman came forward to say how weeks earlier she had seen him (he and his deeds are well known in the community) at Broadway and Commercial (a popular hangout for this population of youth) with a young First Nations girl. She called the police, but they said there was nothing they could do until he committed a crime.

I hate him. I really, really hate him. Actually, I hate a society that is so complacent that we would allow him to exist. It is our fault he was free to pick up two girls in a park, fill them with booze and Ecstasy, and let them both die. If it were a First Nations sex offender targeting rich white girls from West Vancouver, that guy would never see the light of day, let alone get near another female youth.

I've always wanted to write a film about those youth, but everything I come up with either sounds like *Dangerous Minds* (with a science teacher) or an After School Special, where everything turns out hunky-dory.

Last night, I had a dream of Martha yelling at me, "You want to make a movie about me? This was my life. Not fodder for entertainment!"

That's not it, but it is about me. I can't tell you the number of extremely dangerous situations I got myself into during my alcoholic years. I even went home with a biker once when I was eighteen. I snuck out before he woke up and somehow found my way home. Still can't remember how since I had no idea where I was and there were no cell phones back then. Maybe I took a cab, or a bus? Seriously, I can't remember.

What I do remember is sterilizing myself in the steaming shower, gagging as I scrubbed every place his mouth had been. Curling into a ball on the floor, "Why am I alive?"

Not particularly thankful, just curious.

This is still a question I ask.

Maybe it is to tell Martha and Kayla's story. Maybe it's to share mine.

11

Cocoons are for Moths. Butterflies have Chrysalises

March 5, 2012

I was having a pretty good day yesterday, almost feeling myself again, but then last night I had some drinks and dessert and today I feel depressed. It's like I'm creating things to feel bad about. I'm doing all this work and then I self-sabotage it. I create things to bring me down.

Carlos told me once I was addicted to feeling guilty. Like when things start going well, I seem to do something to make myself feel guilty. I always hated admitting when he was right.

March 6, 2012

I ended up having a great day yesterday. It took a lot of work to change the momentum of my mind, but I was determined. To help out, the Universe provided me with glorious sunshine and a new student named Stanley. Stanley is in Grade 2 and the teacher at his school is having issues with him. He is super-active and bright and imaginative; not a good fit for public school. He gave me a hug as soon as we met. He's so cute. I'm so lucky.

March 7, 2012

I am so excited to write. I am so grateful for my life, my passion, my job, coffee, Grounds, where I live, music, Spring Break and the Vancouver Women in Film Festival that WIFTV puts on. It is going to be a great weekend and I'm going to be a full on participant! Two years ago volunteering for this festival was a springboard for my career and I want to give it all my support and positive energy. Woo hoo!

Stanley and I did some arts and crafts today. Good to know my science degree is being put to good use. He made caterpillars out of cotton balls and stick-on googly eyeballs. I made butterflies out of pipe cleaners and ribbons. It was his idea. He loves caterpillars. I didn't tell him I was becoming a butterfly this year, but I think he might've thought it was cool. I suggested we make a cocoon to show the intermediate stage.

"Cocoons are for moths. Butterflies have chrythalithes." He corrected with the cutest lisp ever. *Thanks a lot, science degree.*

Stanley made four caterpillars by the time I barely finished one butterfly.

He smiled at me, "They don't have to be perfect."

I looked at his crooked chains of cotton balls with lopsided eyes, "Yours are."

Later: What just happened? What just happened?

The Indianapolis Colts have just released Peyton Manning... *WTF!*

March 8, 2012

Happy International Women's Day!

The reason I first decided to write this book was to chronicle the year I became a woman and what that meant to me... I've kind of gone off on a tangent. Maybe this weekend and being at the festival will help me refocus.

Later: Tonight was the opening of the festival, which we have combined with the Spotlight Awards Gala (which honors women in the industry as a whole), and Deboragh Gabler's Legacy Awards (which are for the 3 best BC short films in the festival). A night of honoring inspiring women and their incredible work. I love WIFTV. I love what we do. I am so proud to be vice-president of such an incredible organization. The best part of being vice-prez, is you just get to sit back and enjoy the show.

March 9, 2012

Happy birthday, Lee!

Holy shit! I am way too young to have a nephew that is 20 years old. I can't believe this amazing gift has been in my life for two whole decades.

Tracy was pregnant with Lee the first time I moved to Vancouver. I had just turned 19 and was desperate to get my life on track. My parents bought me the ticket. The plan was to go for eight months until I would, hopefully, start university in the fall. I lasted three weeks.

I was lonely and it rained every single day, but the big reason I wanted to come home was because I wanted to be there when Tracy gave birth. I promised myself if I came back I would make that little baby proud.

In order to do this, I would have to make some major life changes; from my shameful drunken behavior to my excess weight. I came home and the bulimia began. By the time Lee was born, six weeks later, I had lost 20 pounds, by the time he was one month old, I had dropped another ten. I wanted to lose weight fast so he wouldn't be embarrassed I was his auntie. Why in the world I thought a newborn baby would care if I weighed 115 lbs, I have no idea, but that number meant everything to me.

The ironic thing is that it was my love for Lee that set me on the extreme journey of trying to be perfect, which only fueled my self-loathing. My desire for him to be proud of me led into a decade of shame.

The greater irony is that I never knew what positive pride was before Lee. He inspires me continuously. Just the way he lives his life with strength and humor. He also gives the best hugs. Just as you separate, his hand lingers on your back and gives a little rub.

Whoa. I just had an amazing moment. I'm at Grounds writing this and a lady just walked in. I looked up and we smiled. Then I glanced around at the elderly man at the coffee station, the cyclist at the cashier, the barista at the espresso machine and I had a profound awareness of this deep connection between all of us. Ripples on this ocean of energy looking at each other like we are separate waves, oblivious to the mass we share beneath. We are all connected to each other through the Source. We are all family.

Elliot's words rang in my ears. "If you go back far enough, we are all related."

Usually a cliché, but because he says it matter-of-factly as a way of explaining away why him and I are so similar, its truth resonates. I am so grateful for him, all this learning that has come my way through him and this moment of gorgeous clarity.

I feel amazing today! I had a healthy Friday night and am reaping the benefits today. Going to write for a few hours and then back to the film festival. I'm there to support others and I'm so excited to do so. *Yay!*

I am starting to experience the separation of the levels. The boundaries are blurring - my inner world versus the outer world. The outer world is my playground and my inner world is my sanctuary. This is very freeing.

The main theme of *Happiless* is that you can't find happiness 'out there' but I'm going to take it a step further now. You can't find anything you seek: love, abundance, safety, respect... out there, it is all inside. Anxiety arises when you try. It is a message letting you know you are off track, that you are looking in the wrong place.

March 11, 2012

Two nights in a row I stayed home and made the healthy food and drink choices! I'm so proud of myself. I am joyful, loving, abundant and peaceful!

I did some EC'ing, and not surprisingly a bunch of stuff came up around my ex-uncle leaving my auntie for another woman after 35 years of marriage. My whole family was shocked and confused. I trapped some 'heartbroken' ones for my aunt, but also because Carlos refused to promise he would never betray me. He would say he could promise in the 'now', but who knows what could happen in the future. I hated him for this.

I also watched the film that is winning the award I sponsored and will be presenting tonight. I didn't decide the winner, but am happy with the choice: Desiree Lim and her film *The House*.

I'm already festivaled out, though. Why do we have to do the closing awards on a Sunday night? I just want to stay home and drink beer and eat nachos. My Sunday night reward. I know the healthier choice is to go to the awards, but I really don't want to.

9:30 PM: I just gave out the Sharlene Chartrand Screenwriting Award! I'm not quite sure what was going on with me earlier. Tonight was a lot of fun. In Mary's speech, she told the story of how the awards' sponsorship idea all started with "Rachelle Chartrand putting her money where her mouth is", which was very overwhelming, because I didn't expect her to do that. She is so supportive. Mary is such a classy, elegant lady, and I'm not just saying that because she always has nice things to say about me.

March 12, 2012

I threw up last night. Full-on bulimia-style.

I wasn't going to write about this, but I have to get it out of me where it is eating me up and threatens to appear again. It wasn't planned, although a binge was... I just couldn't stop eating. *Couldn't stop...* What does that even mean? My body was in control. That is not possible. My body cannot attack itself. My mind controls my body, but why would it want to do this?

Besides for one time in Korea, it's been TEN years. I am so confused. That time in Korea happened the same way. Seemingly out of the blue. I was eating a bowl of cereal, then two, then I was gone. I told Carlos that night, because I promised him I would never lie about it.

Addiction thrives on lies... and loneliness.

Yesterday, at Grounds, I was telling Erik how I *used* to be bulimic. "Oh, it was 10 years ago, blah, blah, blah.'" I'm not saying I'm bulimic. I'm not an action or an addiction. I did something last night and I need to leave it there. I've been thinking a lot more about it with journaling and clearing. Maybe it has just brought up a bunch of deep shit to the surface where I can wipe it out for good.

I left the theatre after giving my mom's award and missed the closing film because I was tired, but deep down I wanted to be alone. The weird thing is I was feeling so proud after Mary's acknowledgement, but just wanted to bolt.

Maybe seeing the vision of my highest life is scaring the crap out of my ego or maybe Mary's recognition in front of the audience triggered something. It was very emotional.

HALT: Never let myself get too Hungry, too Angry (or any emotion), too Lonely or too Tired. I haven't thought about that acronym in a long, long time.

I am brave. I am courageous. I am love. I am joy. I am abundance.

I refuse to believe this is a step back. It is part of the process. I'm sure the caterpillar feels tired before it breaks through, wondering if it ever will. No. The caterpillar doesn't worry about it. It just does what it needs to do moment to moment, which is usually nothing.

6 PM: I had a great visit with Charlie and Christina. Her and I have a lot in common. I told her about some of the processes I've been doing. We also talked about the importance of a safe environment. The caterpillar builds a cocoon, I mean chrysalis, to protect itself. I need to do that for the next little while. I'm so sensitive to people right now as it is.

Spring Break! A time of renewal. Perfect time for me to do the ten-day Vipassana meditation at-home-retreat I've been meaning to do for years. I did the official one in Merritt about seven years ago. No talking, exercising, journaling, reading, nothing but meditating for ten days. It was the most intense experience of my life, and one of the most important. It turned me inside. It also turned me into a vegetarian.

In addition to meditation, they played nightly discourses - video tapes of S.N. Goenka teaching some of Buddha's philosophies as well as guiding you through the meditation process and some things to expect. They have the set of CD's at Banyen Books, which I finally bought.

One key aspect is that you are not supposed to leave in the middle of the retreat. On Day 6, I understood why. I was ready to leave my husband of 4 years to go back to my ex-husband who I had not spoken to for 2 years, and was now married with a family, and beg him to take me back. Declare we had made a huge mistake and were meant to be together. On day 7 that feeling had passed.

These ten days will not be that strict, of course, only a few hours of meditation a day and lots of Emotion Coding. I also want to get lots of writing done, but will have to limit the number of people I speak to and take no action - inspired or otherwise. I am protecting myself from outside toxins in all their forms at this very delicate stage. Any emotion, attachment, desire that arises, I will just observe it and move on.

I am also protecting the outside world. Carlos doesn't need any random phone calls!

12

My Personal 10-Day Meditation Retreat

<u>March 13, 2012</u>

Day 1 of this my... I need to come up with a cool, catchy name for this retreat.

I was pretty low condition at the beginning, but I battled through and am really pumped. It will be up and down, but I'm sticking with it. I cleaned my home. I love my home. It is so perfect for this process - a beautiful, supportive, cozy, safe, pink chrysalis. I'm being very diligent with what I let into my world these next ten days - only love and support and joy and abundance and peace.

Later: If ever I doubted the Emotion Code, never again. I now have visual proof it is for real. For the past 15 years or so I have had this weird discoloration on my eyelids, mostly concentrated near the inner corners. Depending on the day or my health, it has ranged from a yellow tinge to bright orange, but it is consistently there. It is unsightly and I hate it.

I have researched potential causes and asked every doctor I've come into contact with, but it seems to be some rare disorder no one has ever seen before. The only person who offered a theory was the make-up lady on the episode of *Stargate: SG-1* I did six years ago. She said we have little glands on the inner corner of our eyes and that there are probably toxins built up there, but she had no idea how to get rid of them. *Toxins trapped in my eyelids. Awesome.*

Today they were really dark, I think because I haven't been sleeping. I asked, "Do I have a trapped emotion causing the yellow above my eyes?" And I did. Dozens! Mostly self-abuse, which isn't surprising considering they first appeared halfway through my decade of bulimia and are always darkest after a week in Alberta.

After releasing about twenty of them, I went to the washroom and looked in the mirror. They were a lot lighter, but I thought it was probably just wishful thinking. I did ten more, but this round they were 'defensiveness'. I just checked again and the yellow is gone. Completely! I really can't believe it. I mean, I was hopeful they would get lighter, but they have disappeared. After 15 years of carrying this crap above my eyes, it's all gone.

Later: Just listened to the first Goenka discourse CD. I'm excited for this unique experience. Observing my breath for a minute, then an hour. This afternoon, I will go onto the next stage, which is focusing for an hour on the area just below my nostrils. Just being aware of the sensations. I'm only doing 2 one-hour sessions a day. I'm also doing intense clearing and other energy work and I do need to interact with the world.

March 14, 2012

Day 2 complete! The major emotions I EC'd were 'guilt' and 'shame'.

I was a thief. It is really hard for me to write that as integrity is something I now value deeply. These are ugly secrets I have kept hidden for a long time. Carlos was aware of a lot of them, as some of the events were when we were together. Yeah. This wasn't just stealing clothes from stores as a teenager or loose change from my parents' dresser.

I knew full well what I was doing was wrong, I had a conscience, but I didn't think I had a choice. There was rent to pay. The real disgust came from the fact I had gotten myself into the situation. I was a teacher with a University degree. I was smarter than that. How could I care more about avoiding a domestic dispute than my own integrity? How could I steal instead of telling my boyfriend to get a job?

I hated myself so much, but I was a master of detaching my heart and mind from my actions. I just drowned the guilt in booze and puked out the shame.

Don't get me wrong, I have not forgiven myself, or to be honest, Carlos for contributing (or not contributing) to the dire situation, but I am so grateful for these releasing techniques. These emotions are stale and not making me a better person. They are holding me back and keeping me stuck. EFT, Emotion Code, yoga and meditation have come into my life for a reason.

I am so grateful. Most people my age are re-evaluating their life and sensing there is a part of them that is bigger; a beautiful, limitless, wiser part of themselves that wants to be free, but have no idea how to release it or the time and solitude to do so. I have all three.

Granted, I have this time because I was brave enough to let go of the life that was holding me back. Brave enough to face a clean slate. I say brave, because as romantic as a clean slate sounds, it is filled with immense pressure of not fucking up again. Maybe this is why I haven't gone on a date since I left Carlos. I'm scared of fucking up my second, sorry, *third*, chance.

I do have a lot more shit to bulldoze through than most people, but instead of going on a trip or reading and watching movies my whole Spring Break, I am doing this work. *Why?* Because I have had a glimpse of the life I am meant to live. Once you see this, this vision of your highest self living your most loving, abundant life, well, there just ain't no turning back.

The pain pushes until the vision pulls.

The butterfly whispers gently to the caterpillar, encouraging it to spin itself a chrysalis where it is safe and magical things will happen.

March 15, 2012

Day 3 complete of... I really need a funky title for this retreat.

Clare and I went to see *Monsieur Lazhar*, a Québécois film. It was really good. Amazing performances. A little creepy because there was a caterpillar/chrysalis/butterfly theme. It's weird how the word 'chrysalis' keeps popping up when I don't ever remember seeing the word before. Thank you, Stanley.

Clare is one of my dearest friends. Our parents have been friends since I can remember, but we only became close after both moving to Vancouver. I'm actually 10 years older than her. I used to babysit her and tease her she was a brat. She was. Now she is a subtle mix of sweet and sassy and one of the only people I could hang out with during this retreat.

Two things to reflect upon:

1. On the way into the movie, I was telling Clare about all the energy work I've been doing recently, as well as my visions and intentions for this retreat. At one point, going up the escalator, she had a blank look on her face.

Thinking I had gone too far, I joked, "Am I the craziest friend you have?"

She deadpanned, "No. I'm scared of escalators."

I haven't referred to myself as *crazy* in a long time and I immediately felt guilty. It diminishes me and my journey and my power. Besides, her blank look had nothing to do with me. She was just holding onto the rail for dear life.

2. After the movie, I told Clare how the director's mom had seen the play and told him he *had* to adapt it to film. Clare sweetly said she heard the same story about *The King's Speech*.

Memory is a very weird thing and really should never be trusted. At least not mine. Especially when talking about people and events. This is why I should not write nonfiction. Even with this book, how much can you believe? I promise I am being truthful and open, but everything is from my perspective and based on my untrustworthy memory. It is my perspective from a time when I was a different person. If there is one thing I have learned from the Emotion Code, it is that memories are colored by emotion.

March 16, 2012

Day 4 complete! What a day of epiphanies!

Two major ones about my first Vipassana retreat years ago:

1. I now know why I ended up in India. When I arrived on the Merritt compound in February 2006, I never had the slightest interest in India - except for western-style curry. Seven months later, I was living there, teaching ESL, riding rickshaws, wearing Punjabi suits, visiting temples and eating the most delicious, nutritious vegetarian food of my life.

Goenka speaks a lot about India. I think during the original discourses, I must have become drawn to that fascinating country and culture. One of the most amazing experiences of my life and I never made that connection before.

2. I think I had a glimpse of my vision back then and my ego freaked out. Five months later, I was seeing a psychiatrist. I'm not blaming the retreat, I had major issues before I sat on a mat, but that experience was like a portal into this mindset of peace and love that I never knew existed (except when high on E).

One moment, I was convinced I could save the world; the next I couldn't see a world worth saving. One moment I felt like I could fly; the next I was crashed on the bathroom floor.

One serving shift I'd be chatting up my patrons and loving life; the next I was distraught at being a 33 yr-old waitress serving beer and nachos. Hopeless I had yet to become a movie star.

To add to this was the guilt of not appreciating what I had. I had a job and a husband and an adorable puppy. I had a family that was no longer ashamed of me.

Guilt and hopelessness: the perfect recipe to drink, which only adds to the depression.

One day, I plopped myself down behind the library. Two homeless guys strolled by pushing a cart of empties, laughing like they didn't have a care in the world.

"Man, they've really got it figured out. Life shouldn't be this hard. Maybe I should just collect bottles and hang out at the beach."

That seemed like it would be too much work. I mean, it was only 9 AM and they already had a full cart. I curled in a ball, the words 'hopeless' and 'homeless' swirling before my eyes.

"What if I just never got up?" I imagined myself morphing into a bag lady. "I'm sure someone would bring me a blanket. Another Good Samaritan might bring me a burger, but I'd have to tell them I'm vegetarian. Maybe Carlos would bring Simon to visit me. I'm sure the library won't like me living here, but I promise not to bother anyone. I just want to rest."

I was dead serious, so I went to the medi-centre.

In the examination room, I blurted, "I think I'm depressed."

The 70 yr old substitute doctor replied, "You're not depressed."

"Really? I'm identifying with homeless people."

"But you're laughing."

"I'm laughing 'cause I'm crazy."

He started writing me a prescription for anti-depressants.

I cried, "No. There is more to this than that."

I told him about my swings of euphoria and despair.

"You sound bipolar."

Awesome. You were just going to prescribe me anti-depressants and now you think I'm bipolar. Do you think you should ask a few more questions before you whip out that pad of paper? He referred me to a psychiatrist. I had images of lithium injections and lobotomies.

That's how I met Dr. Pez. My first appointment with him was mostly a get to know you. How do you sum up 33 years in 50 minutes? I called him Dr. Pez because he was petite and sat perched in his armchair listening to me babble on, nodding his head slightly.

Finally, I stopped yammering. A moment of stillness, then his mouth opened and *pop*, "Who are you to save the world?"

He wasn't judging, he was challenging. I suspect he knew what was going on at a deeper (or higher) level, but that I wasn't yet ready. I had to work through a lot of shit first.

I let go of the vision then. I'm ready for it now.

March 17, 2012

Later: Day 5 complete!

I started listening to these pre-recorded group coaching calls that go with the online *Law of Emergence* program I bought from Derek Rydall. Basically, it blows the whole Law of Attraction model out of the water. He uses the metaphor that if a caterpillar (see?) was to attract everything he wanted he would attract more of a caterpillar life, but the caterpillar was always meant to be a butterfly and everything he needs is already in him, he just needs to emerge.

Today, I listened to his guided Timeline Meditation:

Lying down, eyes closed, in a very relaxed state, imagine a timeline stretching into the past and into the future. Then rising above the present moment, bring forth a recurring negative emotion - a fear, resistance or limiting belief you have had for a very long time. Allow yourself to really experience it and intensify it, then ask, "When did I first experience this?"

Float back along the timeline, trying not to think of the answer, trusting that you are going exactly where you are meant to go. Finally, drop down into your timeline and look around. *Where are you? What is this event when you first felt this way?*

At the onset of the meditation, I wasn't sure which I should do first. I have so many recurring negative emotions. I was completely in my head, so I just listened to my breath and relaxed deeper and then it emerged - my fear of my amazingness. *Huh?* I tried not to judge.

Okay. When did I first experience this?

I floated back days, weeks, months, years, further and further into my past. There was a tinge of anxiety of where this would take me, but I just kept breathing, kept relaxing.

Then I dropped... into the backseat of that car.

At first I thought, "No, this is wrong, I had issues way before this." I chose to trust.

For the first time ever, I actually *remembered* it. Even the next morning, if it wasn't for the indisputable evidence left on my panties and the aching between my legs, I wouldn't have known I had lost my virginity the night before. I had zero recollection.

But there I was, lying on my back, skirt hiked up, panties around my ankles, cheap upholstery scratching the back of my thighs, wasted out of my mind at fourteen years old with a seventeen year-old penis pounding into me; not nearly coherent enough to say "no"... even if I had wanted to.

Any glimmer of amazingness I had left after that, disappeared in the days to follow, once the rumors got out.

Bloody Slut - that's the cool nickname I was given. What made the event even more awesome was the guy wanted nothing to do with me, except to ask for his jacket back. You may be thinking, "What a jerk?" But I actually don't hold any ill will against him. As far as I know, he did nothing to perpetuate the rumors, was just as drunk as I was and had to go over to his friend's the next morning to clean up the mess left behind in the car.

Twenty-five years later and I'm finally cleaning up the mess left behind in my heart.

Part of this meditation isn't just to relive it; it is to see the real purpose. How did this event serve my higher purpose? This didn't come to me during the process, but at the beach later. God, I love the beach. This event changed everything for me. After that, I became an incredible liar, a master denier. I could look people right in the eyes, even my friends, and deny it ever happened.

It taught me that people lie out of fear. Fear of getting in trouble, fear of losing face, fear of losing love, fear of people believing you are a Bloody Slut, or worse, believing it yourself.

This desire to help people know their true worthiness would not be burning in me if I didn't know what it means to feel completely worthless. Not just that night but many others just like it.

My purpose - to help others know their power, could never be realized unless I knew what it meant to be powerless. But I now know my power. I am one of the bravest people I know. I face my fears. And I have faced my fear of my amazingness. Fear and love cannot coexist. I must learn to love my amazingness. No, allow myself to love my amazingness.

<u>March 18, 2012</u>

As I was falling asleep last night, I had a vision of me as a caterpillar shedding my layer of skin, the Universe lovingly peeling it off piece by piece. I am in my chrysalis. I am safe. No matter what happens in the outer world, I will love and care for myself. I am undergoing a metamorphosis. I am protecting myself from outside toxins, in all their forms, at this very delicate stage. Any emotion, attachment, desire that arises, I will observe it and move on.

I am ripping off the shackles of my misery. I am shedding my past. Not suppressing it or ignoring it, but letting it go. I am grateful for every single moment of my past. It was necessary for me to go through those times to learn, grow and strengthen. I have developed this incredible insight into compassion and pain and why we do the things we do.

Reverse Paranoia: I believe the Universe is conspiring for my highest good.

Later: Day 6 complete! Goenka says Day 6 is the hardest, but it wasn't so bad. Not at all like my first one (when I was leaving Carlos for Matthew). I thought for sure I had lost my mind.

I also did some clearing around Carlos. Holy shit, I have a lot of trapped emotions around him. Trying to stay equanimous. Just observe, "Oh, that emotion is interesting." The timing of this is perfect. I am doing all this releasing of past emotions, but not having any judgment on them, just being grateful I am able to let them go.

I've decided to let go of this idea my coffee shop crush is my Soul Mate. I don't even know him. He may be a smoker. Besides, I have a history of creating illusions around men.

Matthew: the Ideal Husband - 'Beaumont's Most Eligible Bachelor', Carlos: the Ideal Partner - 'The Most Talented Director I Know'. Both times I fell in love with the idea of someone, their potential. That wasn't fair to them or to me. Not surprising they ended in divorce.

What is the most romantic illusion of all? Labeling someone my soul mate.

Letting go of the illusion to make room for the reality.

Later: I just watched *Crazy. Stupid. Love*, not a movie I would ever watch except Ryan Gosling is in it. It's about fighting for your soul mate. ARGHHHH! Damn Universe!

2 AM: Inspired Idea! I should write my Soul Mate a note. Just an easy, breezy, *Hey, how ya doing?* note. He mentioned many times which condo he lives in. Maybe subconsciously his higher self knew I would need to find him at some point. I'll give it to his condo manager. After my meditation retreat of course... I am on Day 6 after all.

March 19, 2012

Day 7 complete! I woke up this morning and exclaimed, "I am ready to grow and develop in whatever ways I need to in order to fulfill my life's purpose!" Then I laughed my ass off. Thank you Universe. I've rediscovered my sense of humor.

Tonight's Vipassana Meditation was intense. I could feel the Saṅkhāras (mental formations) rising and they are not pleasant. Working to just observe. When I did the first retreat, it was always the most intense around my throat, a mixture of being nauseas and strangled. It took a lot to stay equanimous as I passed over this area. I think it was from being bulimic for so long. I also tried to choke myself with a belt when I was thirteen.

This time, they are the most intense around my head, especially on the bridge of my nose. When Celina and I were in our car accident and my head hit the dashboard, my nose got dislocated. I still have a bump on it, maybe that's why.

Derek has also introduced the idea of the shadow. Weird, as the first time I ever heard about it was a month or so ago. That's not true. I remember reading about the theory in my studies of Carl Jung, but always just glazed over it. I now know, without a shadow of a doubt (ha ha, I'm so funny), that I have many and it is time to bring them into the light. That's why this process keeps popping up and why it is resonating with me.

Our Dark Shadows are the parts of ourselves that at one time we labeled 'bad' so shunned, the flipside are our Light Shadows, or our Masks. These are the traits we praise ourselves for. Simply put, whenever you declare, "I am NOT that" you know you have a shadow. If you pride yourself on, "I AM that", well, my friend, you've got yourself a mask.

First shadow that came to mind, the thing I find most despicable in others, that I declare, "I am not", is being judgmental. I pride myself on not being judgmental.

Derek's Shadow Process: *Lie down and relax, eyes closed, just listening to your breath. With every breath, just let go a little bit more. Imagine an elevator. Step into it and press 'down'.*

Anxiety rushed in. I was scared and wanted to stop, but heard a voice, "Be brave."

Down farther and farther.

"Why do I need to be brave? I am going deeper into me. What am I afraid I will find?"

Farther and farther.

I could feel my heart beating faster. I imagined I was going down into a dark place full of demons. Not external monsters that will try to hurt me, but personal demons who have been wreaking havoc from within.

The doors open to your personal sanctuary.

Shannon Falls, Squamish. Luscious vegetation and a mesmerizing waterfall. Derek was guiding us to a place of safety and beauty. Why did I assume going inside would be a place of danger and ugliness?

Call forth your shadow. You can use a nickname to lighten the process, if you like.

I called forth my Judging-self but nothing came. Not even when I called out, 'Judging Jodi'. I tried my 'I'm not good enough' shadow. Nothing. Why don't my shadows want to come out? I could feel myself trying to force it, which just brought me out of it. I tried to reign my mind back in, but it was already gone.

In meditation, in yoga and in life, as soon as you force it, you are no longer doing it.

Derek quote: *Don't feed a pearl to the swine.*

Not sure why I just thought of this.

March 20, 2012

Happy Vernal Equinox! Today is the 1st day of spring, so I decided to plant a seed... I wrote the note. Well, actually I wrote and rewrote it three times to make sure it was casual, uncontrived and, of course, breezy.

Hey! How have you been? I miss our visits! Did you give up caffeine? Did you break both your legs playing hockey? Were you banned from Grounds after an unruly incident?

If any of the above are true and you would like to hang some time, here are some options:

You could a) phone or text me at... b) email me at... c) become my Facebook friend or d) follow me on Twitter (just kidding, don't do that, it would be creepy)

Hope to see you soon!

Totally breezy, right? Whatever. Either he'll think I'm crazy and want to run like hell or he'll know I'm crazy and want to hang out.

This is by far the most romantic thing I have ever done. I wrote it on pink flowery paper and slipped it in an envelope. I don't know his last name, so I just wrote his first name along with the only other piece of information I have: the small Alberta town he's from.

Standing outside the condo building, my Soul Mate's home, I'm overwhelmed with a flow of electricity. I have not felt this alive in years! The only problem is I can't find any sort of contact information for the residents. No buzzer or anything. What do delivery people do? I peek through the front gates, side lobby and parkade. Nothing.

Should I ask someone who lives here? Please don't let him walk out right now.

Being romantic rocks.

I got home and Googled the name of his complex. I tried calling the management company, but couldn't get through. Giving up, I went to the library and the doubt, resistance and vulnerability started spewing. Thank God I wasn't able to deliver the letter. I promised myself I wouldn't take any actions, inspired or otherwise, until the end of the ten days and this is why. I am in my chrysalis and this is a vulnerable stage. It is not the time to invite someone in. I cannot worry about time. Time is an illusion. If my Soul Mate is my soul mate, the Universe will conspire to bring us together, just like it is conspiring for me to live my purpose and passion.

Later: My parents stood me up on our Skype call two days ago and haven't replied to my email or text. They could be kidnapped by banditos and I'm not even joking. Retired people can be so irresponsible!

I tried meditating and experienced a lot of resistance - wandering mind, drowsiness. I know this is all part of the process and I am trying to be fucking equanimous, but shit, it's hard.

More than I want to change anything external, I want to emerge as my true identity.

Day 8 complete!

March 21, 2012

7:30 AM at Grounds: There is this chick who always comes in to wait for the bus. She never buys anything, just sits here playing games on her phone.

BEEP. BEEP. BEEP. So annoying! Just breathe. Be aware.

Hmmm... I wonder how long this feeling will last?

She left. It's gone.

Later: I tried the Shadow Process again. Going down the elevator was more relaxing knowing I was heading somewhere beautiful. I did feel anxiety over wanting it to work this time, but just breathed and kept going down the shaft until the pressure was gone.

The doors opened. I called forth 'Coward'. A hunched, scrawny, eternally hurt weasel came out. She must've noticed the shock on my face, because she started to slink back into the shadows. I have pushed this part of me deep into the dark, especially as I've created my 'I'm-the-Bravest-Person-I-Know' mask.

How can I bring her into the light?

Listen to her.

I whisper, "I'm sorry. This is my first time. Please, come talk to me"

She crept forward, "Being scared and vulnerable in dangerous environments is okay. I can keep you safe. True bravery is not the lack of fear, it is asking, 'What is the seed of this? What is the reality of this?' And then deciding if it is protecting you or holding you back."

Wow, my Coward is so wise.

A flash. Arriving in New Delhi, India at 1:30 AM by myself. The ESL company that hired me had arranged for someone to meet me at the airport to drive me to my hotel. I was not comfortable with this, but didn't want to seem scared. I decided to think of it as an adventure. I always wanted to get off an international flight and have someone there holding a sign with my name on it. There was something really romantic about that for some reason.

My someone turned out to be a cab driver. I could see the headlines: STUPID CANADIAN WOMAN DESERVED HER FATE!

I nodded at Coward, 'Okay. I will listen to you."

Since I was already in my sanctuary, I thought I would see if there was a Judging shadow lurking in the dark. I wasn't convinced there would be, as I only really judge Patriot fans and pit bull owners, but I have definitely created an 'I'm so open-minded' mask.

"I am arrogant in my open-mindedness," I boasted to Erik once.

He squinted at me, "What the hell does that mean?"

"It means I think people who are not open-minded are ignorant."

His eyes widened, "Yeah, you're fucked."

I called out for Judging Jodi. *He* came out. I was surprised it was a male. I once dated a guy named Jody. He was super nice, but I didn't treat him very nicely. I always felt bad about that.

Judging Jody revealed two things: 1. I judge. We all do. I judge people who are unhealthy. Not admitting this has made me a hypocrite. Instead, I should show the person love and compassion knowing it is a lack of self-love/compassion that is the root of the problem. Besides, I am not as healthy as I like to believe. 2. Being judgmental of people who are being judgmental ends the conversation.

I asked my shadow, "How can I love and accept you so you can be an ally?"

Silence.

"What's positive about being judgmental?"

He disappeared.

Later: Day 9 complete! I had an amazing two-hour walk at the beach. Glorious sunshine. I realized a positive to being judgmental. By being aware of the thoughts, instead of shunning them, I can explore my own projections. Judgments are always projections of fears or parts of myself I don't want to acknowledge which just creates more shadows. This is why I am so judgmental of judgmental people. I am judgmental.

<u>March 22, 2012</u>

My Personal 10-day Meditation Retreat is complete! Time to get drunk. *Just kidding.*

I'm leaving my Soul Mate his note today. It is an Inspired Idea coming from a place of self-love. Any fear that arises will go away. Any doubt that arises will go away.

I finally Skyped with my mom and dad. They're fine. Just livin' la vida loca.

My mom said she always feels so good after talking to me because of how happy I look. She had tears in her eyes. For the first time in my life, I understand the whole 'as a parent you just want your child to be happy' claim. I never believed it before. Today, I saw it.

Later: Ahhhhhh! I did it. I left the note for my Soul Mate!

I finally got through to the property management place. The man who answered said he couldn't give out the contact information for a resident and I felt like a stalker. I told him I had a letter to deliver and he said I could leave it with the owner of the little bookstore on the main floor of the complex. The *fantasy* bookstore - how perfect is that?!

When I walked in, the place was empty, thank God. I didn't want to have to explain what I was doing in front of anyone. A lady finally came out from the back. I asked if she by chance knew my guy. She said she did, but his first name being quite common, I needed to be sure. So, I described my Soul Mate in detail. Tall, dark and handsome... I giggled to myself, *I might as well call him Prince Charming. She does work at The White Dwarf Bookstore; she probably wouldn't bat an eye.*

"Oh sure, I know him. I'll make sure he gets it." Then she threw my future in a drawer.

Of course, now I'm going through monstrous fear and doubt.

No. It was an Inspired Idea that came from a loving place. Besides, this book really needs a plot point. This year has been way too internal. I need some action!

Dear Rachelle Butterfly

<u>March 22, 2012</u>
Dear Rachelle Butterfly,

I'm sorry I have not been creating a life that fulfills my purpose. I have had a glimpse of it now, but I know I cannot do it without you. I promise to rearrange my life to welcome you.

You are love. I will be more loving in each of my relationships with family, friends, past participants and strangers. I will treat myself with love. I will treat my body with love. I will love my mind. I will love my home. I will love animals. I will love my car. I will be open to give love and receive love. Love is my true nature.

You are joy. I will laugh. I will open up to joyful events. I will fill my heart with joyful memories. I will fill my body with joyful nutrition and allow it to enjoy joyful activities, experiences and sensations. I will look for joy all around me. I will listen to joyful music and watch joyful movies. I will enjoy life. Joy is my true nature.

You are abundance. I will be generous with others. I will be open to generosity from others. I will observe the abundance that is all around me. I will meditate and visualize being rained down on with abundance. I will remove all resistance to giving and receiving abundance. Abundance is my true nature.

You are forgiveness. I will forgive those who I feel have hurt me. I will forgive myself for hurting others. I will forgive myself for hurting myself. Forgiveness is my true nature.

You are creativity. I will be open and supportive and appreciative of my creative side. I will create. I will write, dance and sing. I will share my creative gifts. I will open my mind and heart to the creativity of others. I will meditate on creativity. Creativity is my true nature.

You are peace. I will create peace in my home and in my mind and in my relationships. I will create peace through releasing, yoga and meditation. Peace is my true nature.

I am love.
I am joy.
I am abundant.
I am forgiveness.
I am creative.
I am peace.
I am grateful.

Time is an Illusion

March 23, 2012

Morning Meditation: I stand on the balcony of my dream home sanctuary across from Locarno beach. It has a stunning view of downtown. I raise my hands and let the golden light flow over the sand. It spreads across the ocean and blankets the city. Spreading my love through Vancouver. Canada. The World. Sharing stories; inspiring others to do the same.

Shadow Process for Liar.

I asked 'Liar, Liar, Pants on Fire' why I created her.

She answered, "As a child, you didn't feel unconditionally loved. You were always afraid of getting in trouble, so lied. The first time you heard, 'Every time you lie, the nail goes deeper into Baby Jesus' hands' I was born."

Her gifts? She has helped me be compassionate with someone who lies.

Carlos. I suspected he was lying to me numerous times. It made me sad he couldn't be honest with me, that he didn't trust my feelings for him.

Fuck that. It pissed me off every single time. I was not at all compassionate. I judged him big time, which is hilarious because I was lying to him, too. I had a fucking eating disorder for crying out loud. I thought it was Law of Attraction. I was a liar, so I attracted a liar. Now I realize there is a whole other layer to it. The reason I hated him when he lied to me was I was projecting my own liar; that part of me I detested.

The only way I can truly feel compassion is if I am able to integrate LLPOF. Not change her, but love and accept her. Yeah, this is going to be a tough one.

I worked on my 'I am spiritual not materialistic' mask, as well. This split stems from all the negative choices I made in order to get money: stealing, lying, waitressing at places that made me feel low about myself, fighting with Carlos (being with Carlos). One of the lowest moments of my life was going to the food bank in Kelowna. I have deep resentment towards Carlos for making me go, because he was 'too embarrassed', even though I was the one working three part-time jobs.

I am both spiritual and material. They are both energies. My Higher Self chose my body to experience the physical world. Bulimia and alcoholism caused a split not only between my body and mind, but also with my spirit. These fissures are an illusion and I can regain my awareness of my wholeness. I am going for a walk at the beach now with all parts of me. I am love and abundance. Spiritual side is love and abundance - that is obvious, now it is time for my physical side to experience this love and abundance as well.

Later: I was cruising down Broadway, windows wide open, Flo Rida blasting, singing along full tilt, when a car passed me and honked.

I yelled out, "Woo hoo, springtime!"

Then I realized, maybe that's not what he was honking about. I was so wrapped up in the glorious moment that anything that came in was colored with joy.

Two years ago, when I was wound up in anxiety, I drove around pissed off most of the time. If someone honked, I was like, "What the hell is your problem? Relax, will ya?"

Wow. Perceptions and projections are powerful.

March 25, 2012

"Time is an illusion."

It really pisses Elliot off when I say this. I love to warp his brain. Yesterday was especially fun.

"The past and the future only exist in our minds."

Elliot retaliated, "I get how the future isn't real, but the past is real. It *actually* happened."

I smirked, "How do you know?"

"Because I can remember it?"

"What if you couldn't? Does that mean it didn't happen? Or better yet, what if I was able to implant a memory into your brain, would that mean it *did* happen? Have you ever had a dream that seemed so real you actually believed it was real? Even recounted it later as an event. Or a nightmare so visceral you woke up sweating with your heart palpitating?"

He was silent, but the wheels were spinning. I knew this was not the end to this conversation. Sometimes I think my time with Elliot has just been one long 7-month ongoing conversation... with a break here and there to multiply integers.

Later: I just went through an intense few hours of extreme doubt around my note to my Soul Mate. Even though I promised myself I wouldn't second-guess the decision, I have. I am grateful for all these releasing techniques and meditations, but by spending an hour trying to release through EFT and EC, am I creating an aversion to the experience, which will only make me more miserable?

I went for a long walk on the beach and just sat with that and meditated. Just being aware of it. I know it is my ego. Only the ego can be hurt and be scared and be in and out. I know this has nothing to do with my Soul Mate. For one thing he hasn't done anything... at all. It fascinates me how doubt can make me want to run and hide when I don't even have anything to run from!

Nothing outside of myself can make me feel anything. The only meaning something has is the meaning we give it. It is my choice to feel something according to the perspective I choose and the stories I tell myself. And, boy oh boy, can my ego create some doozies in order to make itself right. My ego is dying and it is scared. It keeps me delving into the past for proof that I'm not healthy in relationships, that I'm stronger and better on my own.

My ego blabs, "See. You're obviously not ready if you are going through all this and you don't even know what's going on or even anything about him for that matter. He could be a smoker for crying out loud!"

The answer is self-love. Blah, blah, blah, I know, but it's true. I am whole and complete. This does not mean I am better alone, it means I'm good. Everything is good. No need to freak out and self-sabotage, which I did *not* do last night. Yay, me!

My Higher Self knows the bigger picture. All is good. No need to panic. The ego is shortsighted and comes from a place of lack and fear. It believes in the illusion. It created the illusion. It is the illusion. My Higher Self knows better. I have had the glimpse of the vision of my true divinity and it is awesome and comes from a place of love and compassion.

The Universe is conspiring for me to live my highest purpose through my passions. How can I not trust that?

March 26, 2012

Stanley and I were sitting on the floor reading a book this morning, when he said way too matter-of-factly, "My teacher doesn't care about me."

I'm sure she does, or at least I hope she does, but having a overcrowded Grade 2 class, there is no way she could be expected to embrace his gorgeous uniqueness. I have never had such a creative, curious student, but I can see how it would be hard to appreciate him with 30 other seven year-olds. He is a handful one-on-one.

Stanley must sense the reason he comes to me for an hour each day is his teacher needs a break. Heart-breaking. I hope he senses how much I care about him.

March 29, 2012

Morning Meditation: I had a vision I was a sunflower - a big, beautiful sunflower. I was floating along, smiling brightly, gathering other sunflowers to follow me. My soul mate (also a sunflower) joined me and we held 'leaves' as we encouraged others to bloom and face the sun. This time my soul mate wasn't my Soul Mate, though... I probably just didn't recognize him disguised as a sunflower.

Something unexpected has emerged. I was reflecting on an area where I continually feel in survival mode and, of course, men came up, specifically being disrespected by men. This is a huge trigger for me. Just the thought of being disrespected by a man boils my blood.

I did the Timeline Meditation, assuming it would bring up all the times I put myself in shameful circumstances; that this male-trigger was really a projection of how I have disrespected myself, but what I discovered was quite shocking.

I disrespect men.

Whoa, even writing that causes a surge to run through me.

The exercise dropped me to a moment when I was babysitting and talking on the phone to Minh (a brief boyfriend I had in Grade 8). I am embarrassed to say the only reason I was dating him was to get close to his friend, Tony. I liked Tony a lot.

I had a flash of writing in my diary, confessing I was going out with Minh because I didn't want to be alone. I wanted a boyfriend and thought being with him would make Tony jealous. I knew Minh liked me, but didn't respect his feelings at all.

Now, the cause of this insensitivity goes back way further and I'm trying not to judge myself, but it definitely colored my choices moving forward in regards to boys. I was boy *crazy*.

When I went with my best friend and her family to Expo '86, we met 100 guys in six weeks. I made a list and was so proud when we hit one hundred. In school, I always liked at least five guys at a time. I flirted to get what I wanted even if it was just some attention. It usually worked, but when it didn't my ego was crushed.

I remember thinking guys didn't really have feelings. If I'm going to be honest, I'm still not sure they do. This is ridiculous, I know. I am surrounded by super-sensitive men - my father, uncles, brother-in-laws and many wonderful guy friends.

The truth is I never believed guys had real feelings for me. It just felt better to think they didn't have feelings at all. I think one of the reasons I was meant to work with youth, was not only to develop the compassion to forgive myself for my past, but to work one-on-one with sensitive young men. The beliefs were created when I was a pre-teen and cemented as a teenager.

After the embarrassment of my second sexual experience, I was bitter. From then on, I unconsciously pursued other girls' boyfriends. It soothed my bruised ego if a guy paid attention to me or cheated on his girlfriend, proving my belief they had no feelings while feeding it, too.

Both Matthew and Carlos had girlfriends when I first pursued them. I've had zero respect for men around sex. Including my husbands. I accused both of them numerous times of just wanting to get off. I used sex to lure them into the relationship and then later as blackmail - the promise of it to get what I wanted and its denial as a form of punishment.

None of this was conscious. My own relationship with sex is much more complex, but nonetheless, I believed for them it was an act they were biologically unable to function without and I capitalized on it. *Wow...* I never realized this.

I am consciously making the choice to respect every single man I meet. If they are living in their ego or shadow I will show them love and compassion, but still respect them and their journey. Respecting them enough to listen and to tell the truth. Most of all, respecting them as teachers as they will be showing me a part of my ego I am denying.

March 30, 2012

I had a phone chat with Shauna Hardy Mishaw, the founder and Executive Director of the Whistler Film Festival, about WIFTV doing a mentorship with them. It is going to be even more awesome than I thought. Whistler is by far my favorite festival and I am so pumped to create an opportunity for one of our members like what we have planned.

Okay. Busiest writing weekend ever. Focus! My goal is to get this draft of *Making of a Faith Healer* done. I am a genius screenwriter!

I did some EC'ing yesterday around any emotions that are blocking me from getting *FLOW* optioned and I had two: 'frustration' and 'rejection'.

As confident as I think I am when it comes to my writing and this script, past rejections are still holding me back. So annoying. The 'frustration' events were all in connection to *10:01*.

10:01 was a short film Carlos and I made when we lived in Kelowna. It was about a rich trophy wife who was having an affair with a butch lesbian who sets her younger lover up for the murder of her husband. I played the lesbian. I cut my hair short and dyed it auburn. The film opened with a very erotic bedroom scene where the other actress was, um, pleasuring me under the sheets and I have an orgasm. I cringe when I think of it.

I worked out (and binged and purged) relentlessly to deal with the pure panic of having to appear naked. I explored my curiosities around women. I wanted to be authentic. I wanted our kissing to be authentic. I immersed myself in the process; my way of rationalizing playing a role I suspected deep down was a ploy Carlos used to finally see me with a woman.

The frustrations around this film run deep, deep, deep. It took way too long and way too much money to make. The film was shot the weekend after September 11th, 2001. Yes, that September 11th. As you can imagine, there was an awful energy around those last days of prep. Not to mention the soul-sucking surrealism of the shoot.

Carlos is an extremely talented director. First and foremost, I have to say that. His story-telling genius, attention to detail and visual style could compete with any director. I'm not exaggerating, he has a gift, but as the producer of this film, and the girlfriend financially supporting him while making it, his perfectionism and disregard for money drove me crazy.

We were fighting incessantly and the tension was unbearably thick. I was having major doubts about us. I was extremely stressed and depressed, drinking and puking daily. I felt stuck. I was scared he was using me and just going to dump me as soon as he was successful, so I did the obvious thing: I asked him to marry me.

The night I popped the question, I was drunk. I had just come home from work. One of the bartenders had written a poem for me about my auburn hair. I was smitten. We flirted. He kissed me good night. I went home and proposed to Carlos.

I think part of me was hoping this would be the grand finale. His refusal would give me an excuse to leave.

"Sure. I'll marry your ass."

It was the middle of November and Carlos thought we should do it while we were in Alberta for Christmas. I agreed. Needless to say, everyone was shocked speechless. My mom was the only one to honestly voice her concern, asking us to wait until the spring. I rewarded her with a, 'Why can't you ever just support me?' It was an awful phone conversation. I made my mom cry, spewing accusations and judgments that had nothing to do with Carlos, but everything to do with my first divorce.

Once the date was set, my family was amazing. We were married by a Justice of the Peace at a hotel in Nisku. I wore black. Carlos always teased me that I actually married the JP, because that's who I said my vows to. I never looked at Carlos once the whole time. I told him it made me uncomfortable the way he was staring at him. It was true. I feel bad about that.

My parents hosted the reception in their home with a gourmet dinner for 25 guests. It was quite wonderful. Carlos' parents came from Calgary. His grandfather and his girlfriend took a train from Ontario. Another 30 friends joined us after to celebrate the night away.

After that, I created a new illusion of Carlos and I. We were going to take Vancouver and the Canadian film industry by storm - him the uber-talented director; me the glamorous actress. And it would all start with *10:01*.

After a year of re-shoots, ADR (we had to redo the audio of the entire 20-minute film), post-production and thousands of dollars, it was finally complete. We were very proud of it. It was perfect timing as we were moving to Vancouver because Carlos had received a full scholarship to Vancouver Film School.

But first we took a trip to Alberta to transfer it back on film.

We showed it to family and a few friends. Almost everyone loved it (FYI my dad did not watch the first few minutes). Almost everyone. One person said he was disappointed in Carlos and the film. That was it. The film never saw the light of day.

I thought I was going to lose my mind.

<u>March 31, 2012</u>

I went to Jerrid and Christina's last night, first for sushi and then to hang out with Charlie. He is so flipping cute. I am so grateful to have a baby in Vancouver I can chill with. I am really proud of Christina. She left her job with the advertising company she worked at and started consulting. It's only been a few weeks and she's already not taking on any new clients and chatted with someone at BCIT about maybe teaching! I love this story, because it is inspiring and proves if you leap the net will appear.

The Universe loves and supports us.

Derek's meditation of imagining living on the Emerging Edge:

"Where am I living in survival mode or holding on to archaic habits? What do I need to embrace or let go of to fully live my vision?"

Judging. I know this is holding me back from living my vision, because a big part of it is to help dismantle the false idea of separation. My ego has stepped in to sabotage my vision with spiritual arrogance. The job of the ego is to hold you back under the illusion of moving you forward. Me thinking I am somehow more enlightened than others is holding me back. My judging others is actually a way of protecting my precious ego and I don't need to do that.

The Timeline Meditation brought me to the moment I opened the letter that said I had been accepted into the Faculty of Engineering at the University of Alberta. A friend was there and her response was, "I guess you think you're better than us now."

This always bugged me, but now I see it from a different perspective. Jealously is based in fear. Part of the process, after you see the event from an enlightened perspective, is to shower it with loving silver light from that moment along the timeline all the way through to the present. The event has new wisdom and all the other subsequent events have changed as well. My friend was not acting from her Higher Self, it was her scared ego speaking and it hurt my ego terribly.

That letter was proof to me, and my parents, I wasn't a complete fuck-up. That even though I made monstrous mistakes, there was hope. I was going to be an engineer! Who would've thought? I didn't end up going that September. I realized that summer, as I was completing my registration, that I had zero interest in actually being an engineer. It was too late to switch programs, so I decided to take another year off, much to the chagrin of my parents.

After that moment, my ego began protecting me by judging others around career choices. It contributed to my fear of success, thinking people would be jealous or want to bring me down or not like me if I was successful. *Maybe more people will like me if I'm a fuck-up.* This was a huge projection I placed on Carlos.

5 PM: I was feeling triggered to binge. I was talking to Christine and Jerrid about being bulimic yesterday. He never knew I was. Our family sure doesn't gossip like I thought.

When I had that bizarre relapse two weeks ago, it was after telling Erik about it. Talking about it must bring trapped emotions to the surface. I decided to Emotion Code the urge and sure enough, a whole bunch of self-abuse ones came up. I released them with love.

15

Wild Rose of Alberta

April 1, 2012

I am here to inspire others to tell their stories, empower them to heal themselves and to awaken the world to the illusions that divide us, all through storytelling.

Inspire. Empower. Awaken.

Purpose vs. Passion: My purpose is why I am alive. My passion is how I live my life.

April 2, 2012

Something is definitely trying to emerge. I had four beers last night, ate a whole pan of nachos, half a tub of yogurt and tons of nuts. *Can you be addicted to nuts?* Yesterday, I actually got my purpose on paper for the first time and I still drank and binged all night. So frustrating!!!!

When I'm out and about, I rarely drink and barely eat. It's not that I am pretending to be healthy in public, but then running home and abusing. I used to do that when I was bulimic. While people were enjoying fries and burgers and pizza, I would nibble my salad, secretly making a mental menu of all the foods I would binge and purge when I got home. This is different. At industry events, I honestly don't feel like drinking and find eating in public awkward. With friends (excluding family and the Beaumont gang), I never have more than two beers; part of it is because I don't want to pay for a cab (which I don't have to worry about in Beaumont), most of it is because I want to stay in control (which doesn't matter in Beaumont).

This is about being alone, my lonely weekends. Beer and wine... still my BFF's.

Addiction is rooted in loneliness. This is caterpillar behavior and this crisis - waking up feeling low and disappointed, is my butterfly-self crying out to let it go. Whatever I think it is giving me, I already have.

April 4, 2012

I introduced Elliot to muscle testing today and it blew his mind - my favorite thing to do. He got all giddy, making me MT everything from the computer screen to my organic broccoli.

Elliot: Why do you only eat organic vegetables?

Me: Because they aren't covered in pesticides. Besides, they taste better.

I handed over a bright green stalk. He took a bite and smiled.

Elliot: That doesn't taste like broccoli.

Me: I swear if they labeled organic vegetables as the regular ones and had a special stand for Cheap Pesticide-Grown Veggies, most people would buy organic.

As he finished off my broccoli, I MT'd my water bottle. My finger went limp. My heart sank. I drink liters of water each day. Tap water. As soon as I muscle test something that is bad for me, the thought of consuming it makes me sick. Like my body has finally been heard and it won't be silenced again. Last night, I did beer and it said up to 3 are good; the 4th is bad. I also did wine and my finger went weak for both white and red. Now the thought of either makes me want to gag. I guess I'm buying a water purifier.

April 5, 2012

I have my first Group Coaching Call with Derek Rydall today! I bought, I mean I *invested*, in the full Law of Emergence program, which includes at least three monthly conference calls with people from around the world. I'm not using time or money as an excuse. I asked the Universe for support and to bring me people I can talk to about this stuff and here it is.

After the call: Amazing! I didn't even need to ask a question, because everyone else's seemed completely relevant to my life.

Today's topic: Lose the Wait.

"Waiting for something comes from a place of lack, but whatever you are waiting for; you are waiting with, so give it to yourself."

An unemployed man asked how he could focus on his vision when he can't find a job. He is too preoccupied with filling out applications and then gets frustrated while waiting to hear back. So interesting... that's how I feel with trying to get my script optioned.

Derek had a cool perspective on applying for jobs, auditioning, or putting yourself out there in any way. If you are in a state of 'needing' the job, you are coming from a place of lack. You are giving something outside of yourself the power to make you feel safe, secure, confident, valued, whatever you think the result will bring you. Instead, in every situation, think of it as offering someone a bar of gold (you, your talent, your service) and it is their choice if they want to accept it. Your worth does not change one iota if they don't hire or accept you.

This is all fine and dandy, but it still doesn't get my film made!

April 6, 2012 - Good Friday

It's Easter weekend. Time for rebirth! It is sunny out, so I'm going to the beach. I used to spend Easter weekend in church, but now the ocean is my altar.

Later: I'm sitting at Benny's enjoying a beer and reading Derek Rydall's book *There's No Business Like Soul Business*. I can't believe Derek was attracted into my life. Yes, I can.

A lady just walked by with her beloved, "Don't you ever buy me a damn Easter Lily. I can't stand them."

My first thought was, "How can you have such negative feelings about a flower?" Then I remembered how I've often stated my dislike for roses. It hurt me whenever Carlos bought them, because I had told him on many occasions I didn't like them. Tiger lilies are my favorite, but I think roses are fake and commercial, but not wild ones... wild roses of Alberta...

Oh my gosh, where has Wild Rose been?

"Who's Wild Rose?" You ask. Well, let me tell you a story about coming face to face with your future on a dark night in the pouring rain.

Rose is an elderly lady who hangs out in the neighborhood. She has curly white hair and wears a bright red ball cap. She is a lovely lady who doesn't really know when it is time to leave. She often approaches people at Grounds and chats their ear off. It can get awkward.

I first met her years ago with Carlos when we lived in Kits. We were having coffee one day and she sat with us. Apparently, she used to be a teacher in Alberta. She went on and on about past students and some of her teaching methods - how she got children excited to read back in the day, etc.

After she left, Carlos looked at me and smiled, "That's gonna be you."

Fast-forward to the peak of my dark days. Whenever Rose came into Grounds, I buried my face in my laptop before she could get a word out. I didn't want to hear the same story over and over again about what a quirky lass she still is, how she was an awesome teacher and how her nickname is Wild Rose of Alberta. I was a huge grump and she triggered something in me big time. I felt bad, because it was obvious she was lonely and hadn't yet discovered Facebook.

On one particularly disgusting rainy autumn night, I was walking down 4th Ave. It was a Saturday night and I was lonely and depressed. I had parked in front of The Cove with the intent of going in to write, but had a huge ball in my stomach. I didn't want to drink, but couldn't think of anything else to do so I just started walking. I slogged for about a mile in the pouring rain in one direction before crossing the street and walking back the other way.

My hood was up and I was staring at the ground, crying. I saw another pair of shoes, so looked up and there in front of me, inches from my face, was Rose in her red ball cap. Our lonely eyes met. She didn't recognize me, but I recognized her... she was me at 80. Carlos was right.

The last time I saw her was about a year ago. My Soul Mate and I were having one of our awesome visits at Grounds, when Rose came up to our table. I had since lightened up and was always happy when he was around. She showed us a picture on the wall of her teaching an elementary class fifty years ago. Rose talked our ear off for about an hour. At one point, she went up to the cashier to borrow a pen.

I smiled at my Soul Mate and whispered, "You're gonna leave, aren't you?"

He shook his head, "No. I won't leave you."

April 8, 2012 - Easter Sunday

I went to Jerrid and Christina's for Easter Dinner tonight, but on my way stopped at the beach for a stroll. I only had my old runners in the car, which are killer on my back, but the ocean was calling my name, so I couldn't resist. It turned out to be a blessing in disguise.

The tide was out. I used to love walking the shoreline when the tide was out. Vancouver beaches get pretty packed, but at low tide, when the waterline is out about a hundred yards, it feels like you and the seagulls are all alone, which I was grateful for today. Since I got my new pink and white runners, I've stuck to the main path, *wantin' to keep 'em all stylin', ya know.* But for some reason today, on this gorgeous Easter Sunday, I was pulled out with the tide.

Strolling along Locarno, a bald eagle soared overhead. I looked up... then sunk down. *Damn sinkholes.* Up to my knees in mud, the suction was so strong I could barely lift my legs out. A couple inches higher and I would've been hollering to the beach for help. I had to wiggle my feet out of my shoes, one at a time, and then reach into the muck to exhume them.

Flashback: the farm, slopping through the outdoor pens in my rubber boots wrestling between the pigs to fill their troughs. They were not a patient bunch and getting stuck in the mud (I pretended it was just mud) was a regular occurrence. The suction on my boots easily overpowered my weak bulimic legs, but I squirmed my way out with as much grace and dignity as possible. Luckily the only witnesses were the pigs, who were preoccupied with the bucket of slop I incidentally spilled in the process.

Back then it was shit-laced mud, now it is seaweed-infused sediment. My life has changed in so many ways.

Sneakers and shins caked in sediment I waded through the water to clean them off. Still about 100 yards from the beach, for absolutely no apparent reason, I began crying, no, bawling, but without tears. All the other sensations and facial contortions were there, my chest caved and my knees went weak, there were just no tears.

Have you ever done that?

I don't mean crying until you drained your tear ducts, done that millions of times. I mean *dry* crying. It wasn't chemicals or emotional toxins that accompanied whatever took over my body, it was love and gratitude. Euphoria. Ecstasy times 1000. It lasted a solid five minutes. I thought about Matthew and Carlos and my Good Friend... each re-triggering this overwhelming, unconditional joy.

The feeling is gone now, but I've had a glimpse of something.

Bar of Gold

April 9, 2012

I did a Wealth Visualization today, where I imagined myself wealthy and envisioned the qualities I would embody - generosity, freedom, abundance, joy, expansiveness.

What activities can I do to activate these qualities and vibrations? Visit neighborhoods and houses near the beach. Park in front of my dream home at Locarno and start my beach walk from there, like I'm leaving my home. It is my home.

April 11, 2012

I was accepted into the Good to Go Program at the Female Eye Film Festival!

This is so amazingly awesome. I was just hoping to be part of the Script Reading Program, but I got into GTG! *Woo hoo!* This is a huge opportunity to not only pitch my script, but my vision for the whole industry. I'm gonna offer my gold bar in all its shimmering glory!

As I was falling asleep last night, I had a thought that maybe nothing is happening with my Soul Mate because things are really exploding with my career. Who knows where I'll end up? Maybe our lives won't fit. It was a quick thought... then I dreamed about him. I hope he doesn't think I'm crazy when we're together and he reads all this. Who am I kidding?

April 12, 2012

I went to Christine's last night to watch the Canucks game. It was a weeknight and I couldn't care less about hockey, but I miss her and wanted to meet her friend Shannon, who turns out is super chill. I told them about my upcoming trip to Toronto for the FEFF.

Shannon told me about this cool accommodation-networky-thing called AirBNB. I checked it out and found a cute and cozy room for 3 nights for the price of one night in the host hotel. It saves me $300! Woo hoo, Universe! I'm so glad I went. A reminder it is time to get out in the world. Expand! Expand! Expand!

April 13, 2012

Ohhhhh Friday the 13th! I need to have a massively productive weekend, so I'm going to spend some time planning and I am definitely having a healthy weekend. I will not self-sabotage this amazingness. My weekend and life are busting at the seams.

Just finished my taxes and I'm not getting back nearly what I was expecting. Maybe I shouldn't have done them on Friday the 13th.

April 14, 2012

It's been three weeks since I left my Soul Mate the note. *Universe, I need a sign.* I need to know if I'm crazy.

Later: Michele came into Grounds this morning and we started chatting about *Arctic Air*. The first season, which was quite successful, is coming to an end and although they haven't officially got the green light for Season 2, they've already started writing it.

I'm a fan of the show overall, especially the very dreamy Adam Beach. I was telling her which episodes I liked best and which I felt didn't work, some of the characters that resonated with me and the ones that didn't. We got into a pretty deep discussion and she seemed genuinely interested in my opinion. Like I'm finally just offering my bar of gold and she accepted.

I was in the middle of analyzing one of the main character's season arcs when I glanced up and standing in the doorway was my Soul Mate.

He smiled. I looked back at Michele and thought to myself, *You gotta go.* All focus was gone. She was talking. I think she asked me to email her my feedback. One of the coolest moments I've had as a writer and all I could stammer was, "That's my friend. He's here."

Luckily, Grounds was super-busy so by the time he had his coffee, Michele had left. I hope she didn't feel like I was cutting our conversation short. I really enjoy our talks.

My Soul Mate tossed his bagged muffin on my table, "Is this seat taken?"

He he he. "No." My heart was pounding so hard I was scared he could see it. "I guess you got my note."

Dimples taking over his face, "You're so brave. I don't think I could ever do something like that."

I thought to myself, *Ha! Brave? I'm scared to death. It's just my fear of regret is so much greater than my fear of rejection.*

He got it a couple weeks ago, but didn't want to just text or Facebook. "It's better in person."

What do you mean? What's better in person?!

He kept saying over and over again how brave he thinks I am... better than crazy!

I just stared at him in a daze. I think I may have said, "I can't believe you're here." But I hope not. I love his ratty camouflage Oilers hat.

We talked for about an hour. He's been super busy. He took up snowboarding in December so has been doing that every weekend. I think he is in his early thirties. God, please don't let him only be 30. We talked tattoos. He has a cool lion one on his bicep. He showed it to me and let out a little roar.

Somehow we got on the subject of him traveling to Saskatchewan as a youth.

I asked, "Oh, for hockey?"

"No. Band."

"Really, what instrument do you play?"

"The bagpipes."

"The bagpipes?! Uh, that's so cool. You're the only person I know who plays the bagpipes. I love the bagpipes. Best part of bonspiels."

"Oh yeah, played lots of those."

We left together. That's the first time I've stood beside him erect, I mean, me not perched behind my table. He is so tall. He must weigh 230 lbs.

On our way out the door, he looked me right in the eyes. He has such a radiant smile; it actually made me quite uncomfortable. I couldn't handle it, so I looked away. He said he would call or text. We hugged goodbye. My forehead touched his cheek. I forgot to smell him.

I called Celina as soon as I got home and started telling her the story about the note when I heard her groan deeply.

Me: Do you really want to know what I did?

Celina: No, not really, but it's kinda like a car wreck. I can't help myself. Keep talking.

Later: The ego is a bastardly beast. Feeling great one moment, then doubt creeps in to ruin the fun. I'm aware of his conniving ways.

April 15, 2012

I am so happy. Not because of anything that is 'happening'. It's not the fruits causing this feeling, although I am enjoying them; it's these deep roots I'm growing. I am being very conscious of feelings, doubts and negative expectations, allowing them to be, but not engaging. They are past ideas that protected me, but I'm strong now.

I didn't sleep well at all, though. Doubt and anxiety like to rear their head at 4 AM. My ego is panicking. He knows he cannot live at the level of great love.

Why do I refer to my ego as 'he'?

Later: My Soul Mate asked me to be his friend on Facebook! When I got the notification in my email I burst into laughter. His last name literally means 'descendant of a deity'.

I promise to only look at his pictures once. I will not Facebook stalk him.

Oh my God, there is a picture of him wearing a T-shirt with a sunflower on it and a caption that it is his 'native spirit'. Lots of pictures of the ocean, lakes, snow covered mountains, i.e. water... H_2O. This guy is so my Soul Mate.

17

Thrashing Thresholds

April 18, 2012

My lower back is killing me. I woke up at 4 AM and was up for 1.5 hours. My body is breaking. I look and feel like I'm 80. Derek talks about reaching thresholds in the emerging process. I've definitely reached one, but I am bursting through. I'm having a breakthrough.

When I was obsessed about my weight, I would size up every single woman I met, even girls, assuming they were doing the same to me. Now it is skin. I've been scrutinizing other women's wrinkles a lot lately. *Whatever you project is mirrored back.* I hate looking in the mirror. I claim to not like getting ready because I don't care about appearances, but the truth is I just don't care for what I see. I want to, though.

From now on I am going to accept the way I look! Wrinkles and all.

Later: It's my Wednesday morning writing session at Grounds and I just saw my Soul Mate walk across the street. It's dark and rainy, and even though he was wearing a coat with a hood, I knew it was him. He's so handsome. I wanted to go say hi, but wasn't feeling my best, exhausted looking and all. Fuck! Didn't I just write I was going to accept my looks?

April 19, 2012

My Soul Mate hasn't called or texted or Facebooked me (perhaps he's following me on Twitter? *Just kidding*). I'm okay, because I have a really good feeling about this and I am working through my own issues. It is bringing up every doubt I have about myself, relationships, and mostly, myself in relationships.

Am I going too fast? No, I haven't been on a date or even remotely interested in someone in 29 months. It is time for me to push through my fears and doubts. *Am I creating another illusion?* No. The story of the first time I saw him could not be wasted on an illusion.

They say every person in your life is a projection of yourself - a window into your subconscious. Well, if that's true, then soul mates are magnifying glasses. It's like every doubt or fear I have is being called forth to speak its piece. I listen, acknowledge, thank it for sharing and let it go. Everything that is bubbling to the surface, I am releasing. For the first time in my life I am not suppressing or hiding and I feel light.

I am not running away. I'm going to work through this fear. Even if we end up just being friends... No, in fact, that's the key: friends first. I want to be friends first.

More than I want to change anything in my outer world, I want to discover and emerge as my true divine self.

Later: Killer group conference call! My visualization vision: Me floating above Canada. Golden beams of light emitted from people across the nation, from the film industry, streamed up to me. The lines formed a red cape around my neck. Then my soul mate appeared and we embraced. Our hearts connected. He didn't look like my Soul Mate, but I'm not judging it.

I actually spoke to Derek this time and was able to ask my question around this heavy feeling of resistance to wealth and abundance. How the idea of 'receiving' overwhelms me. It was amazingly insightful. Apparently, I have a values conflict.

My highest value is being authentic and acting with integrity, but I also value wealth and abundance. The problem is I don't think they can happen simultaneously. I still have so much guilt about the past things I did for money, as well as shame for who I became in relationships.

Derak helped me write a double affirmation to rewire my conflicting values of integrity and authenticity with wealth and abundance.

The more I act with integrity and authenticity and love and honor myself, the more wealthy and successful I am.

The more wealthy and successful I am, the more I love and honor myself and act with integrity and authenticity.

What fires together; wires together.

<u>April 20, 2012</u>

420 - International Weed Day. Piece of advice, don't go into downtown Vancouver on April 20th if you can't handle the smell of pot. Actually, it would be a good idea to stay inside completely. I didn't even know what 'four-twenty' meant before moving to Vancouver and they have whole marijuana celebrations and rallies here.

The Law of Emergence call yesterday has me working through some deep insecurities and fears.

Only my ego knows fear. My Higher Self knows love.

Only my ego has expectations. My Higher Self knows the true story.

Only my ego knows my caterpillar. My Higher Self knows my butterfly.

Whoa, maybe *I* should stay inside for the rest of the day.

This is the last page of my 1st journal... Oh. My. God. I just reread what I wrote at the beginning of the year...

Motto of the Year: Honor the New Emerging Person.

Honor the New Emerging Me

Journal Number Two! It is the same type as the first one, but green - nature, growth, expansion. Green is the vibrational frequency of the heart chakra. In feng shui, green represents harmony, balance, healing and health - physical, emotional and spiritual.

<u>April 21, 2012</u>

Life is right and good. I am on the right path. I'm following my intuition and all is good.

I'm working through some crazy ego stuff. My vanity has been in overdrive lately, and I know why.

I did the Shadow Process on Conceited. It was a brief, unfocused visit, but I asked what it needed to be integrated and it told me to accept how I look and look for the beauty in everyone.

Common sense, right? Well, if there is one thing I've learned: Common sense ain't so common.

April 22, 2012

Holy shit, I did a lot of releasing yesterday. Big stuff around Carlos. Like when we had just started dating and I suspected he spent the night with his ex-fiancé and when he used a classmate from film school to make me jealous and insecure. I didn't even realize I had trapped emotions about that one, but major anger and bitterness came up.

Derek taught us a profound meditation process called Visualization, Vibration and Radiation (VVR).

First you just relax and breathe and relax and breathe. Then recall a time when you felt really inspired or in love (that euphoric experience at the beach when I was dry crying filled my heart) and allow this positive energy to flow through your entire body. Then from this place open up to the vision of your life. Allowing yourself to visualize and live all the amazingness. Feel the vibrations of these qualities - love, joy, abundance, peace (they are all in you). Allow them to grow and expand and intensify.

Then, imagine the Earth as a small pearl ball. Raise your hands and radiate all this energy through your arms and out your hands and saturate the globe. Focus on anywhere there is judgment or unforgiveness, just keep the love flowing. Finally, put your hands on yourself to complete the circuit. Shower all that positive energy and forgiveness back through you.

I worked on forgiving Carlos. So trapped in his ego and shadow and fear. I know who he really is and I bless him with love and true happiness. I know the above events are coming from my perspective, and may not even be true, but I trapped these emotions because I believed they happened and that's what I need to release. Maybe it's me, not him, I need to work on forgiving.

Inspired Idea! I'm at Grounds and gonna message my Soul Mate to come for a visit.

Moments later: Why did I just do that? My ego is, of course, freaking out.

No. I'm trusting my intuition. He's a good person. I can feel it. My ego is scared. Scared of being hurt. Scared of change. I love and care for that part of me that has been hurt. I honor it. It is just trying to protect me, but my spirit came here to experience great love and I need to follow the inspirations and trust the insights. Whatever is missing is what I'm not giving.

I don't want to scare my Soul Mate's ego. I have a feeling he is scared, too. Becoming friends on Facebook brought us out of the coffee shop and into the real world. My ego is scared of his ego, but my spirit knows the truth. My soul knows.

No matter what happens, I promise to love and care for myself.

Later: My Soul Mate messaged me back, but has plans all day. Next weekend! I have no expectations. Keeping it casual. Friends first. Deep down I know it is best this moves super slow. I'm happy I sent him a message. He needed to know I'm interested. Ha! How could he not?

Later: I bought sexy lingerie today! Haven't done that in years.

April 23, 2012

Elliot: It's April 23rd's birthday.

Me: Yes, thank you. That one I remembered.

Elliot: You're five years older than her.

Me: Actually, four years, four months, Smarty Pants.

Elliot: Do you remember the day she was born?

Me: Yep. I even remember the first moment I saw her. I came home and she was lying on the bed wrapped up in a blanket. I lied down beside her and stared at her sleeping. She was so peaceful. Last time I remember thinking of her that way.

Elliot beamed. He likes stories like that.

Happy birthday, Baby Sista!

April 24, 2012

Happy birthday, Dylan! It makes me sad that since I left Alberta almost 12 years ago I haven't been home once for Dylan's birthday.

He's such a cool kid. He reminds me a lot of me when I was his age, except he's super athletic. Okay, that made it sound like I was cool at fourteen, which I most definitely, was not. I'm not sure what it is, maybe it's because we look alike. I have a picture of myself sitting around the campfire with no makeup and a ball cap on. I swear we could be twins.

Actually, maybe I just wish we were alike. Dylan has this incredible presence you usually don't see in boys his age. It's quite inspiring. He also gives the best hugs, different than Lee's nurturing back rub. When Dylan hugs you, you know you are being hugged.

Derek had us do an interesting wealth consciousness activity today. He would start a sentence then we finished it in our journals, without thinking. Just letting our hands write.

If I become really wealthy and successful... Life will become overwhelming and unbalanced.

The reason I'm afraid of becoming really wealthy is... I'm scared I will lose it all.

The reason I'm not letting myself become really wealthy is... because I don't deserve it.

If I become really wealthy and successful... I'm afraid I'll have to let go of my story.

I always accused Carlos of pulling me down. What complete bullshit. Nobody pulled me down. I pulled myself down. This projection work is a bitter pill to swallow. Man, it was so much easier to blame Carlos.

Derek also spoke about how the first thing we do when things 'out there' don't seem to be going our way is panic. This is like quicksand (or a sinkhole!). Fighting it will just sink you deeper. Instead, just observe, "Hello, Fear. Hello, doubt. How are you doing today?"

Oh shit. I think this is what Dr. Pez meant about creating a gap. We were discussing my wanting to quit drinking (again). How I would make the commitment, but then at certain times of the day or in certain places I would just react. Just going about my business and then all of a sudden, it would hit. I would want to have a drink and lose all focus.

Dr. Pez's advice: *Take a moment and breathe, 'Hmmm, this is interesting. I would like a drink right now. Why do I want to drink right now?' Don't judge, just observe.*

Observing the anxiety, observing the fear, observing the doubts, creates a space. Just breathe and notice. Create the space, then put them aside and go back to living my vision. This sends a message to my ego that I'm not playing his game anymore.

April 25, 2012

Morning Meditation: My mind kept going back to losing my virginity. I decided to sit with it for a bit, then allowed the next two experiences to flow in as well. For the first time, in a very long time, I saw those three guys as boys. I never realized this, but as the years have passed I've stayed the same age in the memories, but they've aged, like it was their adult-selves that hurt my child-self. I've judged and held resentment towards these guys as grown men. Today I saw them as boys, because they were boys; boys who were just as drunk and fucked up as I was.

My entire sexual timeline flashed before me. Every 'first time' I've had with someone, I was inebriated. Throughout my marriages, even when I was sober, I was never present. How could I be present with them, when I couldn't be present with myself?

I asked that 14-year-old girl, with her teased-streaked hair, "What do you need to feel loved and supported and safe?"

Take it slow, respect my body; respect the sharing of my body.

April 26, 2012

I had a great day writing at Grounds yesterday. Erik came by and we had such a fun, jocular visit. I am so grateful for our friendship. He has taught me so much about finances and business and was the perfect person to teach me you can be successful and still be a beautiful, abundant person. We may not agree on everything, or on most things for that matter, but that is part of our charm. Plus, he thinks I'm funny. Well, he thinks it's funny that I think I'm so funny.

We talked a lot about how scared guys are around relationships. The weird thing is I didn't bring it up. The conversation just went there. He is definitely in my life for a reason.

I also had an AHA moment yesterday about the whole *I'm not ready* crap.

Since I left Carlos, my favorite cop-out has been "I'm not ready." Whenever someone offers to set me up, "I'm not ready." Whenever a guy has hit on me, "Not ready." Whenever a loved-one has asked me if I'm ever going to start dating, I respond, "I'm just not ready yet."

Lately it has evolved to "Oh, whenever my Soul Mate is ready, I'm ready" or "Maybe my Soul Mate is scared" or "I need this to go turtle slow". These are just cop-out projections.

Like Derek says, "Lose the WAIT." If you are waiting for conditions to be right in order to emerge, you will be waiting forever. I don't want to wait forever. There was a time I needed to hide and lick my wounds, but now it is just fear holding me back. I'm waiting for something external to make me feel ready. What am I waiting for?

I always feel safe when I think of love in the future. When I think of being in a relationship now, I panic. When I push it into the future, even by a week, I feel free. The problem is I'll always be pushing into the future what I'm not comfortable experiencing in the now.

I labeled this procrastinator, or future-shover, a 'Coward'. Wow, this really struck a chord. I've done Coward before, but this was a different shade of the shadow. This time Coward was a little girl with long stringy blonde hair. I asked, "When did this all start?"

A few surprising things came up. Being told over and over again, "When you're older" was a big one. Who would've thought such a simple phrase that millions of parents are saying to their children right now, could actually have this effect: encouraging procrastination?

Tracy being the star athlete and me being a complete clutz was another. Also, being put in the 'special' classes for Grade 5 and 6. I hated being singled out for being *not* good at something, so never wanted to try anything new in case I might fail. Later events just perpetuated and cemented this. Because I didn't want to admit I was scared, I drove this part of me into the shadows and just did what I was sure to succeed at: getting plastered.

I have made courageous choices, of course, like quitting teaching to move to Hollywood to become a movie star. Super brave, except four months later I was waitressing in Kelowna, pretending there was a booming film industry there. Convincing myself I needed to learn more first, get more experience first, my relationship (of a whopping five months) should come first.

I asked my Stringy-haired Coward what gifts she has given me.

By taking the long way around in my career, I have created a strong root system both in my craft and in the industry. I have gained amazing life experiences through these prepping years. Korea. India. Teaching at Youth futures. My fear of giving my dream 100% has made me a much more rounded person, a better storyteller and set me on this incredible spiritual journey.

Re: my second marriage being the biggest cowardly sidetrack...

She smiled, "Some trees need a forest fire in order for their cones to crack open and their seeds to be set free. Carlos was our forest fire."

In.Ter.Est.Ing.

"What can I do to make you feel safe and loved and secure in a relationship?"

I expected her to preach, "take it slow", but she didn't.

Instead, she came in close and whispered, "Tell me I have everything I already need. That I am perfect the way I am. Tell me that no matter what happens, you will love and care for me."

Okay, I can do that.

April 27, 2012

I may be going overboard with this shadow work... a new addiction? Perhaps, but I feel all my shadows are bellowing to be heard and I want to listen.

Today, I did 'Whiner'. Nothing pisses me off more than if someone calls me a whiner. It wasn't as clear a session, because it wavered with 'Scared', but both led me to the same realization: it is time to accept and surrender. I have slipped into that controlling space, thinking I need to fix me (under the guise of healing). This stems from my fear of the Law of Attraction. Afraid of what I will attract into my life.

Today is about surrendering. Surrendering to the magic of life, the magic of how things unfold, the magic of the moment. I am not doing any clearing or releasing today. Today, I am 100% perfect, with all my trapped emotions.

Besides, my forearm is stiff from muscle testing and last night I got some weird answers, like it is a lie my name is Rachelle... time to take a breather. A beautiful, accepting breather.

My life is perfect. I'm perfect.

I'm at Grounds writing in my journal and this middle-aged man just sat down in a puffy chair by the window. He looks like he may have been a roadie in his early years. Turns out he's a guitar teacher/film extra/ construction worker... you can imagine why 'roadie' came to mind.

Sunny's his name. Rockin' people's worlds is his game.

He asked what I was writing. When I told him, he took out a scribbler, like the ones they give you in elementary school, "Yeah, journaling is powerful shit."

It's gonna be one rockin' day.

April 28, 2012

5:04 PM Christine and I just went for a two-hour beach walk! I am so blessed with so many amazing friends. Whatever is the opposite of lonely, that's what I am. What is the opposite of lonely?

After, we went to her place for tea. She has this box of cards with insights and inspirations. She held it out to me and told me to pick one to keep.

All that I need to know at any given moment is revealed to me. I trust myself and I trust life. All is well. Flip to the other side: *Life is simple and easy.*

Oh Universe, I love you so much. How perfect of a parental message is this? Things are unfolding perfectly and I am not supposed to know everything. Maybe if I did, I would avoid experiences that will lead me to my vision. I have had a glimpse of my destiny and it is beautiful and peaceful and inspiring and maybe for me to tune into it, I need to learn some stuff first.

5:00 PM: Well, my Soul Mate is MIA.

I'm working through some major issues here, but I need to let this go for now. I deserve to sleep. The time is not right. This anxiety is not healthy. I am not going to run away. I am going to do the work, but this has nothing to do with him. This is a sign that something in me is trying to emerge. He is just the trigger. I know I am here to experience great love. And I am not able to do that as long as I am filled with doubt and insecurity.

More than I want to change anything in my external world, I want to awaken to my true nature and divine destiny. I am whole and complete and have everything I need. No matter what happens, I will love and care for myself.

I did some shadow work today on my Control Freak. It started with being spanked when I was young. Spanked as a way to control my behavior. That's what spanking is. I swore I would never do that and so pushed the controlling part of me into a shadow. The only reason I would want to control someone is out of fear. This 'having to know' is fear. Love extinguishes fear.

What I am going through here is a gift. I am learning to live even more in the now, accepting the present, embracing and appreciating the amazing NOW.

<u>April 29, 2012</u>

10 PM: I just had the most amazing Sunday Funday! Scott and I met for a beer at The Shack and it was so awesome. I was totally present the whole time. We *also* talked about how guys are scared of girls, especially Vancouver girls, and how hard it is to meet people here. Why are all the guys in my life talking to me about this?

On my way home, Jen texted me to talk and we did... for 3.5 hours!

Beaujolais, one of Beaumont's neighborhood pubs is now a nightclub. Last night, they had a wet T-shirt contest! I haven't laughed that hard in so long. Thank GOD they didn't have them back when I was in my late teens. One less thing I have to Emotion Code about now.

19

Lions and Tiger Lilies and Bears, Oh My!

<u>May 1, 2012</u>

Today was the most beautiful day of my life. I am so grateful to the Universe for guiding me to Derek Rydall. I participated in a group coaching call today and something was freed that has been festering for over 30 years.

I'm actually not sure if I'm going to include this day in my book or not, because it is deeply personal and involves not only me. It involves two people who I love and respect like no others: my parents. I have to write it out, though.

I thought I was going to miss today's call because of work, but I had a couple cancellations and it was no coincidence. I was meant to ask Derek my question. It was about my controlling feelings around manifesting my soul mate. How I can be so 'go with the flow' with every other area in my life, but with this I can feel myself trying to manipulate the situation. I can't trust the unfolding of it. I was all over the place and really stuck in my story, going back to being divorced twice, how all my other relationships are healthy, blah, blah, blah.

Derek was so patient and just guided me back to the theme of the call.

Whatever is missing is what you're not giving.

I sighed, "I get it when you are in a relationship, give what you want to receive, but I don't have a soul mate to *give* to."

He backed up to reflect on relationships in general. "Whenever you are in a relationship to get something, it leads to wanting to manipulate the person to give it to you. This creates codependency. Happy and blissful when you get it, frustrated and controlling when you don't."

This makes so much sense when I look back at my relationship with Matthew and Carlos.

Matthew once said arguing with me felt like stabbing an ice pick in his eye. No matter what he said, it was never enough. I always wanted more and more and more.

With Carlos, I felt on top of the world when he told me I was smart; rock bottom if he teased me I was not. I always wanted him to tell me I was beautiful, but he never would. He would skirt around the issue, "Well, *I* think you're beautiful, but I love you." Like the reason he thought I was beautiful was because his eyesight was distorted by his feelings for me.

I wanted to hear I was beautiful as a fact, not a feeling.

This was a perpetual tug-of-war in our relationship. He knew he was taunting me with a piece of gold. On some level, I think he thought if he ever gave it to me, I'd leave. The ironic thing is if he would have, I probably would've stayed. Vanity is a powerful, addictive drug. Co-dependency? *Oh, oui, oui!*

Derek continued, "What would it feel like if you were with your soul mate?"

Silence.

"Close your eyes and imagine you are in the relationship with him. How do you feel?"

I had a vision of sitting up at a kitchen island and staring into some man's eyes. "Home."

What else? Loved. *What else?* Safe. *What else?* A profound connection with someone. He kept asking, "What else?" again and again until finally my ego had run out of answers.

Then a little voice from deep within whispered, "Appreciated."

I started to cry. The floodgates opened and 30 years of pain flowed out.

Derek was so kind and compassionate; reminding me to breathe, just breathe through it. He started to ask the usual question, "Is there a time when you were young where you --"

"We were spanked." Right away I justified, "I mean, I wasn't abused or anything."

He stopped me, "Rachelle, you were abused. You were a little girl and you were spanked. That's abuse. This is not a judgment on your mom or dad. They did the best they could at a time when spanking was the accepted form of discipline, but to that little girl... it was abuse."

I had already forgiven my parents long ago. We are all on are own journeys. Maya Angelou's quote 'When you know better you do better.' is one of my mantras.

My relationship with my mom was especially strained, but one of the reasons I respect her so much is how she has become the most loving, understanding, supportive, fun-loving woman I know. You should see her with her grandkids. She is so patient and kind and fun.

On a spiritual level, I know I chose my mom to be my mom for a reason. We both learned so much from our relationship, and trust me, how I treated my mom in my teens could definitely be defined as emotional, mental and spiritual abuse.

Derek agreed, but said to be careful of taking a spiritual bypass - where we jump over the healing and get right to the higher understanding. That little girl is still crying out to be appreciated, but instead of looking for it from my mom, I've been trying to get it from a man. Ironically, I have drawn into my life boys and men who made me feel *unsafe* and *unappreciated*.

That little girl is crying and I am listening. This projection of wanting to feel appreciated is that little girl crying out to me. She wants *me* to appreciate her.

I get it. The true meaning of 'Whatever is missing, is what you're not giving' is whatever we think someone else should give us, is actually what we are not giving ourselves.

How can I make her feel appreciated? Take really good care of myself. *What does that mean?* Healthy choices. *What is one specific thing I can do to make myself feel appreciated?* Buy myself flowers. Wild flowers. Tiger lilies. Hmmm... interesting.

Derek ended with, "And how long will it take? As long as it takes."

On my windowsill, between the framed pictures of my nieces and nephews, sits one of myself as a toddler. I found it in a box when Carlos and I split up. I put it there to remind me I was once young and innocent and am worthy of forgiveness.

Living in Vancouver, I don't have very many childhood pictures. In fact, the only other one I have is a printout of my Grade 10 school photo. Tracy scanned and emailed me it this fall for the 'awkward teenage years' collage we put up at work.

I picked up my toddler photo and lied down on my bed imagining that time, the memories of being spanked. I wanted to be there for her. I wasn't this young, though. *Grade one.* I remember my school picture that year. I was wearing a red and white plaid shirt with a cream sweater vest that had a picture of a farm on it. *Next time I go home I'm going to find that picture.*

How old was I in this one? Two maybe? I decided to look at the back of the picture to find out. My mom always wrote our ages on the back of our photos. I opened the frame and there was another picture behind it - from Grade one. The only other picture in the frame.

Now, I'm loving this precious little 5-year-old girl.

After DECADES of self-abuse - the bulimia, the drinking, the meaningless sex, the unhealthy relationships, I will never abuse or punish myself again. No matter what happens or what mistakes I make, I promise to love and care for and comfort and appreciate myself. Finally I know why I did all of it and I will never do it again. From now on, all thoughts, words and actions to myself and about myself are only of love and compassion and appreciation.

My number one priority is to make my little girl feel loved and appreciated and safe.

And how long will it take? As long as it takes.

May 3, 2012

I bought myself flowers! Hanging out in the floral department at Safeway, I felt a bit weird, but not as much as I expected. Mostly the thoughts were around how much I should spend, until a sweet little voice asked, "What am I worth?"

I looked away from the prices and picked the most colorful bouquet of spring wild flowers with three huge tiger lilies poking out. They have added such vibrancy and abundance to my home. The best part is when I woke up this morning and saw them, I was instantaneously filled with love and appreciation.

"I bought those for myself. I fucking rock!"

May 5, 2012

Christine and I went to the opening night of the DOXA Documentary Film Festival last night. The film was *Bear 71*; a documentary about the bears in Kananaskis that are under video surveillance. They are constantly being watched so they can be stopped before coming into Canmore, a city near Banff. Bear 71 is a mama bear and the lead of the film, which basically just follows the tracking of these poor bears roaming around. It was extremely creepy to watch the footage, especially at the end when Bear 71, with her cub eating grain off train tracks, is killed while protecting her baby. The mama bear stood up to a train!

118

CHRYSALIS

That's the final image. Heartbreaking. Their maternal instinct is mind-blowing.

Later: Excellent WIFTV Pitching Workshop. We put one on every year to help prepare people for the Banff World Media Festival in June. Erik Paulsson and Diana Wilson of Crazy 8's hosted the morning, and then Bill Hurst and Caroline Coutts joined them to listen to pitches and offer feedback in the afternoon. I didn't pitch, but still learned a lot.

Biggest take-away: I need to write my pitches NOW! Then practice, feedback, practice, feedback. I've been procrastinating because *FLOW* is a challenge to pitch. It's confusing to pitch the intertwined storylines in a coherent way, but I will get creative and find a way.

I haven't been sleeping again. I am so tired and cranky.

May 6, 2012

At Grounds: I just had a great chat with Michele about my pitch... How I've never pitched before, how I have no idea what I'm doing, how complex a story *FLOW* is and how I don't have a clue how to even start it out. As a development exec, Michele's been pitched to thousands of times. She said her favorite ones have started out with the personal.

She asked bluntly, "Why did you write it?"

I laughed, "I'm a recovering control freak. I used to try to control everything, not only in my own life but for those around me, culminating in an eating disorder, alcoholism, depression, two failed marriages, you know, fun stuff like that."

I debated if I should share the next part... "Then my psychiatrist suggested meditation. I sucked at it, but was determined to make it work. One day, while I was trying to force my monkey mind into submission, the monkey spoke to me, 'The more you try to control me, the more out of control I become.'

I sat down and began rewriting *FLOW*, a script I had started working on a couple years earlier when I was a frustrated actor. The three intertwined stories of this film represent the 3-pronged fork in the road I faced and the paths I could've taken. The film is about letting go."

I chuckled, "About learning to go with the *flow*."

Michele looked me right in the eyes, "Start with that."

Well, it would seem my Soul Mate does not feel the same way about me. In fact, you know what? I'm going to stop referring to him as that. I am going to get the story out of the first time I saw him, once and for all, and then let this illusion go. This is a difficult thing to do, which is precisely why I have to.

Some of the events you are now aware of, so sorry if I repeat myself, but I feel I need to tell it as a self-contained story, so I can close the book on it for good.

Three weeks before my 37th birthday, I walked out on Carlos leaving him and our puppies behind. I stood in that doorway for what seemed an eternity, unable to move. Daphne (Sweety Pie) panting away, Simon (Moomoo Bear) glaring at me, *Where the hell are you going?* We both knew he knew.

I forced myself through the door, my gut being ripped out through my throat.

Am I making the biggest mistake of my life? No. If I stay, I die.

How could making the most courageous decision of my life leave me feeling like such a coward?

Carlos kept the puppies and the friends, which was fine by me. I wanted to be alone, alone as fucking possible. Divorce: not just the death of a marriage, the death of a life.

That first drive along the Sea to Sky highway from Squamish to Vancouver, across the Lion's Gate Bridge through downtown to my new little basement suite in Kitsilano was the longest, most surreal trip of my life. I gagged the whole way.

I don't think my self-worth had ever been lower. And it's been pretty low. I cried every single day for a year. Sometimes begging for the pain to go away, sometimes overwhelmed with gratitude I was free. Somewhere inside I sensed my future held possibility, but my present felt like a well-earned, well-deserved perdition.

All I could do to stay grounded in this world was to focus on writing and teaching. I rejoined WIFTV, wrote (and drank and ate) my weekends away and threw myself into the lives of the youth I taught.

The internal angst and tension continued to build until I had a panic attack trapped in traffic on Lion's Gate Bridge on my way back from a Sunday puppy visit. Looking out over Burrard Inlet, I considered jumping. Not because I wanted to die, but because I wanted to see if I could fly. Once again, I decided to seek out professional help.

Dr. Pez, the most straightforward, spiritually minded psychiatrist possible. I called and left a message, but he never got back to me. I let it go.

There are people with way bigger problems than me. I'll just stay off bridges for a while.

When Martha and Kayla died, that was it. *Snap.* I was in a perpetual state of anxiety. No amount of Sun Salutations helped. I called Dr. Pez again, this time hyperventilating into his answering machine. He got me in on the Monday.

By this point, I had lost all boundaries with the students, talking and texting with them constantly. Even opening myself up to a former student that first weekend who desperately needed my help finding a job so he could pay off some "debts".

Dr. Pez, "At least you had something to do on a Friday night."

Bastard.

We had six sessions and mostly talked about love and relationships, which was bizarre, because I went there to deal with my guilt and grief about the girls. In a round about way, I guess I did.

Divorce can be shattering, but when it is your second, you have little to no hope or expectation of ever finding love. I had absolutely no desire at the time anyways. Like I said, I wanted to be alone, alone as possible.

Yet, there was something inside of me - in the deepest hollows of my dark, dank soul - that was still curious. Even though I didn't believe love was possible for me - I was damaged goods after all, I wondered how and where other people find it.

"As long as you are looking for love it is impossible to find it."

"Huh?"

"You have to be love. Just love, and one day, seemingly out of nowhere, the right person will appear."

I sassed, "Like it's *magical?*"

Silence. And then... "No. It's not magical, but it is a miracle."

His words struck me at an achingly beautiful spot deep within where that curiosity lived. Dare I say a glimmer of hope was born.

As you know, I believe in soul mates, I had a few in my life already. So, I thought, "Hmm, maybe I just haven't met my *romantic* soul mate yet." I shuttered at the word romantic.

That was our last appointment. He said I was good. *Alrighty, if you think so.*

I got in my car and turned on the radio. Michael Bublé's, "Just Haven't Met You Yet", was playing.

Wherever you are, whenever it's right, you'll come outta nowhere and into my life.

Cute, Universe, very cute.

Just like every other uncoupled person that summer this song became my song, my anthem, my mantra. Don't get me wrong, I still wanted to be alone, but whenever I started to judge myself for my divorces, it seemed this song would come on the radio.

I continued to live in my self-induced state of isolation. I had created a mobile bitter bubble around me wherever I went; my usual gummy smile replaced with a scowl. Writing at Grounds, if ever a male specimen dared to smile at me, I would immediately bury myself back into my laptop. I considered tattooing *What the fuck are you looking at?* on my forehead.

If a poor guy did catch my eye-line, and dared to cross it and flirt, the coldness washed over me. I was an icy bitch. I rarely went out, but if I did it was always with Scott and Mike, both like brothers, or my lesbian friends.

Exhausted by life, I took a leave of absence that summer. Before escaping to my parents' cabin for a month, I went to Tennessee to do research for *Making Of A Faith Healer.* On one of my connecting flights, I sat next to a guy from Denver. He relentlessly tried to strike up conversation. *Why are you talking to me? Can't you see I am staring out the window... into fog?*

He was relentless, though, so I coldly answered a few of his annoying questions.

"Tennessee."... "To research a script I'm writing."... "Yes, alone."

He sleazed, "There is absolutely no reason you are alone."

"Really? Try two divorces."

Nothing will shut a guy up like telling him you've been divorced twice.

This two-month break helped immensely with the anxiety, but did nothing to soften the wall around my heart or clear the negativity of my aura. I was content in my dark cloud, until one October morning, sitting in my corner booth at Grounds, I glanced up from my laptop. This guy in a ratty camouflage Edmonton Oilers cap was walking towards me.

He had a radiant smile with dangerously deep dimples. His face was a sliver of sunshine in a dense fog. He actually glowed. He was looking at me. A rush of warmth and electricity ran from my toes, all the way through every organ of my body, even my linoleum heart, all the way up to my face. My mouth smiled. I didn't even have a chance to stop it. It was an instinctual, cellular, spiritual reaction.

He turned away to the coffee station.

What. The. Fuck. Was. That?

My eyes were watering and my heart was pounding. And then I listened. The song playing in the background? "Just Haven't Met You Yet."

True story.

It would take him six more smiles before speaking to me. The day he did, he just turned around abruptly and asked, "So, what are you always working on here?"

I smiled, "I'm writing."

He teased, "You writing the next Harry Potter?"

We were friends instantly. I wish we were still friends. Illusions are sure tough to let go of, especially when they have dimples like weapons of mass destruction...

Okay. Enough. *See ya, Soul Mate.*

Two minutes later: I literally just closed my journal, was gonna leave, but decided to make a quick visit to see what was going on in Facebook world.

The first picture on my feed: Josh (formerly known as Soul Mate) posted a picture... of a bear! A pic he took yesterday of one wandering in the wilderness near Whistler. It looks like a surveillance photo. Are you fucking kidding me?!

I posted a comment.

Soooooo weird. I just saw a documentary about bears under video surveillance in the forest... Are you a secret wildlife spy? Cool.

We can be friends again. He doesn't need to be afraid to leave his condo.

Later: Why is the Universe trying to fuck with my mind?

So, I leave Grounds after posting my little comment on Josh's picture, turn the corner and guess who's crossing the street? Josh. Coming from another coffee shop...

He sees me. Fuck. Now he's never going to want to leave his condo. My heart pounds in my throat. Okay, this does not need to be awkward.

I call out, "Oh my God, this is so weird! I just posted a comment on your bear picture."

He smiles that glorious smile as I proceed to give him a play-by-play of the entire *Bear 71* documentary. How creepy the footage was. How amazing bears are. I ramble on and on until a realization rises, *Am I seriously talking about bears?* I listen. Yes, yes I am. I'm talking about bears. Please stop talking about bears. Nope. I'm on a roll.

"Momma bears are absolutely fearless. You should've seen..."

Josh just keeps smiling. *Wow, she must really like bears.*

Okay, Rachelle, you are a great conversationalist. Change the fucking subject. *To what?* I don't care, anything. I scan all mental files. Nothing. Just bears. Maybe I could compliment him on how awesome his eyes look in his baby blue shirt. *Is that ketchup down the front of it?* I eye the lion tattoo on his bicep ... The moment passes. I check back in. Yep, still talking about bears.

"When I lived in Squamish, a momma bear lived in the woods behind us. I always worried my puppies might get caught between her and her cub. I mean, if a momma bear will stand up to a train, imagine what she would do to a Shih tzu." I giggle nervously.

"Was it a brown bear or black bear?"

"I'm not sure."

He goes on to tell me the difference. *Oh great, now he's talking about bears.*

"Brown bears are the ones you need to worry about."

My eyes widen, "Really? Wow, that's so interesting."

We stand in awkward silence. He says something about maybe hooking up soon, "You know, go for a beer or something."

"Sure that sounds nice." I put my hand on his bicep, my palm covering his lion tattoo, my thumb on his ketchup-stained T-shirt, and smile, "See ya, Josh."

I walk away.

When I get home, I notice he commented on my comment. *Wildlife spy...interesting, sure I'll take that job!* We're friends. Thank you, Universe.

Wisdom as Old as Hills

<u>May 8, 2012</u>

A man bought me flowers today! Okay fine, it was Sam and he just hung geraniums out my door, but they are beautiful and life is all about perspective.

I had a dream last night I was getting ready for a party and struggling with some things - clothes, time, etc. Then my dad called me boring. *Me? Boring?* He was right. No more.

<u>May 9, 2012</u>

I told Erik yesterday Christine and I were thinking about working on a TV project together and he made it sound sexual. I was so pissed off. He's such a pervert. He realized he was being an asshole and blamed it on being in Vegas. *Seriously, you are 45 years old, 4 days in Vegas is not going to change your values.* I'm still pissed off.

Erik and I argue quite a bit... like siblings. Don't get me wrong he's extremely interesting and we have great conversations, but, man, he can press my buttons. *Sand in my oyster.*

Later: Carlos just phoned me.

His grandfather passed away and didn't know who else to call. He wanted, needed, to tell someone and it must've taken a lot to call me. I'm actually quite touched and grateful. I loved his grandfather. He wrote letters. Whenever he called, he asked to talk to me. He was kind and funny and I loved talking to him. I'm sad he's gone.

It's almost a cliché to say we don't appreciate our elders, but clichés are clichés for a reason. I think some elderly people feel unfulfilled because they have all this life experience and wisdom and no one to share it with. As a child you are told to 'respect your elders' which just seems like one more thing you're supposed to do. As a teenager you don't think anyone over the age of 18 knows anything about anything. By the time you reach adulthood, you may be open, even eager, to receive all your grandparents have to share, but by this time either they've passed away or the relationship has. Especially nowadays, when generations are not separated just by years, but by great distances.

I think one of the reasons people are lonely is we don't have this multi-generational environment to grow and thrive in. This is also why I think so many people need to go to therapy, when all they may need is advice from an elder. Wisdom is timeless. Maybe this is why I moved in with Sam.

Carlos and I chatted for a bit. It was different. It was nice. We caught up on things, career mostly. He teased me about Josh - I'd forgotten I told him last summer about "this guy I met at the coffee shop."

When I got off the phone, I was overcome with this feeling of confidence, not something Carlos usually brings out in me. Then I realized, it wasn't him who was different... it was me. When we talked about *FLOW* getting into the Female Eye Film Festival, I didn't water anything down or jokingly self-deprecate or give him credit for helping me with the script. I just said what was happening. I stood in my power without even trying.

He did help a lot with *FLOW*, though. I miss his input. I've been wishing I had someone like Carlos to read *Making of a Faith Healer*, but I know that would be a huge mistake.

This phone call was huge for me. A test I didn't know I was taking and I passed.

<u>May 12, 2012</u>

I am hiking the Chief today! It's been awhile, but I'll just take it slow and steady.

The Stawamus Chief is a granite monolith just outside of Squamish. When I lived out there, I hiked it twice a week. Up and down to 1st Peak (there are 3) took me about 2 hours with a rest at the top. The puppies loved it there, too, but at the end I chose to hike it in solitude. I do my best thinking when... *Inspired Idea!*

A Summer Chief Challenge: I'm going to hike the Chief 20 times this season. *Woo hoo!*

My sleeping is not what I need it to be. I wake up at 4:30 AM with my heart racing. What am I anxious about? I know it is trapped emotions causing this, because with every one I've brought up in the past couple of days, I feel my heart and chest releasing, relaxing. This is not in my head. It's visceral.

I can also feel tension in my back and neck, especially when I wake up. This awareness is powerful. I'm having a breakthrough. I will continue doing the work, moving through this threshold and most importantly, loving and caring for my body while it's going through this.

One of the things Dr. Bradley advises against is muscle testing around relationships, but I asked about Josh anyways. I had to know. It agrees. He is my Soul Mate. *What is a girl to do?* It also said Jennifer and Elliot are my soul mates. I have eight in all, but have only met these three so far. I was surprised Celina and my Good Friend aren't, and Jon Bon Jovi. I was sure he was one.

A question Derek always asks is, "What would you need to become, in order to be okay with never having what you want?" This is so confusing to me, because being in a relationship is a big part of my vision. How can I be okay with my vision not happening?

A day in the life of my vision always has me waking up in *our* bedroom. We have white bedding, which I would never imagine having before, and the door to our balcony is open, crisp ocean air blowing in. We make love before starting our day chatting over coffee and breakfast in *our* kitchen. I then either go into my office, which overlooks the ocean, or if it is nice out, sit on *our* patio and write all day.

One of the reasons I've resisted dating is because I didn't feel I could have both a successful career and relationship, but in my vision they are intertwined.

Maybe I'll try to visualize being alone in my dream home and see what that brings up.

After: That was lame. The difference between visualizing and being open to a vision is like the difference between trying to figure out a problem and letting the answer reveal itself. Allowing *AHA* moments. I'm not questioning my visions anymore.

May 13, 2012

Top of the Chief: *There is wisdom held in this mountain and I am open to it.*

As soon as I started, tension fell away from my jaw... I didn't even know I carried stress there. Oh, yeah, I grind my teeth at night. *Why did I not make that connection before?* With every meter I ascended, I could feel my whole body loosen up, my mind, too.

Now, as I scan the Sea to Sky corridor, Howe Sound and over to the Squamish neighborhood where Carlos and I and the puppies lived... hmmmm... an epiphany...

Carlos was the greatest gift the Universe has ever given me.

I'm not sugarcoating or trying to put a positive spin on a negative situation. It was extremely painful at times, and if it wasn't my 2nd marriage, I would have bolted a lot earlier, but because of pride, fear and commitment to becoming the best wife I could be [whatever that means], I stayed. Maybe the reason I battled through wasn't the most honorable, but it set me on this path of authenticity. When it comes to our time together, I've gone from regretting, to resenting, to accepting, to appreciating. Wow. Powerful.

This is going to be the best summer ever - the summer of love.

May 14, 2012

When I awoke at 4:30 AM this morning, instead of fussing, I lied there. I listened to my heart beating, not trying to slow it down, just honoring it. I thanked it for doing such a great job keeping my blood flowing.

My heart smiled shyly, "Awe shucks. No problem." and then giggled. God, I'm weird. Scratch that. *I am unique.*

Today is Mother's Day and I did something special this year. I hope my mom agrees.

As you know, my mom and I have had a very up and down and all around relationship. There were times of extreme strain. She hurt me and I hurt her. I spent years blaming her for my pain and then carried guilt for many more knowing I was to blame for hers. Blame and guilt are toxic emotions to try and build a relationship on, but we did it. Our story is proof of the power of forgiveness, so I emailed her a gift card to Kiva. I want an entrepreneurial woman halfway around the world to benefit from our love. We are all connected.

6:30 PM: What a gorgeous day! I just visited Scott and his brother, Kyle, at the beach. I'm so proud of myself for texting Scott. My fun, social butterfly is emerging.

Thank you, Dad, for visiting me in my dream and calling me boring.

Later: So, I asked myself, "Rachelle, what do you *really* want to do to celebrate your 40th?" *Inspired Idea!* A Beaumont Hall Party!

I'm going to have a 40th Birthday Party for myself when I go home for Christmas. Actually, it's gonna be a Thank-You Party for everyone who helped me make it to forty. I could go on a trip or buy myself something, but gathering all my friends and family, well, it's just perfect. I know most people wouldn't want a 40th birthday party, but I do. I want to have a huge celebration, not in my honor, but as an expression of all the love and appreciation I have for my friends and family.

Don't get me wrong, I love that I am doing this for myself, as well. I deserve it. Whatever it costs, I am worth it. This is my 40th birthday present to myself. Let's be honest, there was a time when I wasn't sure I would make it, or even wanted to for that matter, but now I am immensely grateful I did.

May 15, 2012

One of my students, Trevor, has OCD and it is really getting on my nerves. Sometimes I feel he uses his perfectionism as an excuse for procrastination and it drives me crazy. I know, I know, this means I am a perfectionist, too.

I used to be a pessimistic perfectionist, like him. I would rather not do something at all if it couldn't be perfect. One of the reasons I procrastinate cleaning is to avoid the frustration of not getting something spotless. Although I am definitely more accepting of flaws [whoa, writing that just made me uncomfortable, maybe I'm not], now I'm more of an optimistic perfectionist, especially with screenwriting.

Ros finished reading *Making of a Faith Healer*. I first met Ros in Kelowna when I acted in a short film she produced there. Our paths crossed the first few years I lived in Vancouver, but when I went back to teaching and moved to Squamish, I pretty much left the industry. When I moved back and was looking for a way to re-enter, I volunteered for the Women in Film Festival, mostly because Ros was festival chair. I owe her a lot. She suggested I run for the board, which has been incredible, and gives me advice regarding screenwriter. She's a writer, as well, and we often read each other's work.

It's taken her a few weeks to read *Making of a Faith Healer* and I was nervous all day because her email didn't have any comments, it just said we should meet. When she read *FLOW* her response came within a day along with the feedback, "Genius!"

We met last night to discuss. She said it was rich and layered, with such great characters. Creative insecurity is so funny. She gave me some constructive feedback, too. There is still a lot of work to do, especially around the main character, Alexandra. I know what I need to do, but not quite sure how to do it. I need to take a couple days to percolate.

May 16, 2012

Ana is going to be at the Female Eye Film Festival, too! Yay! I am so excited that I will know another person in Toronto and in the 'room'. So much love and support to give and receive. I have so much work to do. Visualization, Vibration, Radiation, and Emotion Code all the way, baby. I have so many tools. I am so grateful for the Universe's love and generosity. We make great co-creators. I can see how it is conspiring for my greater good.

<u>May 17, 2012</u>

Monday is Victoria Day. 'May Long Weekend' is traditionally the first party weekend of the summer, but I'm spending it differently: Executive meeting, Telefilm event for Bill Hurst, rewrite *Making of a Faith Healer*, hike the Chief, Emotion Coding, Law of Emergence work...

Today, I am cleaning, mowing the lawn and tying up loose ends before my spectacular weekend. I love my home. I love that I live in a house and not an apartment. Sam is so amazing. He offered to tear up half his backyard so I could plant vegetables. *Why am I so lucky?*

<u>May 18, 2012</u>

I'm at Galileo's in Britannia Beach! It's been 2.5 years, but they still remember me.

Galileo's was my 'Grounds' when I lived in Squamish. They have the best coffee, muffins and most importantly, vibe, so this was where I set up shop every Saturday morning.

I went on an EC releasing rampage yesterday around dating. At one point I exclaimed, "Oh my God, this is endless!" I asked how many I had left. It said 15, so I motored through with love and compassion and there were exactly 15. Weird. I even asked just now and it said 'none'.

Apparently, I only have 65 trapped emotions left in total! I'm so excited. I can do this. I can release them all this long weekend. My heart is so full and I can feel myself vibrating at such a high level. I am living my purpose, my vision, and love is a part of that.

I was walking through Safeway yesterday and saw some sunflowers. They reminded me of my vision. I bought them and they add sunshine to my home. I am a sunflower that inspires others to move towards the light.

21

Friday Fête avec la Toilette

<u>May 19, 2012</u>

I had an amazing day yesterday! Wrote at Galileo's - forgot about the stunning view of Howe Sound from my corner perch, hiked the Chief and went to the Bill Hurst retirement.

Bill has worked for Telefilm for years and is extremely respected. I don't really know him, the first time I met him was just a couple weeks ago at our pitching workshop, but he is a huge supporter of Canadian talent and WIFTV, so I wanted to return the gesture. It was held at a downtown pub and I went with Carolyn, our Executive Director.

I saw my buddy Jason James. Jason is a producer and director in town. He's super smart and talented, but most importantly he is one of the loveliest people in the industry. He's got his sights set on LA, though. Hmmmm.... we have to plug this talent drain.

Had a nice little catch-up session with John Dippong, too. John also works for Telefilm and is another huge supporter of WIFTV. I first met him two years ago, when I organized the pitching sessions for our film festival. We hit it off immediately. Whenever I see John, I seem to talk his ear off. I try not to, but I just can't help myself. We have similar views when it comes to the industry and he is so supportive of me as a writer. After *FLOW* won a screenplay award at the Canadian International Film Festival, he offered to read it. I thought that was incredibly generous of him and his feedback was invaluable. This was an older draft, which was much more of a drama then it is now. Whoa... I just remembered... one of his comments was how all the male characters seemed like jerks. This surprised him, because he didn't take me as a man-hater.

Note to self: never do a re-write while going through a divorce.

Carolyn and I then went to the Executive meeting. I love those ladies. Mary mentioned something that really bothered me, though. A member complained to her about the festival awards being sponsored by individuals and how it was tacky to have awards named after people.

I truly believe I sponsored the screenwriting award from a place of love, not ego. I was looking to tithe. Now, would I have done it anonymously? No. So I guess there was a bit of ego involved. The ego aspect for me is that I like to inspire people and to be inspired. Hearing somebody else do this would inspire me.

Why did this really bother me? Insecurity? Wanting to feel appreciated?

What kind of person always needs to feel appreciated? Needy. Ouch.

My night ended cranky and I think deep down this is why. No, I know it. My frustration did motivate me to clean my bathroom, though. I finally spent a Friday night scrubbing my toilet. Dr. Pez would be so proud. He was right. It made me feel a lot better than binging or drinking.

May 20, 2012

I did it. I have no more trapped emotions. It took two extremely intense hours, but I did it. When I think of the hundreds of emotions I've released over the past 3 months, literally hours and hours, I am so overwhelmed with love and appreciation - for Dr. Bradley, the Universe and myself; also to the guy who wrote that *Power vs. Force* book. I should really read it again.

I feel like I've gone through ten, no twenty, years of therapy. Actually, I don't know if therapy does the same thing. Talking is important to gain insight, but unless you release the stagnant energy, you could be talking forever.

The last three emotions were self-abuse, self-abuse and depression, not surprising, but the weirdest experiences were when I had about ten left.

I first wandered around my suite a bit, no biggie, I often need to take breaks mid-session. This time, though, when I sat back down in my EC Chair, an intense sensation of spiders and snakes washed, no crawled, over me. Like they were all around me. I didn't 'see' any, it was completely visceral. I felt like I was paranoid at best, losing my mind at worst. I thought I was having an Ecstasy/speed flashback.

In a panic, I asked about snakes and it led to 'terror'. I saw a flash of a snake striking! I've never had 'terror' before and the feeling was awful. Fuck, I wanted to crawl out of my skin.

I then did it for spiders and there were two: both 'terror', as well. Quickly released.

Holy shit, fuck, that was intense!

After they were all gone, I went to the bathroom and washed my face. I looked in the mirror and the dark circles are way lighter and my eyes seem greener. If ever I thought Emotion Code might be a hoax, this proves it is not.

May 21, 2012 - Victoria Day

There were two suicides in Edmonton this week: a 22-year-old girl and a 24-year-old boy. Separate incidences. I am sending all my love and blessings to those families, and to the souls of those young people. They just didn't know it could get better.

I was there... a few times. The only difference is I failed. The greatest failures of my life. Those two young people did not die because they had less support than me or because I had a greater desire to live. They just succeeded where I failed. I want their loved ones to know that. That in order to support someone there has to be a connection, but it is impossible to connect with someone who is disconnected from themselves, which is the fundamental delusion when you are suicidal. It's a delusion, because survival is the primal desire of all living beings.

The last time I attempted suicide outright, I was 18 years old. Jennifer and I were living together and I took a bunch of sleeping pills one night when she was out. I wrote her a note and went to sleep. When I woke up, I glanced over at my full-length mirror and shook my head, "You fucking failure. You should've taken the whole box."

Why didn't I? I now know there was a part of me that wanted to live, but at the time I felt like a big chicken-shit. I stuffed the note in my sock drawer, so I wouldn't have to write a new one when I got up enough courage to try again. A few weeks later, Jennifer found the note. I was so incredibly embarrassed. She reached out to me with love, but all I could think was, *She must think I am such a loser.*

I never tried again, but four months later I was back living at my parents' home alternating between starving and barfing; the beginning of a ten-year journey of attempted suicide.

Wanting to kill yourself, slowly or instantly, peacefully or violently, is insane. This is not a judgment, it is an ugly fact, but with it comes a beautiful truth: there is a cure - reconnection with thyself. I am living proof.

I am so grateful for my life, every blessed moment of this incredible journey.

I am so grateful for my clean bathroom.

My life is perfect. Perfect. Perfect. Perfect.

God bless those families.

You're Beautiful

May 24, 2012

I posted on the Law of Emergence Facebook page a question about my sleeping issue and Derek replied. One of the things he said is that at this time, after sleeping for a few hours, it is the perfect opportunity for my spirit to talk to me... when I am open to hear what it has to say.

So this morning, when I awoke at 4:30 AM, before even opening my eyes, I gently asked, "What would you like me to know?" I can't remember the answer exactly, it was kinda surreal, but it was that there is a great love in me trying to emerge and to just let it happen. It is not about attracting love, but making it welcome. I felt so at peace and just fell back to sleep.

One of my favorite Derek metaphors is the radio analogy. The music of our highest vision is already playing; we're just not tuned into it. The distance between where we are and where we want to be is not one of space and time, but one of frequency.

Derek's post also asked me to look at my limiting beliefs about my body that this sleep-deprivation is bringing up. Okay, I admit it - I don't want to look old. I'm insecure because Josh is younger than me. I'm not sure how much younger (please don't let him be 30), but this is why I think he's not interested in me.

I have to remind myself this has nothing to do with him, poor guy, this is all projections of my own fears about looking old. I realize I don't even know him; he's just the first guy I've liked in a long time. He's a catalyst for the expression of all of these insecurities I haven't had to face hanging out alone in my basement suite.

Later: I saw the puppies today! Carlos texted me completely out of the blue. He's in town shooting and had a couple free hours, so was taking the puppies to Spanish Banks if I wanted to come say hi.

I haven't seen him since August, the last time he was in town. We had met for coffee and he really pissed me off. I told him I quit Youth Futures, making the huge decision to work part-time and pursue writing full-time.

He nodded, "Yeah, I wish I could find a way to play hockey full-time."

I was so mad. Like him playing Alberta beer-league hockey is the same as me being a professional screenwriter. He never played hockey the whole time we were together... *Argh!* He works in the industry. That is how he makes his living. I was fuming, but even worse, it was the first time I doubted my decision to quit my job. I doubted myself as a professional screenwriter. This is the power he had over me. This is the power I gave him.

Driving along Marine Drive to meet them, I was extremely anxious, my stomach wrenching the whole way. *What am I doing? I'm happy. Why am I setting myself up to get pissed off?* It's one thing talking to someone on the phone, when you don't have to see them or have them see you. Being there for him because of his grandfather's passing was nice, but authenticity has become so important to me and I don't want to be in a situation where I have to pretend.

Still, something was guiding me along the swerving ocean-side road to the beach where we had hung out at as a family years ago.

Daphne was all over me. Simon was aloof. Carlos tried to get him to play with me, but I didn't want to force him. We did have a moment when I cuddled him and we looked into each other's eyes. He knows I love him. He knows I always will. We always had a connection.

Simon was born outside a Buddhist Temple in Korea. Need I say more?

Carlos is a great dad. I always knew they would be better off with him and I was right.

It was super windy, so we sat in the car for a bit... so weird being back in the Yaris with him. The last time we were, was the last time we had sex. Today, we just had an amazing talk.

He is seeing someone new. Lindsay. She's a director, too. Actually, he worked on a short film of hers years ago when we were living in Kelowna. I remember the project. He got the gig through a friend from Edmonton and they shot in Nelson. I never met her, though.

He smiled, "It's funny because it's like she is the *me* and I am the *you* in the relationship."

"Be careful with that, Carlos. That's how I felt when we started dating... like I was *Matthew* and you were *me*. I felt it was my penance for hurting Matthew." I never told him that before. "Don't enter a new relationship from a place of guilt."

We talked about my fears about guys - the belief they are all cheaters. He looked at me shocked and said, "I never cheated on you, Rachelle; never even thought about it."

I needed to hear that.

Carlos was a really good friend today; showed me how I am projecting my fears on Josh. Fears he feels he is responsible for. Carlos carries a lot of guilt about our relationship, but today I told him he had nothing to be sorry for. I held him back, too, by not allowing him to grow.

"There's nothing to forgive. We were meant to be together and we are meant to be apart."

I mentioned how I only hang out with 50-year-old single women and 30-year-old taken guys.

"You are better than that, Rachelle. You deserve to be with someone."

He told me I was a great wife. He told me I was beautiful.

I laughed, "Ha! It only took me 12 years, but I finally got you to say it!"

He shook his head, "Not telling you... that was my own shit. And I will always regret it."

"Don't. If you'd given me what I wanted, it would've been like giving candy to a child. I would've just craved more. Only I can give myself what I need."

We hugged. The puppies must've been confused. I can't believe the timing of this visit. I just released all the trapped emotions around our relationship... plus my epiphany on the Chief.

I truly appreciate Carlos in my life. I hope he knows this. I think he needed this visit, too.

Oh shit, I will be pitching *FLOW* in exactly one month and I have SO much work to do!

Four more weeks of insanity and then watch out Vancouver and surrounding area, I am going to unleash a side of me you never thought you'd see!

I have absolutely no idea what that means.

23

Reflections of a Naked Dancer

<u>May 26, 2012</u>

The Chief was dead yesterday, which was good, because I needed the quiet time to reflect. I'm trying too hard. I can feel it. I want to have fun!

I don't need to find things to do to have fun. If there was one thing living in India taught me, it is you can have fun doing whatever you are doing, even if it is talking to someone who doesn't understand a word you say. I learned that from my driver. *What was his name?* Oh yeah, Vikram!

Every day, to and from work, Vikram would drive along explaining the world of Ahmedabad. Grinning from ear to ear, he would point to the monkeys and the camels and the random coconut stand, sharing the most hilarious anecdotes - him not knowing a word of English, me not knowing a word of Gujarati or Hindi or whatever the hell he was speaking. I would just sit in the backseat giggling away. He's the funniest man I've ever met.

Jokes are cultural; humor is universal.

Remembering Vikram hurts my mouth. My lips are so dry I can barely smile. There is something fascinating going on here. These past couple months, I've been more concerned with my looks than in years. Maybe I should look deeper at my attitude about my age. I think one of the reasons I haven't had an issue with turning 40 is because people tell me I don't look it. I like it a lot when people are surprised by my age, but what if they weren't? Then would I have an issue? Why was I (am I) so scared of Josh knowing my age?

I'm focusing on creating the conditions that are congruent with my vision. Having fun, feeling sexy. I masturbated manually (i.e. sans vibrator) for the 1st time in years and it was awesome. I slow danced with my grade one picture. Holding her over my heart to a love song.

May 27, 2012

Clare is by far one of the most beautiful ladies I know. Yeah, yeah, inside and out, but seriously, she is gorgeous. She is ten years younger than me and usually goes out for roles ten years younger than herself, but still she looks at people's wrinkles around their eyes. I usually do, too, but since my lips have been going through this catastrophic drought, all I notice is how moist and supple everybody else's are.

8:00 PM: I am dancing buck-naked in front of my full-length mirror to the MuchMusic Countdown! Oh my God, everyone must do this.

This is not ego; it is glorious.

This is not narcissism; this is acceptance.

Small breasts equal less stretch marks.

I am not a girl anymore. I am a woman! Hear me *roar*! Rawrr-purrrrrrrrr.... Okay maybe I'm a girl-woman. One step at a time.

An Ode To Polysporin

<u>May 28, 2012</u>

Sadie's 5th birthday! When Celina was pregnant with her, I was a little concerned I wouldn't feel the same intensity as with my other nieces and nephews or that I would have to somehow share my love between them, but the moment Sadie was born, my heart just grew.

My lips are falling off my face. Could I finally be breaking out of my chrysalis?

<u>May 29, 2012</u>

7:16 AM: My lips are so tight I can't speak. Pure agony. *How am I supposed to teach if I can't talk?* Desperate, I call Celina. She's a mom. She'll know what to do.

"Use the oil from the side of your nose. It's a natural moisturizer."

"Really?" My finger instinctually gives it a try.

"Yeah, or your armpits."

Silence. She bursts out laughing. So do I. My lips crack.

"Fuck off. My lips are one big paper cut."

She prescribes Polysporin. I ransack my place looking for some, digging deep in old Squamish boxes I have yet unpacked. Nothing. *The First Aid kit in my car!*

I pull it out from beneath books and jackets and hiking gear (I really need to clean my car). Nothing but gauze and band-aids. I glance at my hand. Red dots. My lips are BLEEDING, but I'm late for work. I feel like crying. I consider a band-aid... No, that would look ridiculous.

Later: Here's a teaching first: modeling the adding of fractions while simultaneously trying to stimulate the clotting of blood with a tissue.

I canceled the rest of my day. Not only were my lips in emergency mode, my whole body was shouting, *Go home and stay home!* I even missed the BOD meeting, the first one since joining the board two years ago. I watched TV and read and drank tea. I did no work and didn't even consider it. I just vegged out on my bed, perpetually slathering my lips with Polysporin. I had a one-hour semi-nap and reflected on my wholeness.

May 30, 2012

Oh my God, I just Facebooked Josh! I don't know what came over me.

I still think we should go for a beer sometime.

I am opening my life without limits. I am not putting anything on hold anymore. I'm scared he won't respond, but my fear of regret is so much greater than my fear of rejection.

May 31, 2012

Josh messaged me and agreed we should meet for a beer. It's just a beer. I'm not getting ahead of myself. Expectations and fears: both illusions that ruin the fun. I'm happy though, really happy. I'm glad it is scheduled days ahead, so I can prove to myself I can still focus and be committed to my career goals.

Thank you, affirmation.

My lips are healed! (Perfect timing)

Thank you, Polysporin.

25

Rachelle and the Broccoli Blues

June 1, 2012

Ahhh Ego. You are such a sneaky little sucker, aren't you? Your goal is to hold me back while giving the illusion I am moving forward. Josh sent me his schedule and my mood immediately dropped. Not because of anything he wrote; it just didn't meet my expectations - not enough exclamation marks and happy faces. I really do want an open, easy, 'go with the flow' life in all aspects. I'm just not used to this. I don't know how to act.

Yesterday, out of the blue, Elliot asked, "Do you overanalyze things?" He's so funny.

June 2, 2012

It's Nicole's 40th birthday! I wish I could see her today. I had flowers delivered to her school in Fort Saskatchewan. I hope she got them.

Great Chief hike yesterday. It was pouring, but I still did it. I've committed to my 20 Hike Summer Chief Challenge and I can't let a little rain hold me back!

I reread my message to Josh. I pretty much gave him only one for sure option (Saturday night) and a maybe (Sunday afternoon). Who am I kidding? As if I have any other plans. Playing it all casual didn't work out so well.

No. I wasn't playing casual. I tried to manipulate the situation. I gave Saturday night as my availability, because, well, I wanted it to be a *date*

with all the potential an evening date holds... if ya know what I mean.
My lips are healed... if ya know what I mean.

I have hockey Saturday night, so it will have to be Sunday. Let's play it by ear.

I hate playing it by ear. When will I learn? I don't want to start this off manipulating. Every single time I've liked someone, I've manipulated it from the get go. It may have worked for me in the short term, getting what I wanted, but it has always failed in the long run.

That is not what I want and this is not who I want to be.

Later: This writer who I met through a mutual WIFTV friend wanted to read *Making of a Faith Healer*. He asked a couple times, so I finally sent it to him and he just emailed me that it needs A LOT more work. *A page one rewrite as we say in the biz.* He suggested we meet to discuss his notes. He has experience in the subject area of faith healers and would love to help me out. Seriously? I never even asked him to read it. He asked to!

Inspired Idea! I should donate blood.

June 3, 2012

Today is a great, great day. After two and a half years of coffee talk, Josh and I are finally going for a beer. I woke up at 4:07 AM and was feeling major doubt. Let's be honest, it was full-on anxiety. My heart was beating out of my chest and I never even had chocolate last night. I was preparing myself for Josh canceling on me. I knew I was putting energy into a future event that hadn't even happened yet, but old habits die-hard... especially at 4 AM.

Oh my God! I just realized Matthew and I got married seventeen years ago today.

June 3, 1995, at the ripe old age of 22, I promised to be with Matthew forever. Hilarious. Of all days for Josh and I to go on a date, I mean, for a beer. Well, it would be awesome to give June 3rd a new label: The 1st time Josh and I hung out!

My pitch for *FLOW* is coming along way better. I was too focused on approaching it synopsis style and it felt stiff. Tell a story. A pitch is just telling a story.

Carlos is reading *Making of a Faith Healer*. I may very well regret this, but the script needs it. I need to know his perspective. He is a master of 'show-don't-tell' - a visual poet. I also trust his feedback will be honest, brutally honest. This is where my trepidation lies, but I will keep my precious ego out of this and do what is best for the script.

8 PM - What an amazing day! Too much to go into, but basically I spent until 2 PM drenched in doubt about Josh, expecting him to blow me off. I was actually upset with him and he hadn't even done anything! I EFT'd for about an hour, did a second yoga session and was trying to meditate when he texted me.

Hey Rachelle! Josh here, I got a couple hours if you want to meet for a pint somewhere.

Giggle, giggle. He's so cute. I'm so 15.

We met at Elwood's and talked for 2 ½ hours. He is so nice and cute and we have so much in common. And he's 37! Two years is nothing. Most guys who talk to me are in their late twenties, so this makes me very happy.

He's so dreamy. I'm so 15.

We talked football and which team I should go for now that the Colts have deserted Peyton Manning for the younger stud. No matter how much I try, I'm just not feeling the Broncos. I'm feeling pulled back to the Titans.

We talked careers and about following our intuition. He said he lost himself in a relationship once. That's the first time relationships have been brought up and I quickly changed the subject. I'm still not ready to tell him I'm a deux-fois-divorcée.

We talked about how much we love Vancouver and how we both hate reading fiction. We talked Big Rock beer. We both love the Alberta micro-brewery. He drank Grasshopper and I drank Traditional Ale. We hugged good-bye at the corner of Broadway and Trutch (I forgot to smell him again) and we said we'd do it again soon. He's going to Montreal next weekend for a stag, but we'll touch base after that.

It's been so long since I have felt this way. Years. It's nice. No matter what happens, it just feels good to like someone again.

He's so yummy. I'm so 15.

June 4, 2012

Elliot: So, what's the name of your book gonna be?

I shrugged.

Elliot: *Rachelle and the Broccoli Blues?*

God, I love that kid.

I told Donovan what my book was about (sort of) and he said I had a tsunami of money coming my way. God, I love that kid.

I am so happy. Yes, of course, hanging with Josh is part of it, but it's me. I am happiness. Yesterday was eye opening - thinking negative, expecting the worst, trying to protect myself, projecting my doubts and fears - I spent 10 hours in this self-imposed state for nothing. What a waste of time and energy.

I can't believe he's 37. Hilarious. Again, me projecting an issue I didn't even know I had. No, I don't have an issue. My ego was trying to create an issue, an excuse, to keep me stuck. I can't believe he's read Eckhart Tolle! I brought up 'the ego' and he finished my sentence on how it's main job is to hold us back, a prehistoric remnant created so the caveman wouldn't go out and get eaten by a Saber Tooth tiger. Honestly, this guy is so my Soul Mate. Oh yeah, right, I promised I wouldn't call him that anymore.

This is going to be the funnest summer of my life! I have a lot of work to do over the next few weeks, but the moment my pitch in Toronto is complete, I am going to suck every last ounce of summerness out of this summer. I have been a fuddy duddy work-a-holic for way too long.

A little summer lovin' would be the icing on the cake. I've been a fuddy-duddy celibate for waaaayyyyy tooooooo long!

June 6, 2012

Inspired Idea! I'm going to see my first NFL game! Woo hoo!

Justin has season tickets to the Seahawks and I bought the Titans/ Seahawks preseason game off him. I feel it's a sign I should go back to the Titans being my team. They started it all, after all. Now, I get to see them live! Only thing is I have no idea who I am going to go with.

It was Youth Futures' grad last night. I didn't get there until late, so had to sneak in during the speeches. A few of the students saw me right away and called out my name. It caused a mild disturbance. I loved it.

The night was pretty emotional, as it always is. Even though I don't teach there anymore, those fuckers will always hold a very special place in my heart.

The staff went out for drinks after and it was just like old times. I forgot how much we laughed. I laughed so much it gave me a headache. Mostly we laughed about the students... and me on fieldtrips with the students. Like the time I chased two male youth down English Bay Beach in my high heels and skirt screaming at the top of my lungs to try and stop them from running a flock of Canadian Geese into traffic. Or the time at the zoo, when I almost lost another youth to an Arctic Wolf when he decided to dangle his jacket in the pit while I was off daydreaming. Good times, good times.

I swear that job ignited my dark sense of humor. You have to have one in order to work with at-risk youth. You have to have one to trick yourself into going into such a stressful job each day. The darker your sense of humor, the longer you last.

I'll Decide, Formaldehyde

<u>June 7, 2012</u>

The most bizarre thing happened in my session with Elliot today. We were in the middle of a graphing question, when the x and y-axes rose off the page and merged. I zoned out and then on some surreal energetic level, I felt a crack in reality. Like I broke some energetic barrier and began vibrating at a higher level.

I don't think Elliot noticed. He too was zoned out, but that's not unusual.

Later: I just Skyped with Carlos about *Making of a Faith Healer*. He gave some great feedback, but then said it was like his *10:01*. I was perturbed. There is a lot of history wrapped up in that short film, (shame, regret, guilt - you know, the regular themes of our marriage), but deep down I know what he meant and it is not too late. It is part of the process and me reflecting on why I really want to tell this story and how to bring the emotion out will make it amazing.

He also said the structure was perfect and I have to say, that made me feel good. I take pride in my script structure. Then he said it was *too* perfect. This from the perfectionist who prided himself on noticing each of my flaws! He said it was so perfect it was predictable. *Ugh.* Well, that's all the motivation for a rewrite I need - time to blow the structure a bit.

June 8, 2012

7 AM at Galileo's: It's time to slow down a bit. I just ran a red light on my way to Squamish while jamming to Flo Rida. It was one of those parallel traffic intersection, double light situations under an overpass. I was looking at the far one, when the near one had already turned red. The car behind me wailed on his horn. I am so lucky it was only 6:06 AM.

This was the exact scenario of Celina and my car accident almost twenty years ago, except we were on the overpass. The same overpass I got my DUI on three years earlier. Weird.

Celina was only sixteen and had just got her license. I had been drinking earlier, but this time made the responsible choice and asked her to drive. We were on our way to pick Mom and Dad up at my auntie and uncle's, because they had also had a couple drinks. Funny how even when everyone makes the responsible choice, tragedy can still result. Obviously, we escaped tragedy that night, but it could of easily gone the other way.

After impact, our gold Laser did three 360's. I thought for sure we were going over the edge. Once friction over came our angular momentum and the car stopped, we looked at each other. The fright in Celina's eyes told me there was something seriously wrong with my face.

I wasn't wearing the shoulder strap of my seatbelt, so my head had hit the dashboard.

There are two indisputable characteristics about me: I have a big head and I have big teeth. Both of which did not work in my favor that night. I have a scar below my lip to prove it.*

*Note: this is actually a story I tell children to scare them into wearing their seatbelt. My tooth did go through my left lower lip that night, but the stitches healed it seamlessly. The scar below my right lower lip is due to a drunken wipeout on an icy Beaumont street when I was 16.

By the time my mom and dad arrived on the scene, the police and ambulance were already there. Lying on a stretcher, looking up at them both crying, I thought, "Wow, they are so upset. They must be really drunk."

The car hit right behind Celina's door. A microsecond earlier and my little peach cobbler would've been gone. It makes me sick to think about it. Maybe that's why we got the giggles in the emergency room.

Car accidents are the most baffling thing. Victims have walked away from massive wrecks; others have died from hitting the ditch.

Summer Chief Challenge Hike # 5

I reflected lots about *Making of a Faith Healer*. Brainstormed ways to blow the structure. Came up with some great ideas. Thank you, Carlos! Thank you Chief!

Josh is leaving for Montreal today and I texted him a bon voyage message *en français*. I actually flirted... for the first time in three years. We texted back and forth a bit and, whoa, it is officially on. The word 'panties' appeared in one of his texts. There is no turning back now.

June 9, 2012

I'm supposed to donate blood today and for some reason I don't want to go. I keep trying to come up with excuses. I'm going to force myself, though. This resistance is obviously here for a reason and I want to figure out why. Besides, I promised I would follow all Inspired Ideas.

Later: I did it and I get it. Hooked up to the machine, massive needle sticking in my arm, I listened to the pumping, I watched my blood seep out of my arm, traveling down the tube and filling the bag. It was beautiful. Donating blood is beautiful. It is proof we are all connected. We can literally flow into and through each other. It made me feel incredibly grateful and abundant. I love my life and this is a way to share life and save a life.

Dancing in the mirror naked last night, I realized I want to make love to Josh. I want our first time to vibrate at the level of our relationship. I know it's crazy. Really, I do. I know on an intellectual level there is no relationship (he may not even be attracted to me), but this is the first time I've liked somebody in 3 ½ years. I feel a connection to him even though he's in Montreal.

June 10, 2012

I woke up at 2 AM in a panic. I asked my spirit, "What is it?"

An image of Josh, followed by a whisper: *It's over.*

What? No! That's not possible. It hasn't even started. I never fell back asleep. My heart was beating like crazy. I think he got together with someone. Damn ego. You are just trying to make me feel insecure because he is partying in Montreal, but I'm not listening.

I'll decide when it's over, not you.

I can't shake the message of my spirit, though. I'm trying not to think of him as a pervert.

Beach walk epiphany: We are all perverts. Have fun with it! Sexual desire is primal and powerful. If you suppress it, you'll become perverse and there is nothing worse than a perverse pervert. I'm not joking. If we didn't put such a stigma around sex, we wouldn't have the issues pushing it into the dark corners (of the alleys and the mind), bring.

We are the only species that makes the most natural and necessary act, dirty. I can guarantee you, Simon never felt one ounce of shame or guilt after his hanky-panky pillow escapades. We often caught him surrounded by pillows... he had orgies!

Having worked with teen sex offenders, I can also tell you the damage done by pushing theses thoughts into the shadows. Sometimes, what starts out as confused curiosity mixed in with hormones and mental illness, manifests as unhealthy thoughts. The society tells them these thoughts are evil, re: that they are evil.

Shame is the lowest emotion on the Map of Consciousness. When we push people there, especially our youth, it is near impossible to rise even to the next level: guilt. The Internet doesn't create sex offenders; it gives them a community. It is growing exponentially, and will continue to, as long as youth have a place to go where they feel they won't be judged.

I had one student who inappropriately touched his cousin when he was 14 years old. His family labeled him a monster and chose to press charges. He spent time in the youth detention centre before coming to us. Although the other students didn't know about his charges, he was encouraged to share his thoughts and impulses with the staff. We were able to devise an action plan as he sorted through the guilt and shame. He is on the autism spectrum and has impulse control disorder. One time, he touched me on the knee under the table while I was helping him with math. I very calmly told him it was not appropriate. No shame, no guilt. Just not appropriate. He apologized and never touched me again. I don't even think he realized he had.

Apparently, almost all young sex offenders who get treatment never grow into adult ones. This is what happens when shadows are brought into the light, they disappear.

Emotion Coding brought a lot of the dark things that happened to me as a youth into the light. As much as I know with every fiber of my being that the moment my innocence was shocked out of me by the boy from the neighborhood in that dugout when I was 9, led me to allow the boy from school to touch me in that back alley at 12, which placed me on a path to the backseat of that car at 14, which set the stage for years of meaningless drunken sex with numerous faceless partners, finally ending with two failed marriages, I am glad I kept it a secret.

He wasn't a monster. Whoa, I just realized working with and developing compassion for boys like the 'monster' I described above was a healing gift for an ailment I never knew I had - this deep viral belief that all males are sick perverts. I never got that.

June 11, 2012

I'm on the emerging edge! I am ready to live my vision, my divine destiny. I'm so happy. Not because of anything external, but because emerging feels so fucking awesome. I feel high. I used to drink this feeling away. Then I moved onto puking it away. Then went back to drinking it away. Now, I bathe in it and radiate it!

The anxiety of the actual pitch meetings did poke its head while I was meditating yesterday, but I had a revelation: approach my pitch like a physics lesson. I'm a teacher. I pitch all the time. I love teaching concepts I'm passionate about, trying to engage the youth to hop on the quantum train. Now, I'm pitching/teaching my script and vision which I am insanely passionate about. Just gotta get others to jump on the renaissance train.

June 14, 2012

Yesterday was a fucked day. I saw an upsetting picture of Josh with a girl posted on Facebook (why don't I just stay off that thing?). It is a picture of him in Montreal at the car races with his arm around a girl and she is hugging him. I have no idea 'the story' around the photo and regardless, it has nothing to do with me. We only went for one beer.

I can feel myself waiting for something from him - acknowledgment, reassurance... whatever is missing is what I'm not giving. This is my Little Girl crying out for some acknowledgment and reassurance. I actually just wrote 'recognition' and crossed it out and wrote 'reassurance'. *Freudian slip perhaps?*

Thank you Little Girl for reminding me I have been focusing on my career and a potential relationship, more than myself.

Two more reminders: 1. Expectations ruin the fun. 2. Facebook ruins the fun!

June 15, 2012

Mr. Page-One-Rewrite sent me a huge email ripping *Making of a Faith Healer* to pieces. Did I mention I never asked him to read it? I never even responded to his last email! Why would somebody go out of their way to trash a project they weren't even asked their opinion about?

I'll mine his notes for nuggets of gold at some point. I'm usually pretty good at separating myself from my scripts. It does bring up this need for recognition, though.

Off to hike the Chief! This is my sixth time this season. Keeping promises to myself feels so flipping amazing. Self-worth comes from doing what is worthy.

27

The Pelicans of Lac Santé

June 17, 2012

It's Father's Day and like each and every Father's Day and birthday, each and every year, I've been stressing out all week about what to get my dad. He is absolutely the hardest person on the face of the Earth to buy for. I know everyone says that about their dad, but I will fight tooth and nail on this one. I bought him cheese last year for his birthday... and it wasn't the first time.

The reason he is so impossible to buy for is because, apparently, he only wants one thing: good girls. Our whole gift-giving lives, whenever my sisters or I have asked him what he wants, his answer has always been the same, "Just good girls". The fact he keeps asking for this leads me to believe he doesn't yet feel he's got them.

Richard Chartrand. Doesn't the name just ring with <u>strength</u> and <u>integrity</u>? The name, in this case, most definitely fits the man.

When my grandfather died of cancer way too young and left my mémère a widow at forty with ten kids and a farm in Northern Alberta, my dad became the patriarch of the family. A role he unofficially still holds today. His son-in-laws, past and present, nicknamed him The Godfather, because at weddings, Christmases and every other family gathering, my dad sits at a table in the corner and those who want to speak to him, come to him. He has even been known to wave you over if he has a favor to ask.

To hear my nieces and nephews call my dad *Papa* warms my heart. Especially when Lee, at the age of 20 years old, does. They still hug. It gets me every time.

My dad has one of the biggest hearts, but also loves to tease, sometimes (who am I kidding?) usually, quite brutally. One of my mom's most important roles seems to be apologizing for my dad's offside comments. Having him as a dad has definitely strengthened my ability to handle teasing, although he still knows which buttons to push when it comes to discussing social issues.

Growing up as 'Richard Chartrand's Daughter' was an interesting role to play, which each of us girls filled in very different ways. It's quite amazing how different three sisters can be.

Tracy is the athlete, having won numerous medals and trophies in volleyball, track and field, softball; the list goes on and on. As a kid I was jealous of Tracy and my dad's bond over sports, as I was decisively un-athletic. Tracy was the first one to be picked for a team; I was the last. We both played softball, but while Tracy was sliding into home plate to win the game, I was dancing with the butterflies out in left field.

Celina is the comedian. I don't know anyone who makes my dad's shoulders shake (that's how he laughs) more than Celina. As you know, I feel the same way about her, being her little pocket giggle, but growing up being the cause of a lot of heartache for my dad, I was well aware that Celina was the source of a lot of laughs. Celina was God's salving gift.

I was the chapped lips; Celina was the Polysporin.

I think one thing that helped my dad through all my partying years was that I somehow managed to maintain good grades. I'm not sure how, as I skipped more than I went, got banned from school events and, oh yeah, that time I got suspended for going to Physics class drunk. My 'school smarts' was the one glimmer of hope that maybe, someday, I would get my act together and go to university. Perhaps even get a job that didn't require him to call in a favor.

Elliot once asked me what I had in common with my dad.

I replied, "We both like to laugh and drink beer."

"You say that about everyone in your family. What is something just you and your dad have in common?"

I had to think for a moment. "We both love to nap."

In my preteens, during the glory years of the Edmonton Oilers, I tried to become a hockey fan in an attempt to have something in common with my dad. What actually bloomed was a massive crush on goalie Andy Moog. My interest in hockey waned when Number 35 left the Oilers and finally ceased when, on that dark day of August 9, 1988, Wayne Gretzky was traded to the LA Kings. This happened to coincide with the summer I discovered drinking, so instead of a winter of bonding, it was the first of many seasons of strain for my dad and I.

I can only remember my dad getting angry twice. Both times were at me and they were both about his house, specifically, me having a party in his house. The first was that winter.

I was in Grade 11 and my parents went on vacation. I think they went on a cruise, but to be honest I didn't really care where they were going, just that they were going and leaving us girls home alone for the first time. Seeing this as an opportunity to make some new friends, I had the genius idea of having a party. Not just a party... A *PAR-TEE*. Flyers were spread and furniture flipped (for their own survival - my attempt at being responsible).

On the eve of the festivities, as my girlfriends and I set up, Tracy and her boyfriend came home and threatened to call the cops if the party proceeded. Fearing my fragile budding popularity was about to be destroyed, I left them to bounce away the guests, most of whom I didn't even know.

When my parents returned and found out what I had planned, they were furious. I still remember sitting at the kitchen table that night vibrating with fear. My mom vocalized her anger very distinctly, but my dad just sat at the end of the table staring at me, with utter unmistakable disappointment in his eyes.

He sat there for what seemed an eternity until finally, with unwavering authority, he spoke, "You ever have a party in my house, you can pack your bags."

Now, I was angry. Very angry. Anger, of course, is a secondary emotion. Deep down I was hurt and confused. *How could my father care more about a house than his daughter?*

Never one to learn a lesson quickly, a couple years later I did have a party in my dad's house while my parents were at the cabin. Always one to follow through on his promises, my dad told me to pack my bags. Luckily I was about to start university, so I only had to leave for the weekends they were gone, which happened to be every single one that summer. Living out of the gold Laser was embarrassing, but also a relief. Suffering from a painfully low self-esteem makes it impossible to say no to anyone, especially friends. My being kicked out of the house every weekend solved that problem, but did nothing for my relationship with my dad.

It wasn't until this past December, at the BrainBoost Christmas Party, that I finally got it. The Christmas party was hosted in the beautiful home of the lovely parents of the brother-sister owners. The same home they raised their children in. Vancouver is a very transient city. You rarely meet people who live in Vancouver that were actually born and raised in Vancouver, let alone in the same house, so it is quite a treat to be welcomed into the home of a permanent resident, especially during the holiday season.

As Stephanie, the mom, walked around with a tray of nibblies, I got it. They hadn't just opened their house so the staff could have a place to celebrate; they had opened their home.

It took over two decades, but I finally understood why my dad was so angry all those years ago. I had opened his home to strangers. His *home*.

My family has always had a home. Not just a house, a home. It seems like such a simple thing and maybe that's why I didn't appreciate it, but I am incredibly grateful to my parents for not just providing a roof over my head and a dwelling to come back to again and again... and again, but a home.

In the summer of 2010, at the peak of *that* year, I spent a month with them at the cabin. After a decade of being away, I needed to go home. I needed to be with my mom and dad. I cried a lot. That wasn't anything special, as I had cried everyday for the seven months prior, but there is something about crying in your father's home. I felt safe. My mom and dad hugged, supported and listened to me incessantly. I was unconditionally loved by them. I realized I always had been.

That month got me through the rest of that year. We laughed and napped and watched the news. (My dad watches the news four times a day, something I am committed to change). We sat on the deck overlooking the lake, drinking beer and bonding over the flight patterns of the pelicans. We went for boat rides and mowed the lawn. If there is one gift of that, the hardest year of my life, I am most grateful for it is that my dad and I became friends that summer. Best friends. We're even going to write a movie together, *The Pelicans of Lac Santé*.

Quite a few years ago, my dad's closest friend at the time left his wife of 35 years for another woman. This was a shock to everyone, including my dad. The man's excuse for not talking to my dad about it was, "Richard is black and white." This comment infuriated me. Never has a more inaccurate statement ever been made and it still really pisses me off. I don't need to summarize my past here, but I think you'll agree that it would take black, white, grey and all the colors of the rainbow to be the father of me, to be my dad.

So now, during this, the Best Year of My Life, I am proud to say I have two more things in common with my dad: <u>strength</u> and <u>integrity</u>.

I can finally say, and trust me, I never thought this was possible: I'm a good girl. I'm a very good girl.

Happy Father's Day, Dad. I love you.

28

Good to Go

June 18, 2012

Okay, this is it! Three days and I'm off to Toronto. I am so excited I think I could burst. I know each of the industry guests inside out (when does research become stalking?), and I've made specific goals of what I would like to get out of each meeting. For most of them, it is feedback and guidance, which is a great way to ease the tension. People love to give their feedback. *FLOW* is set in Vancouver, so I don't have any expectations of a Toronto producer optioning it or any of the others offering financial support - they are all Ontario-based organizations.

The Good To Go program is on Thursday, which is perfect. I can rock the pitch sessions; then I'll rock the festival. It looks like there will be some great industry events, VIP parties, networking opportunities. That's my goal: just make connections and build relationships.

'Rachelle's Summer of Fun' kicks off in the Centre of the Universe - perfect!

June 19, 2012

7:10 AM at Grounds: When I ordered my coffee and super-fruit muffin just now, I secretly bought the next person to come in a coffee, too. I haven't done that in, like, forever. Funny thing is the next customer was a coffee shop buddy. The kid at the counter couldn't keep a straight face and neither could I. My friend figured it out and thought it was awesome, so bought the next person one, too. So much fun!

I'm such a weirdo. Last night, I found photos online of all the industry guests I'll be pitching to and made a collage of them on my laptop. Then I took a screenshot. I put the collage full-screen and EFT'd the emotions of 'doubt' and 'stress' as I looked at their faces. I practiced my pitch to them and appreciated each of them for taking the time to be there. I imagined what I want to get from them - acknowledgment, validation, appreciation, respect, connection, but instead that's what I gave them. Flowed it out.

I then visualized how proud of myself I will be when it's all done.

June 20, 2012

Last day before the big pitch-a-roo. I leave tonight on the red-eye, but still have lots to do - running errands, practicing, printing and packing. I want to be very efficient so I have time to meditate, practice my yoga and fit in a beach walk. The perfect day!

Later: I just sent Josh a flirty text. I'm sitting in Grounds and although I have no time to hangout, I texted asking if he was working from home today.

Him: *Yes. Why?*

Me: *I thought maybe I would bring you a coffee and you could show me your bagpipes.*

Him: *Ha ha, that's sweet, but can I get a rain check? I'm taking an online course...*

This is the 2nd time I've texted him inviting him to do something knowing full-well he would have to turn me down. I did the same thing a couple weeks ago asking him to play hooky from work to hike the Chief with me. Why would I do that? Why would I set myself up to be rejected? Why would I put him in a position where I know he would have to say no, but me knowing that ahead of time, I couldn't feel rejected? Why am I making this so complicated?!

9:01 PM: I'm sitting in the Vancouver International Airport lounge having a Rickard's Red. It is de-licious. I am so excited to go have an amazing time and meet a crazy number of people. Both Ana and Amber are going to be there pitching *Sitting on the Edge of Marlene*.

I have honestly, never in my life, been so insanely happy. I feel joyful and loving and abundant. All day I have just been present and appreciative.

Before leaving my basement suite, I wrote myself a note on the same paper as the one to Josh. I placed it on my bed, so I would find it when I get home: I'M SO PROUD OF YOU!

Driving here, I burst into laughter. *I am flying to Toronto to pitch FLOW, the first script I've ever written, to producers, broadcasters, distributors and funders. I love my life!*

Then, I burst into tears. Career-wise this is more than I planned for this year. I am so grateful to life. Not life happening to me, life happening through me.

I know my film inside out. My pitch will flow. That's the name of it for a reason. No matter what happens, it is all perfect. This moment is perfect. Every moment is perfect.

29

Topping Out in TO

Thursday, June 21, 2012

2 AM (5 AM EST): This fucking sucks! My seat is in the second last row and even though it's in the middle of the night, the flight attendants are acting like it's the middle of the day - banging around and having the loudest, most pointless conversations. *Inside voices please!*

I can feel myself resisting sleep, like I'm punishing myself or something.

7:50 AM: I'm on the shuttle bus trying to sleep, but it's so flipping bumpy and noisy and the bus driver won't stop complaining about his job. Fuck, I hate Toronto. I feel like crying...

The driver drops me off at some hotel and I walk down old, decrepit sidewalks, dragging my suitcase. I am grateful my parents bought me luggage for Christmas to replace the humongous crappy green 1970's hand-me-down one.

I find the address of the AirBNB residence. I haul my luggage up four flights of stairs. It's 9 AM and I'm sweating like a pig. *Why is it so fucking humid here?* I feel like rolling up in a ball and crying myself to sleep, right here mid-staircase.

My room is nice and big and I have a fan, thank God. I curl on my bed, but my mind is racing. I am so pissed off. Pissed off at the flight attendants, pissed off at the bus driver, pissed off at myself for taking the red-eye the night before the biggest day of my career just to save $50.

I can't believe I'm gonna screw this up. I don't even want to go. I just want to bail and...

No. I am not doing this! Fuck off, ego or shadow or whatever is trying to sabotage this opportunity for me. I am so sleep-sensitive. If I were going to create an excuse to take me out of the game, this would be it. But I won't. I am aware of your trickery, fuckers. I no longer play with the butterflies in left field, I am the butterfly and I'm sliding into home plate!

I shower. It helps. I do my yoga. I like doing yoga wet and naked. It is refreshing and empowering. I should really practice my pitch, but instead I lie on my bed and VVR and meditate and visualize myself pitching flawlessly. I EFT doubt and anxiety and frustration.

Then I nap. Best one hour nap of my life. I feel like a million bucks. I put on a pleasant professional navy blue dress with little white flowers on it. Classy, no cleaveage.

I love my AirBNB room. It is in an old Victorian house and only a 15-minute walk to the hotel where the industry events of the festival are held. The fresh air will do me good.

I'm off to meet some peeps and rock my pitch.

It's a scorcher - the hottest June 21st in 60 years. Too hot to walk, so I hail a cab. There is so much traffic and construction. A few hours ago, this would've put me over the edge about Toronto, but I am cool, calm and collected. I have lots of time, but from now on I'm walking.

Meet the Funders Panel: A few of the panelists are industry guests who will also be receiving pitches, so I want to get a sense of them and tune into their energy.

Panel Summary - No money for development. Awesome.

4:30 PM: It's time. Months of prep and I am ready. I am Good. To. Go!

The one-to-one, speed-dating style pitches will be held in a conference room. There are about twenty of us screenwriters from across North America lingering outside the door. I peek in and see ten industry professionals sitting two to a table around the perimeter. I recognize some of them from my collage... the others really need to update their headshots.

Just offer them my bar of gold.

They let ten of us in and I take a sharp right. Oh shit. Amber and Ana are gonna pitch right next to me. This could be awkward, especially since Amber has already heard most of my pitch. I look around to see if there is another open seat. Nope. I scan the line at the door. No way.

It works out perfect, because they will rotate counter-clockwise so I will be the first to complete the cycle.

Mark Sawyer, the organizer of the event, is my first pitchee. He is really supportive and asks to read my script. I think he's just being polite, but it's a great way to start, regardless.

Next up is Marguerite Pigott, Head of Creative Development at Super Channel. She is super nice and extremely responsive. Her facial expressions while listening really help feed the energy of my pitch. She asks some great questions about character and tone.

"You are dealing with some serious themes, but have these humorous moments as well."

I offer *American Beauty* as an example.

She winks, "That's what I was thinking. I work with producers, but I'm excited to see this project come across my desk."

Sliding over to Martin Harbury, Film & Television Consultant at Ontario Media Development Corporation, I'm on a roll. He loves my pitch and asks to read the script. He knows it is set in Vancouver, but just loves reading great stories and who knows? Maybe it will end up as an interprovincial co-production.

Wow. Three for three. Maybe Toronto ain't so bad.

The next lady is a director, who I'm definitely going to keep in mind, followed by an agent who loves the script, but only reps writers interested in TV. Not even going there.

Crossing the room to Jinder Chalmers - creator of *Combat Hospital*, I decide not to pitch. I need a break. I could feel my energy waning on the last one and this isn't a project she could do anything with anyways. I ask if I can use our 10 minutes to ask her some questions. Jinder shares some interesting anecdotes and experiences. I like her. She is developing a feature film that is set in Memphis. I don't mention *Making of a Faith Healer*.

I move to the distribution company rep... "How many of you are there?"

I tell him he's about half way and he lets out a huge *sigh*. I feel his pain. I'm sure it is exhausting on their end, too. Not the most motivating way to start a pitch, though.

Next is Marina Cordoni, Vice President of Movies at Breakthrough Entertainment. She's lovely, but doesn't seem interested either.

Hmmm... I think I should go back to the other side of the room.

My favorite rock climbing term was always 'topping out'. Not just touching the edge of the cliff with your fingers, but pulling yourself up on it and taking a look around.

I'm topping out!

Avi Federgreen of Federgreen Entertainment. I really researched this guy and watched as many of the films he's produced as I could, like Michael McGowan's *One Week* with Joshua Jackson and *Score: A Hockey Musical* (which opened TIFF in 2010).

I'm pumped and ready to roll; he's texting on his BlackBerry. I sit there not knowing what to do. I look around at everyone else pitching.

Helllooo. I only have ten minutes... now nine.

I clear my throat.

He looks up, "Oh. Sorry."

I introduce myself and start my pitch. The opening seems stale and contrived. His eyes wander everywhere but on me. I should've worn a cleave-dress. *Just kidding.* Seriously though, where is he looking? Okay, I'm just gonna cut this short and put both of us out of our misery. I streamline my pitch to basically the synopsis. *Okay, I'm done, happy?*

He hands me his card and says he would like to read the script. *Really?* I reach for it before he changes his mind. He pulls it back. Shit.

"Before I agree to read your script, what's the budget?"

Oh great. "About three million."

He hands his card over. "Okay, email me a copy and then send a hard copy in the mail."

As I rise, I turn back, "I loved *One Week*."

He smiles, "Me, too."

I burst out of the conference room. Woo hoo! So glad I'm first to complete the cycle. Some are just starting. Oh the poor distributor guy... he will never want to do this again.

10 PM: What. A. Day. Amber and I went for a lovely dinner at the Biermarket On The Esplanade. Ana had previous plans, so couldn't join us. We had a great visit and barely talked business. She's such a sweetheart. I walked home in the pouring rain. It was glorious.

I just emailed Avi *FLOW* and now I am going to sleep.

Tomorrow begins 'Rachelle's Summer of Fun'!

Friday, June 22, 2014

I just walked up and down and all around a ten-block area trying to find a coffee shop besides Starbucks. The only one I could find was Second Cup. *Fuck, am I in Alberta?* The coffee is weak and the bran muffin is cake. *Why would anyone want to live in this--* Enough. I'm gonna cut Toronto some slack. The last time I was here was November 2009... two weeks before I left Carlos. I was in a completely different headspace and heartspace. I wandered around downtown in the freezing cold, bitter about pretty much everything. Toronto didn't really stand a chance.

I was here because a short film I produced had gotten into a little festival. When I say little, I mean little. The organizer didn't tell me how little, but I should've clued in when he almost blew a gasket when I said I was flying in for it.

As I was flying out of Pearson Airport, I made a pact: no more small, low-budget shorts. Next time I come here it will be for a feature that I've written. And here I am.

This is the first day of the funnest summer of my life and I am chill-axing. It took all my willpower to leave my laptop in my room. I am seriously a work-aholic, but that is going to change. Here. Today. In the Centre of the Universe.

I will get someone to hook me up with a cool coffee shop, but for today I have the perfect spot by the window to people watch before I go listen to the script readings. I am excited to hear *Sitting on the Edge of Marlene*. I don't know much about it besides that Ana adapted it from a short story about a mother-daughter con-team. Ana must be so nervous. I would be.

11:45 PM: *Apparently Toronto Rachelle has a lot in common with Beaumont Rachelle and they plan on teaching Vancouver Rachelle a thing or two about having fun!*

Today was amazing! The reading of *Marlene* went awesome. Ana is so talented and I am pumped more than ever to develop *Happiless* into a feature. I had lunch with Ana, Amber and a couple ladies at the Biermarket On The Esplanade. Toronto actually has very nice patios.

Tonight, there was a VIP Party and I met so many amazing people. Most of the screenwriters are from the states. Many of them have been successful in competitions and festivals there, but haven't had luck getting their scripts optioned. Apparently, it is rare for a festival to have events like FEFF has, specifically the opportunity to pitch. One lady complained that all the industry guests were Canadian, though.

"Why am I here? They all loved my pitch, but said there's nothing they can do because I'm not Canadian."

Why didn't she do her research? I guess not everyone is a research stalker.

I drank a lot of beer, but am super stoked for tomorrow. I asked where the good coffee shops are and everyone laughed, but I am on a mission! *Nighty night.*

<u>Saturday, June 23, 2012</u>

I am opening a coffee shop in downtown Toronto. Seriously, I could make millions just from Vancouver visitors. Yes, I'm back at Second Cup. When I got here, super grateful about life, I decided to buy the next person to come in a coffee.

When I placed my order, the cashier was baffled, "Like someone's meeting you here?"

"No. I'll buy two large coffees and the next person to come in, tell them their coffee is free. But don't tell them who bought it."

He stared at me blankly, but the barista whipped around, "You just made my day."

The guy who got it was stunned. He just stood there looking around like he was on candid camera. This must not be something they do in ole TO.

I've decided to embrace the super-sweet and sticky muffins. I'm lying to myself about what I am putting into my body, though. I have to. The gooiness is crystallizing on my skin.

In exactly six months, I will be turning 40 and into a butterfly. What an incredible year it has been so far. I can't imagine what else could happen. I feel so happy and whole, I'm not sure there is much more of a book to write.

Later: I had lunch with Ana and we chatted about *Happiless*. She is still interested in directing it. She said she really likes my writing. I told her about this book and this year and how I recently took up dancing naked in front of my stand up mirror.

"If I don't want to look at myself naked, how can I expect anyone else to?"

She thought that was just the most awesome thing she ever heard.

I really wanted to make sure we made it to the next event, so kept looking at the time. Ana is so chill and told me to relax. She called me a control freak. It didn't really bother me, though. I pride myself on never being late... and we weren't.

<u>Sunday, June 24, 2012</u>
Back at Second Cup... why ruin a good thing.

I had the best time ever last night, even though it wasn't at all what I thought it was going to be. I was all ramped and ready for another party, but when I got to the hotel lounge, it was empty. *Why am I always so early?* Maybe Ana is right.

I sat at the bar and chatted with a nice lesbian couple who drove in from... I can't remember... some small Ontario town. After about half an hour, I asked the bartender what was going on and apparently the event was cancelled. *Cancelled? Who cancels a party?*

A group of writers came in and said they were going to see a film, if I wanted to join them. *What do you think this is, a film festival? I'm here to par-ty.*

Finally, Dianna and Brad, a husband and wife writing team, and the coolest couple ever, came in. They live in Ann Arbor, Michigan, but Brad is originally from Wisconsin. I love the Wisconsin accent. I have this embarrassing habit of taking on people's accents when I talk to them. French, Korean and Indian are the worst. Sometimes, I'm scared people think I'm making fun of them, but the Wisconsin one is so cute, I couldn't help myself. We drank beers for hours.

8 PM: I'm at the airport getting ready to go home. The closing awards are going on as I write and I'm finding it fascinating I am not there. *Why would I fly home on the night of the awards ceremony, when I don't even work tomorrow?* They give out a Best Screenplay award, why am I assuming I didn't win?

New pact: I will be at the Female Eye Film Festival next year with *Making of a Faith Healer* and I will stay the extra night... because I will win the award.

Oh yeah, and one day *FLOW* will have its premiere at TIFF.

In career, in love and in life, I'm *topping out*.

So long Toronto... you sure know how to show a girl a good time!

I am a Bamboo

<u>June 25, 2012</u>

<u>Summer Chief Challenge Hike #7</u>
My new favorite emergence metaphor: The bamboo.

For years, it doesn't look like the bamboo is growing, but then all of a sudden, it shoots up 90 feet in less than two months. That whole time, when nothing seemed to be happening, it was growing the deep, strong roots needed to support such a massive structure.

I am a Bamboo!

<u>June 26, 2012</u>

I'm gonna text Josh. Enough is enough. Life doesn't happen to you, it happens through you. We are going to hang out this weekend whether he likes it or not! *Just kidding...* kind of.

<u>June 27, 2012</u>

<u>Summer Chief Challenge Hike #8</u>

I feel like I am on top of the world. Maybe it's because I'm sitting on the peak of the Chief overlooking Squamish and Howe Sound, but metaphorically I feel it as well. My perspective has changed so much since I lived here.

I feel like the first six months of this year has been me living in my chrysalis, where an incredible metamorphosis took place. I have let my caterpillar-life go and now I'm bursting out a butterfly. Maybe the second half of my book will just be me flitting around loving and living life to the fullest. Not much drama, but so much fun.

I am free. I am indestructible. I am a bamboo.

Canada Day Weekend (or My Chrysalis Crisis)

<u>June 29, 2012</u>

First weekend of the funnest summer of my life! I want to have a summer love affair.

I texted Josh. We texted back and forth, I tried to flirt and failed miserably, but we are supposed to hang out at some point this weekend.

The WIFTV AGM was the other night and I got re-elected as vice-president. I really want to rock this term. I am a bamboo ready to shoot for the sky.

Later: Josh just texted and we're going to hang out tomorrow! I, of course, want to set a time, but pretending to be all nonchalant, asked if he preferred to make plans or go with the flow.

He texts: *Go with the flow works.*

Argh, why did I give him a choice? I want to make a plan. I want to know what's going to happen. I need to let this go.

He texts: *We can go for a couple pints somewhere close by and then you can come over and I'll show you my bagpipes.*

Ha! Okay, I don't need to know.

This is gonna be the *Summer of Love.*

June 30, 2012

Josh and I are hanging out today! No expectations, just pure fun. Have some beers. Hang out. See his bagpipes. Our texts are so cute. He's so cute. We are so cute. Our friendship is unfolding perfectly. I'm obviously attracted to him, but I want to take it slow and build the foundation. What should I wear? Something sexy and flirty? Not too sexy though. I don't want to drink too much with him. I don't want to have sex with him on our first date.

Is this a date? Oh Fuck. No. We are just hanging out. No big deal.

Breathe. Breathe. Breathe.

5 PM: Josh canceled on me. Yeah. Like 5 hours ago.

Capital "D" doubt is out in full force. Self-Fucking-Doubt to the nth degree.

I jumped out of the shower on top of the world, saw his text and plummeted. He said he had an emergency with a friend. Whatever. I'm out. I never want to like someone again. I want to crawl back into my cave - my chrysalis. It's so much safer there.

He's the one who suggested we hang out today. Yesterday! It's probably no big deal to him. He probably hangs out with girls all the time. He has no idea this is the first time I've put myself out there. The first time I have let myself be vulnerable.

I hate being vulnerable. I fucking HATE vulnerable.

I tried to play it all breezy, texting back: *No worries, I'm easy... going.* Ugh. Why would I make such a self-degrading joke? I'm so pissed... I was having a really awesome hair day.

Okay, this was exactly what I was afraid was going to happen the last time we got together, so if I can work through this for real and not just run and hide (i.e. drink and eat) I know it will be an act of loving myself, so I am going to keep writing and writing and writing.

This has NOTHING to do with him. This is me. As soon as I saw his text, my heart sank, actually, it felt more like a punch in the stomach, but it wasn't that he canceled that bothered me; it was the fear of what I was going to do with the information. *What am I going to make it mean about myself that he canceled on me? What awful things will I tell and do to myself now? How am I going to use this as an excuse to self-destruct?*

The fear of going back to that weak pathetic reject is overwhelming.

All I want to do is get drunk or puke or better yet, both. Obviously, I am not ready.

My God, Rachelle, it's been almost three years since you and Carlos broke up! When the fuck are you going to be ready?

I was just fine before he walked into the coffee shop with those fucking dimples. I was just fine in my cozy little cave. I didn't ask to be pulled out. No, I will not go back there. I refuse to run and hide. This morning I was on top of the world and this afternoon a boy rejects me and I'm crushed. What am I fucking 15?!

Whooooaaaa.... Okay, well, there it is.

When it comes to boys, I am still 15 years old. I think the fact I still call them boys says a lot. I can't believe I am 39 years old and am upset over a... No, I'm not doing this. No matter what happens, no matter what anyone else does, I will love and support myself. I am a bamboo.

I thought it was healthy romantic relationships I doubted, but the truth is I don't really believe *I* can be healthy in a romantic relationship. And since being healthy is my number one priority, I will create and attract situations that will ensure I am never in a romantic relationship.

That's what this is about and it is a lie. I can be healthy no matter what happens externally and I will prove it this weekend!

Today is a beautiful day for a breakthrough. I am turning this crisis into a catalyst.

Thank you, Josh, for ditching me.

Now, where does this doubt come from? I'm going to write with my left hand.

Doubt, doubt, doubt. I doubted I could be loved when I was spanked. How could someone love a bad girl? How could someone love someone that looked like a boy? How could someone like the mouth that ate Tokyo? How could Bobby Zalcik like me? Those girls tricked me and made a fool of me. I felt I needed to pretend to be dumb. I always went for boys who had girlfriends. How do I let go of this doubt? Who loved me? No! It is an inside job. I doubt people could love me, because I don't feel worthy.

Doubter. Loser. Stealer. Tramp. Bloody Slut.

Okay, well, now I know where it comes from, but there is also a great love trying to emerge. It is trying to burst out, but keeps bumping up against this doubt. Is this doubt just my ego trying to keep me stuck? Do I believe it?

I can't believe I'm crying. It's been such a long time since I've cried out of sadness.

Alright, *Doubt*, what the hell are you trying to tell me?

I have MT'd over and over and talked to my Higher Self, and it consistently says that in order for me to be in a loving relationship, I need to let go of my doubt. My highest vision vibrates joy and love where doubt can't live. Joy and love can't live at the vibration of doubt. I am asking for some guidance on this one.

Dear Doubt,

I want to thank you for protecting me. I know you thought I needed protection. I know you thought by keeping my expectations and hopes low, I would be spared disappointment and pain. I know you were created out of pain and disappointment. I am so sorry for that. I know you have acted as a shield around me, but I don't need that protection anymore.

My mom and dad love me unconditionally. They are supportive and love me deeply. I love them deeply. We have forgiven the pain we caused each other, the pain that created you.

My sisters and I are so different, but those differences are no longer the cause of barriers; they are our bonds. The triangle is the strongest shape. We are strong, even though, like the vertices on an equilateral triangle, we couldn't be further apart. The gap from the past is closed. We love and appreciate each other. The pain and judgment that created you has disintegrated and it is time for you to disintegrate as well.

I have the greatest friends in the world. From my girlfriends in Beaumont, who after 24 years are closer than ever, to Scott and Mike and Melissa and Clare and Christine and Erik - they acknowledge and appreciate my uniqueness and love me for it and I love them for all their individual uniqueness. I know that the pain of feeling like an outsider and being rejected and teased created you, but I don't need you anymore. I am confident in my awesomeness.

When Carlos and I broke up, I underestimated everyone from Lee to Grandma, but they all stood by me and loved me. I am worthy of their love and support. Leaving Carlos was the healthiest choice of my life and my family and friend's unconditional support got me through the hardest year of my life. I will never doubt any of them, ever again.

Now, you're in overdrive when it comes to romantic love. You feel like you need to hold on for dear life. I get that. I am grateful for all you've done, truly I am, but it is time I let you go. You are holding me back. You're keeping me stuck in the past and I want to move forward.

I am here to experience great love. GREAT LOVE. Everything I've been through has made me the person I am. I love myself. I am loving and kind and generous and funny and loyal and compassionate and authentic and beautiful and smart and talented. I have unconditional love inside of me that is ready to flow back and forth with my soul mate. Whoever he is.

I am love. I am joy. I am peace. I am confidence. I am whole.

There is nothing to fear and nothing to protect. Love is gorgeous and fun and delicious and wise and foolish and safe and scary and joyous and expansive and truthful and trusting and sexy and confident and whole and brilliant and supportive and bonding and inspiring and provoking and entertaining and educating and witty and challenging and quirky and flirty and hurtful and perverted and unconditional and sunflowers and bears in the woods and a smile in a room and a sliver of light in a foggy life and energizing and lazy and comforting and curious and creative and goofy and bumblebees and intoxicating and dangerous and indulgent and boring and moment to moment and grandiose and romantic and ketchup on a sky blue shirt and raising puppies and soft touches and moist kisses and twirling tongues and making love and primal sex and procreating and family and cooking dinners and drinking beer and long walks on the beach and quickies on the kitchen floor and coffee on the fly and champagne on the balcony and Cheesies in tupperwear next to a big blue chair and cheesecake and secrets made and secrets kept and crying together and crying apart and crying from laughter and crying from anger and even crying on a bathroom floor and hugs... lots and lots of hugs.

Doubt, I'm sorry to tell you, but there is no more room for you. I want and deserve and am ready for all the above and a whole lot more. I am ready for love.

Every single person on the face of the Earth deserves this and owes it to the rest of mankind to strive for it, because really that's what we are all here for. Doubt, you are not just holding me back; you are holding all of mankind back.

I'm letting you go! Goodbye doubt, goodbye doubt, goodbye doubt.

Love,
Rachelle

Dear Rachelle,

At first, I thought I would be able to manipulate you, but now I am actually proud of you. Like an overprotective mother who doesn't think their child will know how to function without them, I thought I was protecting you from crumbling.

You have to admit, in the past when anything negative or painful happened to you, you were the hardest on yourself. My God, you were bulimic for crying out loud! Is there anything more abusive someone can do to themselves?

I know you are strong. I've known it for a while, but I thought I would hang around until I was sure you knew it, too. You deserve love. You are here to experience great love. I disappear in the face of love and you are truly love. I'm not worried about dying, because I am not real. I am just energy and

I am happy to morph into something else. Perhaps, where I was something that held you back, now I can drive you forward.

Energy cannot be created or destroyed, just changed from one form to another. Actually, I'm quite excited. I was getting quite bored in my former role.

What should I become? I guess the obvious thing would be to become belief.
I am now belief
I believe in our vision
I believe you deserve love
I believe you are love
I believe you are safe
I believe you can take care of yourself
I believe in love
I believe love is safe
I believe love is pure
I believe love is expansive
I believe love is trustworthy
I believe love is energy
I believe love flows out
I believe love is whole
I believe you are whole
I believe love is all there is!

Love,
Belief (formerly known as Doubt)

July 1, 2012 - Canada Day

I am so grateful to be Canadian. This is really the most amazing country in the world. I love Vancouver. I am determined to create the life of my vision here. No more waiting!

Yesterday was a huge day for me - the end of the first half of 2012. Six months ago I made the intention to create the Best Year of My Life and, although, it hasn't been at all what I thought, it's been amazing. I worked through some major crap and let go of doubt. I believe. I trust. These are expansive emotions. I choose expansive emotions.

I am not scared of being the fool, because I am a fool. Being foolish is great. It helps me live without analyzing. In the words of the great

Bob Dylan, "You can't be wise and in love at the same time." This takes on new meaning. I'm not scared, because no matter what happens 'out there', 'in here' I am safe and will always love, honor and care for myself.

I want to be a brat today. Ha ha ha... That's what my Little Girl wants. She wants to be a spoiled brat. Okay, Universe let's do this. Let's have an amazing day! I will go out and find a party if I have to. If I can't find anyone who wants to party, I will pretend I am visiting Vancouver. A tourist in my own city! Erik came into Grounds today and we talked about No-Funcouver. I will not accept this. There are people having fun out there and I will find them.

As we were talking, a couple in their 20's came in. She was wearing an oversized T-shirt and sweatpants, but her hair was up in a fancy bun and she was wearing heals. He was in PJ-style attire and obviously extremely hungover. We called them the 'Walk of Shame' couple and made up a whole story around their one-night stand. The guy bought them each a coffee and a muffin and they sat at a back table. The gal tried to create small talk; the guy smiled politely.

Erik said the guy was wondering what the respectable time to call the date to an end was.

He laughed, "Trust me, I know exactly what's going through his head."

I shrugged, "I wouldn't know."

"Bull shit! You've never had a one-night stand?"

"Oh no, I've had plenty. I just always snuck out before the guy woke up. My walks of shame were always solo ones."

7:30 PM: What a bizarre day. Up, down, all around. Many AHA's and a few Oh No's.

I tried to find someone to hang out with, but everyone was either out of town, working on their thesis or not doing something I wanted to do. The past few years, I've been at the cabin. Last year we had a big party with my Uncle Sheldon and my Auntie Claudette's families. There were lots of cousins and kids. It was too much for me to handle. All I wanted to do was hide in my room. I remember talking to my cousin Dana and really wanting to connect with her. We were best friends growing up and were supposed to raise our kids together. Dana is one of the most loving, generous, down-to-Earth people, but I could barely focus on a word she was saying.

This year, I feel like I could connect. I could even party. I have been hiding for 2 ½ years and just because I wanted to have fun this weekend, I expected everyone else to be ready as well.

July 2, 2012 - Holiday Monday

At Grounds: I got caught up in the external world, but I'm back. Today is a beautiful day of love and gratitude. I am grateful for all my relationships exactly as they are. I realized one of the reasons I'm upset about Josh canceling on me is because I hate being wrong. We are friends and I have no expectations. The reality is he had more fun things to do this weekend. He wanted to hang out with his friends and deep down I'm jealous.

I know exactly what the Universe is doing. It's challenging, but I am so grateful it is providing me with experiences, so I can learn to let go and go with the flow. Whenever I have done this, I experience freedom and joy. It is so powerful. I am creating some rich soil and growing some deep, deep, deep roots. My bamboo is going to be fucking 100 feet tall.

Last week when I pitched *FLOW*, I was all, "Oh, yeah, control *used* to be a problem for me. That's why I wrote the script. Learning to go with the flow has changed my life."

My ego heard my pitch and laughed, "USED to be a problem? Ha! We'll see about that."

Later: When I got home, I did the shadow process. I was planning on doing Control Freak, but then 'victim' came to mind and it really struck a chord. So many times I have prided myself on NOT being the victim. I thought about the argument I had with Jen and Nicole at Christmas.

There is no such thing as a victim in a relationship. There are always signs. There is always that first moment when our intuition tells us something is off, but we chose not to listen. If you never have that feeling and the other person turns out to be a user, abuser, cheater or worse, then you need to get in tune with your intuition. If you did hear it, and stayed, living in denial, then you need to look at that, too.

I'm obviously not talking about children here, but I have major judgments about adults who play the victim. It frustrates me to no end...

I called out for Victim, but no shadow emerged. Instead, I was transported to thirty years earlier. Me, as my 9-year old self, standing at the entrance of the baseball dugout gazing out across the field to the bushes where my friend had disappeared into with Chris. I felt the most intense awkwardness. Chris's 12-yr old brother was staring at me from within the dugout.

"Hey, Rachelle. Look."

I looked. For the next 30 years, I will regret looking... maybe the touching that followed wouldn't have happened if I had just kept my eyes on those trees.

I wanted to run, but I was frozen. I wanted to scream, but I was mute.

Frozen, weak, mute. Fucking victim.

I came home that day and never said a word. *Why didn't I tell anyone?* I didn't think anybody would believe me. I didn't want to get him or my friend in trouble. Maybe a little of both. Mostly I was ashamed. *How did I know at nine that this was something to be ashamed of?*

That moment of shock blindsided me and, although, I've EC'd the trapped emotions around the event, that young girl was vulnerable and lost her innocence that afternoon. Choices she made around boys from then on have been rooted in low self-esteem, not just because of what happened that afternoon, but because I have judged her for thirty years.

She wants to be vulnerable and naïve again. Refusing to be either has held me back in all my relationships and kept me guarded. As much as I like to tell myself, and others, I gave 100% in both my marriages, leaving only when I was exhausted, the truth is I never gave Matthew or Carlos the most important thing - intimacy.

Oh my God, I have never been intimate with anyone. To be intimate with someone would mean being vulnerable, but I decided in that moment I would never be vulnerable or naïve again. This has turned me into a skeptic and has even driven me to 'hurt them before they hurt me'.

I promise my 9-year-old self I will love her and support her no matter what. I am listening to her. I will allow her to be vulnerable and naïve. This raises major anxiety inside of me, but I will love this part of me, too.

How long will it take? As long as it takes.

Although I have been trying not to, I have been judging myself this whole weekend. I must be doing something wrong. Labeling my situation 'bad' or 'lacking' on some level, but everything is perfect.

I am flawed. I am vulnerable. I am a victim. I can't believe I'm writing this.

The ironic thing is Josh canceling on me will actually be the best thing for me in a relationship in the long run. The only way great love will appear is if I tune into its vibration. Everything I am shedding and working through this weekend is helping me tune into that.

As long as I keep holding onto my shit, I will keep having the same shitty relationships.

Guided Meditation with Derek: *Recall a time when you have felt unconditional love.*

I usually picture one of my nieces or nephews and allow the unconditional love I feel for them to fill my heart, but today something different happened. I interpreted the request as a time when *I* felt unconditionally loved and there was a block.

When have I felt unconditionally loved? I was feeling heavy and dull, when all of a sudden I felt a bubble in my chest burst and friendship-love emerged. Every friend I've ever had was calling to me, telling me what an amazing friend I am; my future ones exclaiming they are waiting for me to come into their lives. I thought of Clare, Jennifer, Nicole and then my family.

My God, I actually felt love cracking out of my body. A secret, hidden heart-wall burst open. I started bawling bliss. I wasn't sure my face could handle it.

Now, allow this feeling to increase tenfold, twenty-fold, fifty-fold...

I thought I was going to explode. Rays of love shone from every pore of my body. I only saw light for the longest time. I radiated it and bathed in it. It was ecstasy. I allowed it.

Friendship! This is the glorious love that has been yearning to emerge.

Every one of my relationships is healthy, because they are all based in friendship. Friendship is something I used to value, but have not made a priority for a long, long time. This is why Josh has come into my life. He is a projection of what I've been missing. He is all about his friends and having fun and this is what I've been excluding my life. I love you Universe.

Later: I'm a fucking butterfly! I am singing and dancing to the MuchMusic Countdown and I am a beautiful naked butterfly. I'm also a little bit drunk, but I don't care, because this energy in me is trying to get out and I'm not stopping it.

This weekend cracked a crack of my chrysalis and there was a huge part of my caterpillar hanging on for dear life, but I am dancing it off. Thank you Flo Rida!

What a different weekend than I thought it was going to be! I thought the hardest thing about this weekend was going to be *not* having sex. Ha ha ha ha! Honestly, ha ha ha ha... Turns out sex was not in the stars, galaxy or Universe. Am I going to die a born-again virgin?

I'm fucking drunk. And hungry.

July 4<u>th</u>, 2012 - loose leaf paper transcript (I don't know where my journal is)

Happy Independence Day! It is so perfect, because that is actually how I feel. Holy shit, four days of insane breakdowns and breakthroughs. I have never been more grateful to go to work than I was this morning - to get out of my head and out of that weekend.

Last night, I listened to the GCC I did with Derek a couple months ago around manifesting my soul mate. When we got to the feeling *safe* and *appreciated* part, the Little Girl in me started bawling. I've been ignoring her again, but this is not about spanking, it is about that dugout and not feeling I could tell anyone. I did end up telling a friend a few years later, but she didn't believe me. She had a crush on the boy, who was still in my world. There were many incidences of inappropriate, unwanted touching, but she chose to believe the best in him, which meant believing the worst in me. She thought I was making it up.

UNIVERSE, I am open to friends! I am so grateful for every single relationship in my life. Including Josh. He's a nice guy. I think I scared him. I scared me. I was letting someone external affect my validity. Only I can validate myself. If I got what I wanted from him, I wouldn't get what I need, which is to fully emerge.

Just checked Facebook. First pic at the top of my news feed is this Canada Day Collage Josh was tagged in 23 hrs ago! It struck me in my solar plexus - my personal power chakra. *Why would that one be at the top?* It was him and his buddies and a few girls out having a party of a time. I want to get out and socialize. This is the point. This is the gift of the weekend. In all his other pictures, there are never ones of him with girls and now in the past month there are two!?

Yesterday, on my beach walk, I asked the Universe for a sign. It wasn't the one I wanted, but it is absolutely the one I need. I want to create a full INDEPENDENT life. Where I need or want nothing from the other person. I am letting go... breathe... letting go. This has nothing to do with him. This is something inside of me that is trying desperately to emerge. That's why it feels like a crisis. I want to PARTY! I don't think I remember how. That's what was so depressing this weekend. I wanted to party, but didn't know how. I have stifled this part of me for too long.

I don't need to look for the party... I am the fucking party!

Whatever you are looking for, you are looking with. I am the party I've been looking for!

This does not mean I have to drink myself crazy. I don't need to drink to be the party. I *AM* the party. OMG I am having a major breakthrough!!! That Little Girl who became so sad and serious is ready to have fun. I'm not talking about retreating back into my party animal teens. That was for all the wrong reasons: to escape and to impress, this is to expand and to express.

I have been taking life way too fucking serious for way too fucking long. I am exploding with vibrant love and joy and abundance and I don't need to *look* for ways to express it. I can express it in every moment.

If I can't find anyone to go see the Titans in Seattle with me, I'll just go by myself.

This weekend was the midpoint of my book. I thought I wouldn't have anything for the second half. Ha! I guess I needed some conflict, a plot point, a catalyst for a major breakthrough.

I am so grateful for this weekend, including the breakdown Monday night. Thank you Little Girl for the temper tantrum. I hear you. I love you. You do not embarrass me.

Christine... that night having drinks months ago, when I said I was ready to date and she said she would never want someone to diminish this amazing energy I have. I said if I was with my soul mate it wouldn't, but I was wrong. It has nothing to do with the person I'm with. It will only diminish if I let it. I let it diminish this weekend.

32

Bulimic Butterfly

The title of my book should be *Bulimic Butterfly*. That's what happened this weekend. I was a butterfly trying to emerge early. I was putting incredible pressure on myself trying to make something happen with Josh NOW, because I thought I was ready. I wanted to be ready, but I'm not. I've let my old caterpillar-life go, for the most part, but I'm still in this chrysalis and I need to be patient and loving and nurturing. *How long will it take? As long as it takes.*

I barely ate all weekend and weighed 113 pounds Monday morning, less than I did on Friday. I usually weigh 118 lbs on Mondays and 115 lbs on Fridays. I haven't weighed 113 lbs since the peak of my eating disorder. The scariest part... I was proud of myself that I didn't abuse myself by pigging out all weekend, proud of the number, because it meant I didn't lose control, but it was all about control. I was controlling the only thing I felt I could control - what I ate. Or didn't eat. I was starving my Little Girl into silence.

Then Monday night, I ate so much, not really more than my usual Sunday cheat night, but because I hadn't eaten in a week, it was a lot for my shrunken tummy. I also drank 5 beers while having my own private party. The celebration was a lie. It was nothing more than abuse.

I woke up at 2 AM with a stomach filled with anxiety and nachos and yogurt and beer and I puked. I was a little worried, but because it wasn't planned I tried not to make a big deal of it, but deep down I knew. The next day, I Emotion Coded and I had three: defensiveness, frustration and self-abuse. The day after that, I released two more: depression and crying.

The depression and crying were trapped after... fuck, I wasn't going to write about this... I'm so embarrassed... I drunk texted Josh. Something lame about him being such a good friend to his buddy who needed him, I don't really remember, because as soon as I sent it I was so mortified, I deleted it. He never responded. I then spent the next two hours beating myself up about it. I didn't actually cry, which is why I think it got trapped. My Little Girl was having a temper tantrum and I was beating her into submission.

There was a moment, a sliver of a moment, where I thought, *Well, I could just give up.*

When I say give up, I mean *Give Up*, in the darkest of terms. It's been years since that thought has bubbled up. YEARS. But there it was in a flash. I quickly suppressed it, too.

If you crack open a chrysalis early, what would be inside? I'm not sure, but I imagine it would be similar to caterpillar guts, i.e. it would look a lot like puke.

I am in a beautiful vulnerable stage of my development. I need to be very careful of what I let into my life, but more importantly I need to be patient with myself. My metamorphosis should not, and shall not, be interrupted.

What a wake-up call this weekend was. I thought I was going to have this summer of fun with this really great guy, but it looks like I'm on my own. *Alright, girl, let's do this!*

<u>July 6, 2012</u>

I already have a packed weekend with friends. I'm meeting a friend for a TGIF beer tonight down by False Creek, I'm going to the Indian Summer Festival tomorrow for some meditation and to try and meet some like-minded peeps, then some ladies and I are going to watch some stripper movie, plus Christine and I are hiking the Chief on Sunday. It's amazing what the Universe brings you when you open yourself up.

Josh hasn't contacted me. I thought about fear as a primal emotion. Fight or flight. Maybe he's in flight mode. I was definitely in fight mode. I have felt like this ever since leaving him the note, but thought

I was fighting through my ego. In actuality, it was my ego causing a fight. Daring this guy to be with me. Whenever I get scared, I become larger than life, throwing this intense energy at somebody, calling it confidence, but really it's just fear.

That's how I do things: I either hide in a cave or jump off a bridge.

Speaking of making a jump, I am committing to myself that I will move out September 1st. I need to look now, because I'll be in Alberta from mid-August on. It is the perfect time to cleanse and pack. I appreciate my home and will continue to every moment of the time I am here, but I'm expanding. I want to have a place where I can entertain and bring friends together. I want a view of this beautiful city! I'm ready to live where the action is. I still want this area, though, because I love Kits. It's my home.

Hello doubt... How are you doing today? Is there anything constructive you have to offer? No? Okay, thanks for sharing, talk to you later.

Later: Thank you, Universe, for the youthful night! Jen (not Beaumont Jen, a different one I met through WIFTV) and I just drank big beers out of brown paper bags sitting on the rocks by Olympic Village overlooking False Creek. So illegal. My life rocks. No small talk, just right into the good stuff. She said my book sounds interesting, because the butterfly is the opposite of what people expect to happen when you turn 40... Most think you shrivel up. Really? I never thought that.

Love Affair of a Lifetime

<u>July 7, 2012</u>

Today, I was a paradox. Yogi by day; pervert by night.

I went to the Indian Summer Festival. I participated in three meditation sessions and learned a bunch of new techniques. Super cool.

So Hum Meditation

Breathe in... Sooooo... I am.

Where is this breath coming from? Countless creatures breathing from the same source.

Breathe out... Hummmm... All that is.

Where is the breath going? Back to the source.

Breath Meditation

Your breath is the most intimate relationship you will ever have.
Wow. I like that.

Love Yourself Meditation

Enjoy spending time with your inner wise, loving, joyful, gorgeous spirit. Who wouldn't want to hang out with her? I heard a little voice whisper, "Have a love affair with yourself."

Have a love affair with myself? Hmm... maybe this will be the Summer of Love after all.

Yoga Nidra

We did this one lying down, so it was, of course, my favorite. Not really a meditation. Hard to describe. Inner yoga? First you say a silent affirmation, a sankalpa. I wasn't prepared, but then the instructor said it should be your heart's greatest desire, so...

I am in a loving, nurturing, fulfilling relationship with my soul mate.

Then she guided us through a deep body awareness relaxation, similar to Vipassana, and then a bunch of visualizations, finishing with our sankalpa again.

I also took my 1st yoga class! I've been practicing yoga for over 10 years and have never taken a yoga class. After 3 meditation sessions, though, I thought for the 4th one I should do some moving. It was called Fire Yoga and would involve upside down poses... to gain a new perspective. Perfect.

Inspired Idea! It's been a long time since I've had one, since I've allowed one.

I am going to learn to do a handstand this summer. *Why?* It is a metaphor for trusting and supporting myself. The instructor was very cute. Maybe I should get him to teach me.

Then I went and saw *Magic Mike*, a movie about male strippers, with Christine, Tawnya and Christine's friend, Arwen, who it turns out I know through WIFTV. We got there late and the theatre was packed, so we couldn't find seats together. I offered to sit by myself in the front row. Yes, that would be Pervert Row.

I took a look behind me before the movie started and the theatre was filled with women... the average age? About 50! Buncha cougars. Probably the last movie I would've picked, but it was awesome. Funny and fun and exactly what I needed. I shocked myself how much I enjoyed it. A reminder to embrace my inner pervert! It actually had a surprisingly good story, too. I like Channing Tatum. I think I should work with him one day.

July 8, 2012

What an incredible weekend - the polar opposite of last.

I picked Christine up for our Chief hike this morning and gave her a journal I bought her. An 'I'm so grateful we're friends' gift. On the way to Squamish, I was telling her all about the Indian Festival and the different meditations. She was the one who told me about it, but couldn't go. I told her about the intimacy of our breath... she said that really resonated her.

"I think you went to the festival for both of us."

That's how I feel about this book. Not everyone has the time or the space to do all this work, but I can do it and share it with those who want to read it. Maybe that's another reason it's not time for me to be in a relationship. Maybe I'm supposed to go through all this on my own.

Summer Chief Challenge Hike # 9

I usually don't like hiking with people, because I don't want to talk, but it is impossible for Christine and I to be around each other and not blab a mile a minute. As I said, we met on the board of WIFTV. I offered her a ride home one night and we haven't stopped talking since.

Today, I learned how much energy conversations actually take. It was by far the hardest hike I have ever done. Oh, but the coolest thing happened on our way down. I was sharing one of my favorite new life metaphors, just as some hikers were heading up.

"The Universe is like a GPS. It can't correct your path if you're not moving."

A young guy passed right at that moment, "Wow. I so needed to hear that right now".

I love when that happens. Proof we really are all connected.

Later: A hot shower... *Is there anything better after a hike?* I open the window to let in some fresh air. Ahhh new beginnings. I'm wrapped in a plush towel, but the air is cool, so I crawl into bed to reflect on the most amazing weekend.

I breathe in, soooooo. I breathe out, hummmm.

Soooooo... I am. Hummmmm... All that is.

How lucky am I to get to spend this moment with this gorgeous spirit? This gorgeous woman. I am gorgeous. I am sensual. A warmth flows through my body.

I remove the blanket and lower my towel to let the cool air kiss my nipples. They perk up. They have come out to play. I lick my fingers and caress each of them with a smile. They are beautiful. My breasts are small and smooth and perfect. I feel warmth between my legs. I bend them. I spread them.

My finger trails down my stomach and sneaks beneath the towel. It finds the warmth it was looking for. I unwrap the towel, grab a second pillow and prop my head to take a look at my body. My hips are full; my chest is flat. I take a moment to apologize for teasing them, ridiculing them, for the past 25 years. They are gorgeous. Now I am wet.

My clit is hard and yearns to be touched. I comply. I am gentle to start, but am so turned on I press harder. Harder. I like my inner thighs. They are trim and smooth.

I tell myself aloud, "You are beautiful." Over and over again, "You are beautiful." The words I've always wanted to hear.

I don't want this to end. I spend some more time with my breasts and my hips and my stomach and my legs. I caress my neck and my shoulders. Loving each and every inch of me.

My finger finds its way back down and enters me. I explore. I massage my clit with my own moisture. I may not cum, but that is okay. I am patient.

"I love you. As long as it takes. I love you. As long as it takes."

I am throbbing now and with barely a rub, I cum. I cry. Blissfully.

July 9, 2012

Journal Number Three! Same as the other two, but reddish-brown, like wood and roots. Support. Strength. Support and trust - two big themes, both of the Universe and myself. Also, appreciating all the support in my life - friends, family, work, writing, career. I really am blessed.

This journal also starts off My Summer Love Affair... with myself.

Last night was amazing. The first time I made love to myself. *What's the difference?* Masturbating with a vibrator is just getting off, like fucking. Last night, I *made love* to myself.

Later: I just did a striptease for myself in front of my full-length mirror. Appreciating my body and my moves. I am a very beautiful, sexy woman. I am so lucky to get to have this love affair with her.

July 10, 2012

Well, if I ever doubted muscle testing... I was just at Locarno having a late-night picnic with myself. Lying on a blanket, nibbling on organic broccoli, I asked the Universe, "Please give me a sign if muscle testing is real or not, because I kinda feel like I'm going crazy here."

I started reflecting on Doubt vs. doubt. Lower-case 'd' doubt comes and goes, rises and falls. We all have doubt. As long as we have an ego, we will have doubt, that's its job. We can just observe it, *Hello doubt, how are you today? Do you have anything constructive to contribute here? No. Okay, thank you, good-bye.* And then move on.

Capital "D" doubt is more embedded. This Doubt is crippling.

All of a sudden, this fear of failure came up. I have never forgiven myself for leaving Matthew or Carlos. As much as I blame them for not giving me what I needed, the truth is I blame myself for being so needy. Maybe if I didn't always need more and want more, the marriages wouldn't have failed. I wouldn't have been such a fucking failure.

So, lying there on a blanket in front of my dream house, where someday I will live with my soul mate, I talked to me at 25 and 36, whispering, "I forgive you. There is nothing to forgive." Over and over and over again for about an hour. I muscle tested periodically until it said I had forgiven myself completely. I wouldn't leave until I was sure.

Then, for some reason, I asked if I had a trapped emotion and I did. It was weird, because I felt good, very loving and compassionate towards myself. I didn't have the chart with me, but when I came home and EC'd it, guess what it was? FAILURE! My eyes were closed when I narrowed it from 60 to 5, I actually thought it would be guilt, but it was failure.

<u>July 11, 2012</u>

Happy Birthday Tracy! My sister is 42 years young today. Four kids and she looks fabulous. *Why did I just write that?* I hate it when people add qualifiers to complimenting looks. Like, "Wow, you look great for your age."

"Tracy, you look fabulous. Period."

Shadow Process: I call forth 'Fucking Failure' and he bursts onto the scene calling me a stupid idiot. It feels heavy. I know he is right. This isn't about the divorces; this is about the marriages. Instead of my 25 and 36-year-old deserters, he's addressing 22-yr-old and 29-yr-old Rachelle, the two stupid idiots who pressured my ex-husbands into wedlock. He sits back and allows me time to forgive them, but it is hard and I can't do it. I fail at forgiving.

I turn back to Fucking Failure and ask, "What do you need? I will not shame you. I failed Canada Day Weekend, but that is okay. I love myself and respect myself for putting my vulnerable-self out there. Authenticity is key. I didn't fail because things didn't work out the way I wanted, I failed because I wasn't authentic. I failed myself. I am okay with this. I am human and sometimes I will fail. I am not afraid of failing. I am a failure. We all are."

I need you to stop doubting yourself. I am here to show you what you are capable of. I love you, because you never give up.

I will never be able to trust and believe in anyone else as long as I Doubt myself. This has nothing to do with the object of my affection, no matter who he is. My external world reflects my internal world. My

Doubts projected on others are just my inner doubts. The soul uses the mind to 'see' what it wants reflected back. There are literally infinite possibilities of what to see. Everything is a projection of perception. We act off our feelings, but our feelings come from our thoughts and our thoughts are just interpretations of events, colored by our beliefs. Wow.

One way of earning my trust is by keeping my promises to myself, which I am doing, but also by being open to being stupid and a fool and a failure, loving and integrating each of them. Asking what they need in order to be a contributor in my life.

I'll work on this tonight... at the beach.

July 13, 2012

I had a great talk with Celina last night. I did most of the talking... again, which is weird, because I didn't think I wanted to talk about it, but once I started I couldn't stop. I hope she knows how much I appreciate her. She really is getting the brunt of this year.

She simply asked if Josh and I ended up going for a drink and the floodgates opened... I told her everything, well, not everything. I didn't go into the full weekend breakdown, just that he stood me up. Mostly, I told her about the weeks leading up to it - the manipulative texts, setting myself up for rejection, the painful attempts at flirting, feeling like I'm trying to make something happen and so on.

Celina sighed compassionately, "Rachelle, it just shouldn't be this hard."

Exactly. Why is she so wise when it comes to relationships? She has always had her head screwed on right when it came to guys, where I've always just been screwed.

I smother relationships. I can't let them breathe. Like, if I let it breathe, it will have a life of its own out of my control. And how is that working out for me? I just realized something. I was *pursuing* Josh. This is slightly different than trying to *make something happen*, which I was aware I was doing. I hate being pursued, but that is exactly what I was doing to him. Full on. He is the first person I have been even remotely interested in or even attracted to in years and I retreated back to the only thing I knew how to do: pursue.

You pursue a career. You pursue an object. You do not pursue a person. You let a relationship develop and unfold. I have not pursued anyone in a very long time. I have not liked anyone in a very long time. It was just an old pattern. I trust myself I won't do this. I am aware and it is not at all what I want. Yay me!

I'm so sorry, Josh! I won't pursue you anymore. You don't pursue friends.

<u>Summer Chief Challenge Hike # 10</u>

AHA moment about my soul mate. *Whoever he is, he is so much more than my soul mate.*

I know this sounds obvious, but I think I was diminishing him by labeling him as this. He has a whole life separate from being my soul mate. I have this WHOLE life outside of being his. I think that's one of the things that scares me about romantic relationships - the belief I will have to sacrifice part of my wholeness to be in one.

I once had a disagreement with my Good Friend about sacrifice versus compromise. He said sacrifice was part of marriage. I said that's why there are so many miserable married people and so may divorces, because people enter marriage succumbing to this idea of sacrifice.

"You love steak. I love Indian. Compromise is sometimes we go out for steak, sometimes we go out for Indian. Sacrifice is as long as we are together, you will never eat steak again."

Compromise is part of marriage, it's part of every relationship, but in my experience if you have to *sacrifice* something that is important to you in order to be with someone, then you are with the wrong person.

Later: Sam just called to say he's going into the hospital for a few days. He has high blood sugar. I'm really worried. He sounded so old and weak on the phone. Not at all his usual spunky self. I am sending all my positive healthy vibrations his way.

<u>July 14, 2012</u>

Today is my first private yoga session with Nick, the yoga instructor from the Indian Summer Festival. I checked out his website and something about it really resonated with me. *Can you resonate with a website?* Anyways, he has a summer deal: 3 private sessions for $240.

I'm so proud of myself for splurging on this. I am gonna learn to do a handstand!

Trust and support and patience - metaphors for my life right now!

Still Reppin' the A

July 15, 2012

Yoga Nick lives in a funky little bachelor suite in English Bay. It is filled with cool singing bowls and other spiritual books and paraphernalia. He's into quantum physics, too!

One of the reasons I was excited to have these private sessions with him is because I am trying to embrace my pervert. *Perhaps I could have a fling with my handsome young yoga instructor this summer.* How wonderfully cliché would that be?

As soon as I got there he asked what my intentions for the sessions were. I didn't tell him about the fling, but I did tell him I wanted to do a handstand by the end of summer. I told him all about this year and my book. I told him about my birthday vision of becoming a butterfly. How the first few months were shedding my caterpillar past and now I am in my chrysalis under going a major metamorphosis. I can't believe how open I was with him, but I think he actually gets it. He said he would totally read my book. It surprises me how many guys say that.

He's from Alberta, too. Calgary. What is it with me and Alberta boys?

We sat in lotus position on our mats and chatted energy, yoga and meditation. I felt such a deep connection with him - physically, mentally, energetically... *Oh, this is gonna be good.*

CHRYSALIS

As he spoke, I just stared at him smiling; admiring his clear blue eyes, soft mouth, wavy shoulder length hair... his radiant aura... *Mmmmmm.... Hmmmmm... Actually...* (head tilt) *he kinda looks like Jesus.*

Fuck. There goes the fling. Even when I try to be a pervert it turns spiritual!

Looks like I've got another platonic male friendship on my hands. Yee haw.

We did share an amazing hour together, though. He was surprised I've never taken a yoga class. He said I have very good form, which is something I've always wondered about since I learned the poses from VHS tapes and have always practiced alone.

"I think it's because I've done it for so long. I believe yoga is the truth the body knows, so it has just naturally aligned itself over the years."

"You already have the core strength needed to do a handstand. Now, it's all in the mind."

He asked me to pick a word to focus on. "On the mat and in life."

I picked two: Trust and Support.

When I was leaving, and it was time to pay, I handed him the money consciously and said, "I really appreciated today. Thank you for coming into my life."

Then, I picked up a six-pack and headed to Jericho Beach. (Life is all about balance). I met Scott and Kyle and a bunch of their friends. It's Folk Festival weekend, which I usually avoid like the plague, but since I am in party mode I jumped at the chance to go to a beach BBQ.

The actual festival is held behind a huge gated area on the grass, but you can hear the music, and smell the pot, blocks away.

K'naan was gonna be the headliner. I love K'naan... *Still reppin' the S!*

I have no idea what that means, but it's fun to say... Oh, he's from Somalia. Just got that.

When Elliot was trying to figure out the difference between wisdom and knowledge, I whipped out another K'naan lyric:

Any man who knows a thing knows he knows not a damn, damn thing at all.

This boggled his mind - my favorite thing to do.

Anyways, I was super pumped and ready to party, but the vibe of the group was super chill, even though there was this incredible

191

energy all around us. Could be because we were on the other side of the fence; could be because they had already been there a few hours eating, drinking and innocently inhaling the permeating fumes.

Later: Inspired Idea! Tracy and Celina and I should get tattoos!

What better way to commemorate this year than to get tattoos with my sisters. I already have two, one with Jen and one with Jen, Shannon and Kimmie, but I want one with my two sisters. The three of us are so different, in looks and in life; it would be really cool to have this one thing all three of us have in common. I haven't bought either of them their birthday presents yet and this would be so perfect. I hope they say yes.

July 18, 2012

Avi Federgreen phoned me and left a message. His reader read *FLOW* and gave him 'very encouraging' notes. He will be reading it within the next couple of weeks. Yay! I feel so amazingly sure of this. This is happening. He's from Edmonton, too! Hilarious.

I have a good feeling about Amber and Foundation Features, too. An interprovincial co-production would be perfect. This is so happening. *FLOW* is going to be awesome and successful. Everything is unfolding exactly as it should.

The best part is I didn't have to follow-up. I was getting ready to send my 'Just wanted to touch base and see if you've had a chance to read my script' email, but didn't have to. A sign?

July 19, 2012

Happy 40th Birthday Jennifer! I can't wait to see you tomorrow.

I can't believe we have been friends for almost a quarter of a century... actually I can. We've lived a couple of lifetimes and used up a few of our nine lives together. A lot of the dangerous situations I've gotten myself into in the past, Jen was there, too. So, as thankful as I am that I am alive, I am even more grateful she is.

Jen and I actually had an upsetting conversation a couple nights ago that's been with me since. She says I don't listen to her. This really upsets me because I respect her opinion and input so much. I told her how I 'talk' to her all the time when I'm alone and 'listen' to her advice. I often have full conversations with her, without her.

We were talking about relationships and how I have been struggling in this area. She was about to say something, but I cut her off.

"I know what you're going to say, because we've already had this conversation... even if you weren't there." I laughed, but she understandably felt cheated by this.

I was not allowing her to say what she needed to say. I just felt she didn't understand, because she doesn't know the spring I've had. All these processes and releases. I am a different person than I was the last time I saw her. Well, not different, just wiser.

We were talking about *that weekend*. She was giving me advice on something I've already worked through. She was frustrated, but I was agreeing with her! This was three weeks ago and I have already followed all the advice she was giving me. I wanted new advice.

I kept saying, "I know. I know."

"Can't anyone else have an opinion of your life?!" Yeah, she was frustrated.

This triggered me. *Why should anyone have an opinion of my life? It's my life.*

Then last night, I woke up at 4 AM and in my groggy state, asked, "What?"

My Higher Self answered, *Listen to Jennifer.*

Jennifer is my first soul mate and could probably write most of the backstory in this book herself. No one knows the details of my life like her. She is the number one person to reflect back to me something that is going on inside. I know this. The defensiveness arose from me feeling judged in the past, when everyone seemed to have an opinion of my life. This has been a major source of frustration, which is ironic since I open myself up to it by sharing so much. I'm writing a book about my life for crying out loud! Obviously, people are going to have an opinion about my life. Maybe you already do.

Okay. I am going to Parksville tomorrow and I will listen to Jennifer. I bought her a birthday gift, a necklace with a gemstone on it... and a thick black elastic band.

July 20, 2012

Happy Birthday, Alex!

Carlos and I moved away when Alex was less than two months old. He was four when we left for Korea, and to be honest, we didn't really click. I thought he was kind of a brat.

Celina was always shocked at this, "Sweet little Alex?"

I wasn't in a very good place before Korea, but when we got back, for the three months we lived in Beaumont before returning to Vancouver, Alex and I bonded... over brownies.

He was in Kindergarten, so I would pick him up and bring him back to my parents' place until Lee and Dylan got out of school. To pass the time, we started baking brownies. Our ingredients: top-secret.

One afternoon, as he stood on a chair at the counter stirring the choco-concoction, he looked up at me with his big brown eyes, "Auntie, you're fun to hang with."

Who cares about optioned screenplays?

We still bake them when I come to visit. Our ingredients: still top-secret.

Parksville 2012 – Let's Do This!

July 25, 2012

I haven't written for over a week and I feel that sense of being lost. Writing is one of the greatest gifts I have discovered. It invigorates me and makes me feel at peace at the same time. It saved my sanity over the course of that horrible year. It saved my life. I haven't even written in my journal since the day before I left for Parksville, probably because I am feeling major resistance about writing about the weekend.

Hmmmm Parksville... Friday was insane. I was so excited at the airport while waiting for my sea plane, I had a Coors Light to chill me down; reminiscing about the other two times I went to Parksville for Jennifer's Birthday Weekend.

Shannon and Craig have a beautiful house with a big back yard and an above-the-ground swimming pool. Nicole was there this time, but usually it is Jennifer, Shannon, myself and our other friend, Kimmie, who is quite a few years younger than us. I love these weekends because we have the best talks. I'm not sure why, but I just don't have these deep, open talks with people in Vancouver. Maybe because I haven't allowed myself to open up to anyone here, maybe because I haven't allowed myself to get drunk in front of anyone here.

Mostly, we sit around on the back deck and drink, or float on the pool and drink. We usually go out at least one of the nights to listen to live music... and drink. I usually fall in love with the lead singer. We drink a lot in Parksville, but we laugh even more.

My first Parksville weekend was three years ago, a month before Carlos and I separated. It was the first time in a long time I had hung out with the girls and I had forgotten how much we laugh. Laughing with girlfriends is magical and medicinal.

Two years ago, Parksville coincided with the end of my leave of absence from Youth Futures. If there was ever a time I needed to laugh it was that year. I was driving home from the month at my parents' cabin, on my way to the ferry, when Jennifer called me on my cell phone to inform me the four of us were getting tattoos.

"Just little hearts on our wrists with all our favorite colors. You're not allowed to say no."

I hadn't even told her about my new go-with-the-flow-not-allowed-to-say-no motto I had committed to while in Tennessee, but of course she knew. I literally drove off the ferry and met them at the tattoo parlor. Now we all have quad-color hearts on the inside of our left wrists.

Jennifer and I also have matching tattoos on our right ankles - little hearts on vines. What is it with us and heart tattoos? Mine is more girlish, where hers is more abstract. I bought them for us on her 20th birthday... whoa, exactly 20 years ago.

I usually take the ferry to Parksville, but this year I splurged on a plane ticket. The flight over was awesome and I got to co-pilot the plane. I told the pilot how I was going to join the Air Force when I was 18. He laughed. Apparently he didn't believe me, no one ever does, but it's true. I was going to be a fighter pilot. I went through all the testing, but in the end my eyesight sucked. Canada, and the world, should all be grateful for that.

As soon as I got to Shannon's, I took Jen to my room and gave her the necklace. The meaning of the gemstone is 'Maternal Goddess'. She cried. Then she pulled out the elastic band.

As I put it on my wrist, I told her about my 4 AM visit from my Higher Spirit, "It said, 'Listen to Jennifer.' So, every time I say 'I know' this weekend, I have to snap it and just listen."

She tried to apologize for the other night, but I stopped her.

"I love you Jennifer and I am open to advice about my life." She hugged me hard.

We were out on the patio drinking and dancing within two minutes. Shannon's friend, Heather was there, too. She lives in Richmond and is super awesome. We should definitely hang. We tried to decide what we should do for the night, so I, of course, suggested live-music.

"I feel like falling in love with a lead singer."

We went to the Rod and Gun, where I had successfully, although momentarily, done so the last time I was here. He was a rapper, but hey, I'm a sucker for a man with a microphone.

The rock band was getting set up when we got there, so we had a round of drinks. One of the last clear memories I have was when music finally came over the loud speaker. I popped up, clapped my hands together, shouted, "LET'S DO THIS!" and headed out to start the show.

I was already mid-groove, when a male voice boomed, "Check, check, one, two, three."

I looked around at the empty dance floor.... then to my ladies who were laughing their asses off at me. I slinked back to the table and ordered another beer.

The details of the rest of the night will be written in the third person as I only have blurred flashes with the monstrous gaps filled in by the testimonies of eyewitnesses.

Rachelle danced a lot. She remembers getting up on the speaker. She does not, however, remember standing inches in front of the lead singer, who was, uh, trying to sing, and him politely requesting to the crowd mid-song, "Can someone come get the beautiful blonde off the stage?" At least he called her beautiful.

At the table, Shannon nudged Kimmie, "That's one of ours."

"I'll get her." Kimmie removed the blonde from the stage.

Rachelle remembers talking to Jennifer in the bathroom, but wishes she didn't remember the look on Jen's face, "You're too thin. You need to gain some weight."

Rachelle remembers smoking pot in the parking lot. She does not remember lying on the bathroom floor. However, she does vaguely remember puking, nay, dry heaving, at Shannon's; Jennifer holding her hair back and Nicole telling her everything would be all right.

That, Your Honour, was Friday night in a nutshell.

Not shockingly, Saturday I was extremely hungover. We went out for a greasy breakfast then came back to the house and slept for a few hours.

We spent the afternoon on the patio in the back yard and had some drinks, but I took it way easier... and I ate. We had probably one of the greatest talks I have ever had with this group of ladies. I told them about my book, my year, some of my experiences and Emotion Coding. Jennifer knows all about the yellow above my eyes and how I've been trying to figure out the cause and cure for years. She was blown away they were gone. They were all so receptive about the whole thing. Truth resonates, I guess.

They all want to read The Emotion Code book. This makes me so happy and motivated to share it with my family when I'm there in August.

I also showed them the hand trick to show the power of our thoughts.

Hold your palms together with the bottoms lined up. One of your middle fingers should be slightly longer. Put that hand on your tummy and cover it with your other hand. If it is your right hand that is shorter, close your eyes and repeat, "Right hand get bigger." ten times while visualizing it growing. If your left is the shorter one say, "Left hand get bigger." Hold them together again and see what happens.

I never thought I would have this discussion with them. I have such limiting beliefs about people from Alberta, especially Beaumont. I keep them stuck in old thoughts. I underestimate other people's journeys. I can be quite arrogant about my spiritual journey, wanting other people to experience the same things as me. On some level thinking there is only one way to get to the lessons I've learned. I get caught up in my smarty-pants wisdom.

Any woman who knows a thing knows she knows not a damn, damn thing at all.

There's another reason I didn't want to talk about it. I didn't want them to think I was crazy.

Jen laughed, "Rachelle, we do think you're crazy! That's why we love you."

We had a very chill night with a gourmet crab dinner. Then we watched some TV. The ladies wanted to watch some real-life crime show, so I went to bed.

After about ten minutes, Jen came into my room. She curled on the bed facing me. It reminded me of when we lived together, but more intimate. I am opening up to intimacy. She said my way of thinking is so different than what she's used too. I'm so positive. She didn't know about all the processes I've gone through this year and how much I've changed. This was such a tender, honest moment Jen was sharing with me and I wanted her to know how much she means to me.

I told her how I've cheated her by saying 'I know'. Maybe she wasn't giving me advice so that I would hear what she had to say, but so she could hear herself saying it. Sometimes that's the gift of listening. Just listening. Not agreeing or disagreeing. Just listening.

We also talked about my weight. I don't want my weight to ever be a topic of conversation again. For the first few years of our friendship, I was the chubby one and so many talks were about me trying to lose weight. Then I was bulimic for a decade. Now I am healthy. I really am, but I trust Jennifer and if she thinks I'm too skinny, I have to listen. Getting so wasted and puking Friday night scared me. I felt small and weak and unbalanced.

Listen to Jennifer. Oh my God. Maybe this is what my Higher Self meant.

Sunday morning, while the other ladies were sleeping, it was Nicole and my turn to chat. Our conversations are always more on the academic side... occupational hazard. We debated watching the news. She thinks it is our responsibility to know what is going on in the world; I think it just brings our energy down.

No amount of *knowing* about individual global atrocities is going to stop them. I think we need to be careful with awareness. People think I want to live in a bubble, but choosing to not watch the news and to not read the paper does not mean I am unaware. I am well aware of the pain and sorrow and tragedy in the world, I taught at-risk youth and young offenders for four years, but I no longer need to bathe myself in it. I don't understand why we need to know every little detail in order to be aware; I actually think it is a form of self-abuse.

Besides, awareness is not the goal of the news. It is to spread fear and to keep us stuck. Working with those youth and their families, I witnessed how people can get stuck at a certain level of consciousness. I've lived it and I can't help anyone if I am depressed.

No problem can be solved from the same level of consciousness that created it.

Sunday afternoon, we went shopping. Shannon wanted to try and find *The Emotion Code*, but no luck. They are all going to order it online, though.

We went to this hemp store and the smell made me want to yak. I am never smoking pot again. I only ever do it when I'm in Parksville, anyways, which is probably why it affected me so much. *Who am I kidding?* It was probably the eight beers I drank on an empty stomach.

The trip was great, but I felt heavy when I got home. At first, I thought it was just the Sunday night blues, the downer after a weekend of drinking, but then I sensed it was more.

I EC'd for a trapped emotion and I had one: self-abuse, trapped on Friday night. I wasn't really surprised, because the end of the night had started coming back to me. I haven't been drunk like that in over a decade. I was a noodle. I was a larp. I puked hard, just trying to get anything, but nothing, out.

It's hard to feel enlightened when you're hanging your head in a toilet bowl.

36

$\mathcal{I}$ Should $\mathcal{W}$rite a $\mathcal{B}$ook
$\mathcal{A}$bout $\mathcal{W}$riting a $\mathcal{B}$ook

July 26, 2012

I've started transcribing my novel. I am the slowest typer ever. This could take forever.

9:40 PM: I had the idea of texting Josh about Wild Rose of Alberta. I asked Danielle, the manager at Grounds, if anyone had seen her around, but they've been wondering about her, too. A month ago, I would've totally texted him just to create a connection, but part of being healthy is being authentic and acting with integrity AND trusting the Universe.

July 27, 2012

Summer Chief Challenge Hike # 11: An Avalanche of Epiphanies

1. I did an ego check on writing this book. Why do I think my story is worthy? I'm not writing it because I think my story is more interesting, although the pressure of writing a book has helped me create a more interesting year.

This question was triggered by *Eat, Pray, Love.* Do we really need another book like this? Yes! I reread a bit of it the other day. The last couple of pages tell the story of her two years leading up to where the book begins. We have a different story, a different intent, a different voice, but self-love is a common theme and that story can never be over-told.

I hope this book inspires others to share their stories, not necessarily in paperback, but maybe while riding horseback with their daughter or backpacking with a friend or getting a back massage from a lover... Storytelling is as old as fire. It is how we learn. It is how we connect.

2. If you leap, the net will appear!

3. The Sun doesn't stop shining because someone is wearing sunglasses, sun block or sitting in the shade. I am radiation, so I radiate. I am love, so I love.

4. *I really want to go fishing, but why?* I don't want to be responsible for killing the fish. I just want to catch them. I want to be in a boat on a lake. I want to experience the excitement of making the big catch and reeling him in, but then I want to throw it back in. Why would I want to cause fear in a creature just for fun? Then I thought about Josh. Did I scare him because there was a part of me that thought it was fun? Not much of an epiphany, but something to reflect on.

5. *What do I think a soul mate is?* Answer: A person who will accept me, all of me.

Simultaneously, I realized how fulfilling teaching is. I had a really intimate moment with this girl I'm tutoring Math 11 to this summer. The course is very hard and she is only half way done. I can't imagine her finishing it, but she has to in order to be accepted into her program at SFU in the fall. Her test is in less than a week. She was very stressed and on the verge of tears. My God, I remember that feeling like it was yesterday, but for me it was writing essays.

I grabbed her hand and looked her right in the eyes, "We're in this together."

Realization: Teaching is a part of me, but for some reason, on some level, I have looked down on this part of me and made it not as important. I have not appreciated or respected it. Today on my hike I did. I am a teacher AND a writer.

Realization: It is not a soul mate who will accept all the parts of me I seek. It's me.

6. Soul mates aren't just magnifying glasses they are flipping telescopes.

On my drive home, I had one more epiphany. Josh and I are friends, even if he doesn't know it. I do still believe he is one of my eight soul mates, but maybe we are just meant to be friends. I felt a major shift in my whole perspective.

The 'Story' of the first time I saw him, my attachment to manifesting my soul mate this year, wanting a happy ending to the romantic comedy portion of my book... What if this desire to have a romantic relationship is robbing me of the experience of having a great friend?

From day one, that's how I felt about him. That's one thing you will not understand by reading the shenanigans of this spring... we were actually coffee shop buds for a while. I know about his family and friends, and he knows about mine. We have had hours of great conversations about football and fishing and Alberta and tattoos and... I'm gonna stop now.

I wish I could tell him I just want to be friends. Maybe I should write him a note? *JK*.

Later: When I got home, I showered and practiced Vipassana Meditation for the first time in months. It was challenging, but I didn't judge. I was just aware.

Then I made love to myself in front of my full-length mirror.

A couple of observations: First, there are certain angles we are not meant to see ourselves at, especially lying down. Gravity can be so cruel. Second, I noticed a lot of loose skin, especially on my tummy. I didn't like it - body issues, chubby or thin, we all have them and they are equally damaging to self-confidence. I really worked through this. Allowing the insensitive comments of past partners come to the surface and letting go of the attached shame.

Over and over again, telling myself, "You are beautiful. I love you."

That other part of me would protest, "What are you talking about? Look at me!"

"I am... and you are beautiful."

"You're a liar. I have a chest like a boy."

"You're beautiful."

This is going to be an ongoing process, that much is obvious, but I am aware of my thoughts and can observe them as something separate. I know their power, though. Every time I catch myself saying something negative, I say something positive three times. I say the truth.

When I was done loving myself to completion, I stood up in front of the mirror and, this is very hard for me to write, I look *skinny*. My face looks hallow. I think my sleep issues and dark circles under my eyes are trying to tell me something.

The conversation I had with Jen in Parksville came back to me. Then I remembered, "Listen to Jennifer." Okay, it's time to gain a few pounds. Not to change the way I look, I love every fold of skin and my beautiful flat breasts. I love the crinkles around my eyes. They have deepened this year from smiling so much and that's a good thing.

During my eating disorder years, I liked feeling small. I could never be small enough. I felt small last weekend.

Jennifer kept saying, "You're so little." I don't want to be little anymore. I am a woman. I want to have curves. I have no need or desire to be child-like. I am listening to my Little Girl and she is healing. I love her. She doesn't need to manifest herself physically in my life anymore.

July 28, 2012

Now that I'm writing my novel, I have to make extra sure I take extra care of myself and be aware that things may come up. Making healthy choices to trust and support myself.

Going back to what I wrote a few months ago, specifically going back to my meditations and visualizations is fascinating. I just reread my realization on March 29th about how much I've disrespected men and their feelings, even when I was young. Also, that by coming on strong and living in my ego was how I protected myself. It was my way of pushing guys away. Still, I did this with Josh. Learning is sure not linear.

The primal reactions to fear are fight or flight. Some people retreat; I charge in full force challenging you, no daring you to be with me. My 'this is me, take it or leave it' attitude is all a mask, a gladiator's mask.

This is a very special time in my life, and to be honest, I don't want to share it with anyone (except all of you, of course - but by the time you read this I'll be onto a whole new stage of my evolution). I will not be writing the word 'soul mate' for the rest of the summer. I'm taking this time to fully fall in love with myself and write my book. It is bringing up a lot of stuff, including judgments of myself. I know in my heart I need solitude to process and release. I am so grateful that I have that in spades.

How long will it take? As long as it takes.

Later: I'm sitting on the patio at Benny's. It is 5:30 PM and is sunny and beautiful. I'm finally reading *Power vs. Force* by David R. Hawkins and it feels like I'm in Korea; at peace with everything as it is. Nothing to do, just be.

One purpose of writing my book is to show the nature of illness and the power we have to heal ourselves. Why I've chosen to share so much about my past is to show how sick I was emotionally and mentally. I was also a hypochondriac, physically and psychologically - thinking I was diabetic, searching for an answer to why I felt nauseous all the time, wanting an official diagnosis for why I was so fucked up, reading psychology and medical books trying to become an expert on depression.

When that doctor told me he thought I was bipolar, there was a part of me that was relieved. Being clinically labeled 'crazy' actually made me feel less crazy. I was always focusing on the problem, but now by being healthy and making healthy choices and thinking healthy thoughts, I have raised my vibration to where those illnesses can't live.

My depression wasn't cured... it dissipated.

I'm not sure why today of all days I started reading *Power vs. Force*. I've thought about it since I discovered *The Emotion Code* back in February, but I'm so excited. My summer of fun has taken on new meaning. I miss reading. When I started this journey of creating the Best Year of My Life, I really thought it was about building a fabulous external world. Holy shit, was I wrong. Sometimes being wrong is better than being right. *Who just said that?*

This book is reminding me how much I love and have missed physics. Physics is a part of me I love and miss. I am embracing all parts of me including my nerd! God Particle! Einstein! Newton! Holy shit, my summer just took a turn I was not expecting. A part of me has awakened!

How many exclamation marks can I pepper through an entry?!

I'm just so excited to re-acquaintance myself with my Physics Geek. I miss her.

The author, Dr David Hawkins, goes into a whole historical background and proof of muscle testing. *Why is this still not known?* Fuck. I know why. My book is going to introduce it in an approachable, digestible way. This is part of my purpose. Teaching people they have the power to heal themselves. This is why I am here. I am making this mainstream. A new connection to my past and why my major in University was Physics.... another reason to appreciate my whole journey.

I feel so connected to the physics teacher in me right now. Twenty years after starting university, my physics teacher journey has taken a spiritual turn. I always thought my scientific and spiritual sides made me a paradox, but now I see they are one in the same.

Quantum physics is now proving what the spiritual gurus have always said.

We are all energy. We are all one.

July 29, 2012

I can't believe how reading the stuff I wrote in the spring is bringing major shit up. I'm trying not to judge it, but was I whacked or what? Don't answer that. I am so glad I am single while I'm writing this otherwise it would be tainted or I may hold back. I already feel like toning it down so I don't sound so crazy, but I won't. It is part of my journey, and if anything, maybe it will make you feel better about your craziness. We are all crazy.

5:30 PM: Just had the annual WIFTV BOD planning meeting at Mary's. The board this year is, as always, an amazing group of women. They inspire me so much. Mary talked to me about running for president next year. Yikes. The thought scares the hell out of me.

On my drive home, crossing over Lion's Gate Bridge, I looked out over the ocean and smiled. I can't believe the despair I felt two years ago. I'm so at peace. I love my life.

Although, I would still like to fly.

I remembered my vision of a healthy relationship being like water. H_2 and O_2 are completely whole and stable on their own, but when they come together they make H_2O. Water is the most amazing, and anomalous, compound... I must fully be O_2. I am completely shedding the idea of being in a relationship. Not out of fear or closing my heart, quite the opposite. I am going to completely open it and awaken to my wholeness. Only when I am 100% at peace with being single for the rest of my life, will I be whole enough to be in a relationship.

What an expansive epiphany... then "Just Haven't Met You Yet" came on the radio.

8:30 PM: I'm having my Sunday Night Solo Dance Party and Hedley's "Kiss you inside out" video was just on. This song always makes me want a boyfriend, but as I was dancing in front of my mirror, I started to sing it to myself. Like *I* was singing it to *me*. The lyrics have new meaning:

I wanna know you inside out. I'll spend my life trying to figure out.

So pertinent to where I am on my journey right now and my summer love affair with myself. I'm gonna try with my other favorite dance songs and see where it leads me...

David Guetta ft. Sia: "Titanium"... Absolutely.

Rihanna: "Where have you been?"... Yep.

Usher: "Scream"... Kinda, I guess.

Flo Rida "Whistle"... Um... no.

July 30, 2012

According to the Map of Consciousness in *Power vs. Force*, I calibrate at the level of Love - exactly 500. The next level is Joy at 540. The key to rising to Joy is unconditional kindness and compassion to all life, including one's own. Compassion for all? Yikes!

I have been at every level. This year even! I can use my past experiences to gain compassion and explain why we all should. No wonder I had so many trapped emotions! I needed to release them, so I could rise. That's why I'm reading the book now. I wasn't ready before.

Most interesting is that you can be at different levels in different areas of your life. No wonder I feel different about romantic relationships.

I can't believe the Universe guided me back to this book... to help conquer this final frontier with power versus force. It's funny, because *forced* is exactly how I would describe my relationship with romance.

What level was I at when I first read this book years ago? 320 - Wow, I've come a long way. This is the level of willingness. It's true. It was my willingness to rise that set me on this journey. I think most people vibrate lower in their romantic relationships, because as a society we create a lot of shame and guilt, the lowest vibrations, around sex, which is the number one distinguisher from all our other relationships. It is impossible to be intimate when you are filled with shame. You can't be intimate with someone if you can't look them in the eye. I have never been able to look a guy in the eyes. I couldn't even look at Carlos while we said our vows.

Later: I just read a posting on the LOE Facebook page - a guy responded to another Emerger's post about reading signs: *Be wary of external signs. If an alcoholic sees three pubs in a row, is it a sign he should have a drink?*

A Fool Over Failure

<u>August 1, 2012</u>

While I was just getting ready, my least favorite thing to do, I paused. I looked at myself in the mirror and was overcome with love. Not the narcissistic or conceited love I've always been afraid of, but the purest spiritual love. I could see it radiating around my body, my aura illuminated. I felt a surge of tingling from head to toe. I had a spiritual orgasm.

If I can experience this, anyone can, without pharmaceuticals. Pharmaceuticals rob people of the spiritual growth... and the orgasm.

8:55 AM: I just saw Josh. I was standing outside Grounds talking on my cell and he crossed the street. He totally avoided me. I'm not sure why, but I think it's funny. We are funny. I am rising to acceptance. Acceptance on every level, and it feels so good. I have a feeling we will just run into each other someday. Start all over as friends.

So weird. Carlos just texted me. He wants to chat. I automatically thought, "He must want to borrow some money." It's probably time to let him grow into a new person.

2 PM: Well, Carlos didn't want to borrow money.

"I have something to tell you and I didn't want you to find out through the grapevine."

"You're getting married."

He laughed, "God, no!"

"What then?"

Silence. I knew.

"You're going to be a father."

"Yeah."

"Holy shit!" My legs turned to mush and I collapsed on the bed, "Ya coulda told me to sit down first."

"Oh, you're not sitting?"

"I am now. Give me a second."

Shock - utter, unreal, surreal shock. Not sure I've ever been more shocked in my life. The only way I could've been more shocked is if you told me *I* was pregnant. Then I shocked him.

"Congratulations!" I meant it.

There is a baby coming and that is always a good thing. I know he did not plan this and I also know what the idea of being a father means to him. He needs support right now, if not for him, for his new girlfriend and their baby.

I honestly felt pure love and compassion. It just flowed and flowed. It was the most, *what's the word?* Flowing experience.

Carlos whispered, "Wow. Well, that's not the reaction I was expecting."

He thought I'd be upset with him. One of the reasons we initially broke up was because I wanted to have children and he didn't. He said it was because he was too selfish. Not that I would ever have argued his selfishness, but that's not why he didn't want to have kids.

"Carlos, you're a great father to the puppies. You're gonna be a great father to this baby."

"Thank you. I needed to hear that."

Later: I'm lying at Locarno and I feel resentment building. I know it's not about Carlos becoming a father. *What is it?*

Moments later: I just EC'd Carlos cheating on me. Deep down, I've always suspected he did. I think he lied to me in the spring when he said he didn't. There were specific situations and relationships that created huge speculation. I realize muscle testing may not be an exact science. I know it is not proof Carlos cheated on me, but that's not the point. The point is, I thought he did, but ignored, buried and trapped the fear, anger, panic and pride that accompanied the belief.

I want to make sure I allow myself to feel whatever comes up now and not suppress any emotions around this. I don't feel like I am, but I could be protecting myself. There is a part of me that feels like a fool. That's okay though. I am a fool. I can love my fool.

What do you need to feel loved and appreciated?

Those fucking losers! Who the fuck do they think they are? He was lucky to have me and it is ridiculous he would look elsewhere, especially to her! I can't believe I didn't trust my intuition. I chose to be a fool over a failure.

His insecurities projected on me from the start. "I know I married up." Goddamn right you did!

I'm feeling very petty right now and that's okay. I am petty. I am a human being who was cheated on and I am feeling fucking petty. My ego wants them to know I know, but why? I don't really want to have any connection with them.

Okay. Now what? Breathe. Breathe. Breathe.

Not forgiving someone is like drinking poison and thinking it will make the other person sick. How do I forgive and let go? Compassion is always the answer. How can I feel compassion for someone who I believe cheated on me with the worst possible person in the world?

Ugh. The truth is... I wanted him to cheat on me. This was such a long time ago. He was stuck in his ego, but so was I. I wanted the drama. I wanted the conflict. I wanted to be a victim. I wanted him to feel guilty about something. I wanted a way out.

Carlos is going to be a father and I don't want to have negative feelings for him. This is a new start for him. I can forgive him, not from a place of superiority, but from a place of love.

I can love him for real this time.

A higher spiritual context? Carlos has been my greatest teacher and there is a lesson here. I needed this to happen, because if I can authentically love and forgive and have compassion for him, I can for anyone. He is still a catalyst for my growth. This is huge. I will not suppress.

We did not have a healthy marriage and we both contributed to that. I knew his weaknesses and I worked them. Not consciously, of course,... oh shit, fuck, who am I kidding? In the end, I knew exactly what I was doing. That's one of the reasons I knew it was time to go. I was acting like a colossal bitch on a daily basis and I hated myself for it.

Another painful truth: I saw so much potential in him and tried to change him from the get-go. That wasn't fair or authentic. I contributed to *his* low self-worth by not accepting him 100%. Making him feel low, however passive aggressively.

I have to forgive myself. When you know better, you do better.

My God, this has been a long day. I'm going for a walk now.

38

FLOW

<u>August 2, 2012</u>

A few weeks ago, I forgave myself for marrying and divorcing Carlos, but at 4 AM this morning, I finally did it for staying in the marriage so long. Beginnings and endings are their own traumatic thing, but actually <u>staying</u> in something so unhealthy, was a different choice I needed to forgive. Not only for the obvious reasons, but because below the surface there was a disease of dishonesty, lack of trust, inauthenticity and I knew it. In fact I contributed to it by pretending I was okay, that I didn't know what was going on. I knew. That's why I asked the question on the beach. I wouldn't have asked the question, if I didn't know the answer.

Part of me stayed in the marriage out of pride, not wanting to be a twice divorcée, but I also stayed to punish myself.

The summer before moving to Korea, things were really bad. The only time we felt connected was the night we tried Ecstasy. That night, I stared into the mirror, the first time I had ever looked right into my eyes, into my soul. I saw the insanity of both my marriages reflected back at me and asked, "Okay. What is the common denominator here?" The answer: Me.

In that moment, I decided I was going to become 'The Best Wife'. Two days later, a stranger who lived on the floor above us gave me the book *Awakening the Buddha Within* by Lama Surya Das. There began my incredible healing journey.

Ironically, the commitment to save my marriage is what ended it.

Later: Avi wants to option *FLOW*! He wants my GOLD!

He called and left a message. I called him back and he said he wanted it. Weirdest experience ever, because I had to tell him I was meeting another producer (Amber) on Saturday, so asked if I could have the weekend. Ha! I'm such a shaker.

This is the moment I've been waiting for, for... years. I think I'm going to blow a gasket. All this inner work I've been doing, letting go of my resistance, VVR'ing, opening up, allowing, visualizing... I know all the work has not made this happen, but has made it welcome. Never in a million years did I think my trip to Toronto would end up with me optioning my screenplay.

Thank you, Universe! I can't believe how quick he made his decision. I just pitched to him five weeks ago. This is warp speed in West Coast terms. My film is going to get made!

I called Celina right away and she was so excited for me. She's been an eyewitness to the struggles of my life. We couldn't talk long, because I was on my way to my second private yoga session. I didn't think to tell her to keep it a secret until papers were signed.

My session with Nick was amazing. We sat and did our connection check-in. He's read *Power vs. Force* (of course he has). I told him about my script getting optioned and that he was the first person I've told face-to-face. He said he was honored. He asked me to close my eyes and to focus on the feeling I would have if everything were happening *now*... just like Derek does!

Then we brought it on the mat, into my handstand. As he held my legs up and encouraged my toes to reach for the sky (I love how he pronounces "skyyy"), he asked me to focus on the *feeling*. What would it feel like to be able to do a handstand? What would it feel like if I *were* doing a handstand?

Strong. Supported. Trusted.

I focused on my breathing, allowing this energy to flow into all areas of my body, especially the tight places. My hands planted on the ground; my arms long and strong.

I support myself. I trust myself.

Then he let go. And there I was, in the middle of my own personal Jesus' bachelor pad, doing a handstand.

When my feet finally, gently, fell to the ground, I gave Nick the biggest hug. I just shared one of the most profound moments of my life with this man I barely know, but there was no one else on Earth I wanted to share it with.

As I floated down the hall, he called after me, "Rachelle. You inspire me."

I looked back, "Thank you."

I strolled down English Bay basking in the glory of this day, the glory of my life. I can't believe this is all happening the day after I find out Carlos is having a baby.

Yes, I can. Life is funny like that.

Once settled in my car, I turned on my cell phone. I had a whack of texts from a bunch of people wondering what was going on. I was so confused, until I read the one from Celina.

Oops. I think I messed up. I posted on Facebook how proud I am of you and there have been a bunch of replies and questions.

I laughed. She is so funny. It turns out the post was pretty vague:

Soooo proud of my big sister! Just goes to show you're never to old to make your dreams come true!

My sister never posts anything, so people must've thought it was big news.

I commented: *She's just proud of me because I learned to do a handstand today. And who you calling old?!*

When I got home, I Skyped my parents, because I wanted to tell them 'face-to-face', too. They were so cute. The moment I told them - their reactions, questions, everything, was exactly as it was in my vision. They are so proud of me, which feels amazing and I love it, but it does not at all come from a place of need. It's just the icing on the cake.

Making them proud was something I strived for desperately, tearfully, because I felt like a disappointment for so long. I realize this has, and never did have, anything to do with them. My soul was calling for me to rise to a higher vision. The pain pushes, until the vision pulls.

My Little Girl wanted ME to be proud of her. And I am. I am so flipping proud of myself.

Later: I stand naked in front of my full-length mirror and state matter-of-factly, "This is the way I look. This is the way I look. This is my physical body."

I scan my body up and down, careful not to linger on the 'good' parts or the 'bad' parts; not labeling some things pretty, some things ugly.

"I love you. I appreciate you. I am sorry I abused you for so long."

It is awkward. I crumble. I cry.

How long will it take? As long as it takes.

<u>August 3, 2012</u>

<u>Summer Chief Challenge Hike # 12</u>

I've been reflecting a lot lately on why I've been drawn to working with teenage boys. I think it's because, like I said earlier, I have held onto past events, but made the participants into men. Teaching young men, I've realized they are not insensitive, quite the opposite.

Whether at-risk or privileged, preteen or young adults, all the boys I've worked with have one thing in common: they are supersensitive. In some cases, more so than I was at their age. Their seemingly 'insensitive, only after one thing, out to hurt me' personas were just projections of mine. For decades, I've believed males had no feelings, were heartless even. I've attracted situations to prove me right. It was my own form of reverse sexism. I know this is ridiculous now, but that's the nature of limiting beliefs. They are limiting and rooted in ridiculousness.

These were projections of my own guilt and shame. Thinking men were incapable of true intimacy and deep love; it was me who was incapable of intimacy and love.

Well, today I had two separate male encounters that tested my new understanding.

I started the hike much earlier today because it was already hot at 9 AM. The only people I saw on my way up were two groups of 4 guys coming down about a half-hour apart.

First group: clean-cut, mid-thirties.

As I approach them around the swerving path, I can hear one of the guys relaying some war story about a drunken night out on the town, blabbing about how insanely rad it was.

Just as he comes around the bend, chest puffed, he blurts, "Then the sluttiest girls ever--."

We meet face-to-face. *Do men actually use the word 'sluttiest'?*

His friends see me. "Oh my God! I'm so sorry!" They turn to him, "Fuck man, you're such an idiot." They razz him relentlessly. He shrinks.

I make light of it, covering my ears, "La la la la." As I move on, I smile, "Ya gotta be careful, the trees have ears."

His buddies continue bugging him down the trail, but he is silent. So am I. *Why did I make light of this extremely disrespectful comment? Why did I not stand in my power and tell him what I thought?*

Then I realize... I'm not angry. He was in the forest with some buddies telling this ridiculous story completely from his ego. As I continue up the mountain, I radiate compassion to him and his friends. In that moment, his reaction to me, his friends' reactions, were a mix of awkward embarrassment and, shockingly, respect. His silence spoke volumes.

My reaction opened the experience up for him to reflect. Had I backlashed in judgment, it would have given his ego something to fight, something to push back on. I feel as though we may have shared an enlightening moment together.

I also spread love and compassion to 'the sluttiest girls ever'. Been there, done that.

Second group: About two thirds the way up, I run into another group of guys, same age as the first, but a little rougher around the edges.

The first 3 guys of this posse just smile and say hi. The fourth one sticks out. He is shirtless, but has some sort of chest-shield that looks like it is holding ammunition. As I get closer, I see there are a dozen mini-water bottles strapped to his chest. As he passes me, he leers, "You look fan-damn-tastic."

I burst out laughing. As I bless him down the path, I mutter aloud, "Wow, that was the worst line ever. I hope he doesn't use that when he's trying to pick up girls."

A few months ago, heck a few days ago, I would've used these events as proof of my low opinion of men. The experiences are different, the first funny, the second sleazy, but I feel total compassion and love for both.

My sessions with Nick have helped. He is such a beautiful man, physically and spiritually. I look him right in the eyes and he looks back. It is not sexual, but it is intimate. I don't know how to put it into words, so I won't.

I have a third male experience on the hike down. A Doberman with the biggest balls, trots in front of me and won't let me pass. Not yet sure of the higher spiritual meaning of this one.

Water Noodles

<u>August 4, 2012</u>

OMG, Celina just told me the funniest story. Well, funny for me, not for her. If someone ever makes a movie about my life, Kristen Wiig needs to play my sister.

The whole family was at my grandma's house in Parkside, the miniscule Saskatchewan town my mom grew up in. They were all sitting out on the deck, which overlooks my grandma's garden, a bush and then miles of flat field, when Sara emerged from the bush carrying her latest discovery.

Celina, watching from the deck, couldn't quite make out what Sara was holding.

Squinting, she called out, "What is that?"

Proud as can be, Sara responds, "A dead snake."

"Are you kidding me!!!" Celina ran inside bawling. She sat rocking in the TV room with her eyes shut tight.

My mom kept telling her, "Open your eyes."

When she saw a snake at the cabin last year she did the same thing, but closing her eyes didn't block the image out, it sealed it in.

I have a theory about this.

When my sister was fourteen, she was flashed while on a family ski vacation. She had been in the hotel pool with Janelle and Cassie, but was heading up to the room by herself. She met this man in the stairway and he, uh, exposed himself. She was shocked and traumatized, but also terrified, because the girls were still in the pool. She didn't know what to do.

I think her phobia of snakes stems from this incident. My own fear began after I had been flashed. I know it sounds ridiculous, 'the one-eyed snake' seems a bit on the nose, but sometimes this is how the brain works, especially if it is the first time you see a penis.

I also think the fear is about a lack of control (you can't control a snake). Being flashed is unexpected and steals your power. It makes total sense she shuts her eyes; she was 'visually' molested. Celina never asked to see what she saw.

My mom begged, "Celina! Open your eyes."

Sara and Sadie were standing there, confused by the state their mom was in.

Celina finally told them about her phobia. It is time for her to get help. The Universe is telling her it is time. I'm there in two weeks and I think she'll let me Emotion Code her.

<u>August 5, 2012</u>

I can't keep up with my life! The energy pumping through it is exhilarating.

Yesterday, leaving the library on my way to meet with Amber, I drove south on McDonald. As I was turning right (west) onto Broadway, I noticed a black car stopped at the red light heading east. The driver was this mysterious guy wearing a black hat and dark sunglasses. As I turned into the lane next to him, I noticed a bundle of bright colored tubes protruding from the backseat of his car.

I thought to myself: *Who's the guy with all the water noodles?*

The driver looked at me. *I know those dimples.* Josh.

I yelled, "Oh my God! How are you doing?!!" My face radiating at about 100,000 Watts.

He just smiled. I had to drive off, because the bastard behind me was honking.

Why am I completely incapable of playing it cool in his vicinity? So embarrassing. I texted him how funny the exchange was. We texted back and forth a bit about how fun and busy our summers are. Awkwardness over. We're friends. So cool.

I knew we would run into each other someday and it would just be fun and casual. Okay, maybe this wasn't casual, but it was definitely funny.

My meeting with Amber went awesome, but they have a lot on their slate. She doesn't know when they will even be considering new projects for development. I'm going with Avi and am so excited. Amber is excited for me. I believe she really likes the project.

Then I went to donate blood and these kids washed my car for free! I've been procrastinating washing it for two months. Give and receive.

I called Celina and gave her the rundown. "Maybe I should wait until Monday to contact Avi. I don't want to seem desperate."

"Don't play games, Rachelle."

I emailed him right away.

Then I went to Jericho Beach and met Scott and friends for drinks and the fireworks. I am in love with this city. *Is it possible to be in love with a city?*

The Pride Parade is today. I am so grateful I live in a city, and country, where people are free to love who they love. My wonderful friends, Nichole and Melissa, and Fiona and Jocelyn, have taught me so much about relationships - about the power of friendship first.

The first six months following my split with Carlos, I hung out with lesbians a lot. One night, we were out dancing at a straight bar (the goal of the night was to find me a one-night stand - such good friends), but I could not find one guy, in the whole place, I was attracted to.

One of their lesbian friends hit on me, though. I can't recall her name, but she was extremely sexy and sensual and she kept trying to hold my hand. I was so flattered. Lesbians never hit on me. She complimented me and danced close and I was not at all uncomfortable.

That night, lying alone and inebriated on Nichole and Melissa's couch, I ruminated, "Maybe I'm gay. That would explain so much."

I mean, seriously, would that not explain a lot? The next morning, sober and hung-over, it shocked me I even considered this. I knew, without a shadow of a doubt, I needed to be alone for awhile... and that I have zero interest in ever having a one-night stand again.

I shocked myself in another way that night. I ate chili-covered nachos from 7-Eleven. I always wondered who would eat meat from a machine - the drunk and confused, that's who.

Asphalt Awareness

<u>August 8, 2012</u>

FLOW is going to be a movie. Avi already has an action plan, which includes approaching Vancouver producers to do a BC/Ontario co-production. He said he'd get me the option agreement within the week.

It came last night. I love the way Torontonians work. It is printed and now all I need is a witness.

Later: Just mailed the agreement! I was sitting in Grounds wondering if I should just get Danielle to sign it, but then Erik walked in. Perfect. His wealth-conscious hands vibrated into my first film deal. Then my health-conscious hands applied Polysporin onto a cut on his back - my love vibrating into my good friend's wound.

August 9, 2012

I was driving down 4th Ave, coming home from the beach; frustrated I've been in a funk. I feel like I should be more excited about *FLOW*. Everyone is so excited for me, but I... I don't know. *Why can't I let myself enjoy this?* I was snapped out of the daze by a huge black squirrel on the road. It had been run over.

Half of it was stuck to the asphalt, the other struggling for dear life to get free.

August 10, 2012

Summer Chief Challenge Hike # 13

11:42 AM: It is a foggy Friday in August and I am alone at the top of the Chief... except for the chipmunks. On my way up, with every step, I focused on appreciating the rocks for their strength and support. Now, as I sit atop this mighty structure overlooking Squamish and Howe Sound, I am overcome with gratitude for the strength and support the Universe has given me.

I vocalize my appreciation aloud, "Thank you, Universe."

I wonder if the chipmunks think I'm crazy, but shrug it off, "Thank you, Universe!!!"

Lying spread eagle, eyes closed, deeply connected to all that is, a chipmunk kisses my thumb. This reminds me of the squirrel on 4th. It makes me sad.

I am love. I am the Universe... A Peter O'Toole quote comes to mind. "When did I realize I was God? Well, I was praying and I suddenly realized I was talking to myself."

I talk to myself all the time. Maybe I'm God.

<u>Saturday, August 11, 2012</u>
9:15 AM at Speedy Brakes: This is a weekend of firsts.

First #1 - Last night, I went kayaking. It is something I've always wanted to try, but never found the time... never made the time. I went with Christine, Amber and Tracey Mack, another friend I met through WIFTV. Amber and I shared a kayak, because it was both of our first times. So relaxing. Vancouver is, seriously, the most stunning city, from all angles.

First # 2: I am going to Seattle.

First # 3: I'm going to see the Tennessee Titans! My first NFL game. Christine is coming with me. She is such a great friend. She's not at all a football fan, but is coming to experience this event with me. She said she wouldn't miss it for the world.

I have to get my oil changed before we leave, though. The past couple of weeks I've been feeling weird driving, especially on my way to and from Squamish. I feel uneasy, even a bit reckless. I'm driving faster, changing lanes more; hyper and erratic; quick and jerky.

Catching myself, "Slow down, Rachelle! Drive carefully. Be conscious. Mindful."

Am I being self-destructive? Wanting to cause an accident.

Last night and this morning, I was super-anxious about driving to Seattle with Christine. I want to keep us safe, so I'm going to get my oil changed. I feel I need an oil change. Can you *feel* when you need to get an oil change?

Later: I need new brakes. It's going to cost $1000. A grand, unexpectedly gone. I'm actually dealing with it unexpectedly well. My brakes have been squeaking for about a year, but at my last tune up the guy said they were fine, so I've just turned the music up.

I love my car - my cute little eco-friendly Yaris. It keeps me safe and allows me so much independence. In feng shui, your car represents independence. I am grateful I have $1000 to keep it, and my independence, healthy.

The mechanic said, "You probably wouldn't even notice it in the city, but if you were on the Coquihalla, whoa boy, you'd be in big trouble."

I leave for Alberta on Wednesday... on the Coquihalla.

Thank you, Universe, for keeping my friend and me safe.

41

The Titans

August 12, 2012

9 PM: Where do I start? It's been 12.5 years since Music City Miracle -- the first NFL game I ever watched. I can't believe it's taken me this long to see my first game live, but it was well worth the wait.

The three-hour drive to Seattle went smooth as silk with my brand new brakes. Christine and I talked non-stop the whole way there. We stopped at Trader Joe's on our way to the hotel to pick up supplies: beer, wine and Sante Fe Salads. We sat by the pool, had some bevies, ate our salads and gabbed some more. Sometimes I wonder if we'll ever run out of things to talk about.

One of the things I am most grateful for this year, is how Christine and my friendship has blossomed. At one point she was telling me a story, her legs dangling in the pool and I just stared at her. She really is one of the most beautiful women I know. Not because of her thick blonde hair or her crystal blue eyes or her disgustingly long eyelashes, but because she is just so... beautiful. I just don't know another word to describe her.

We got ready for the game. Since it was super hot out, we wore shorts and fancy tank tops to start, but I was so excited to wear my # 27 Eddie George Tennessee Titans Jersey - a 30th birthday present from Carlos. I brought my Titans visor for Christine. She's such a good sport.

We asked the hotel clerk to call us a cab. He laughed, "You're not gonna get a cab tonight. It's game night!"

Uh, yeah, a pre-season game.

"But if you want, you can take the limo outside."

Christine and I glanced at the Towne car outside and then at each other. "Why not?"

Oh my God. The drive there was INSANE. When Vancouver was in the Stanley Cup final, I avoided downtown like the plague, but I can't imagine it was as crazy as this. I'm not talking about the riots after Game 7; I'm talking about the celebration before Game 1.

Seahawk fans are awesome. The whole city was a party - horns honking, music blaring, traffic jams, thousands of people in navy blue and fluorescent green streaming the streets, tail-gate parties on every corner... and this was just a pre-season game!

We decided to stop for a beer at The Hawks Nest. The place was packed. Every single person was wearing a Seahawks jersey, so Christine and I decided to wait until we were in the stadium before putting on our Titans gear... where there would surely be security guards.

We were right. No one bugged us. Not even me in my oversized jersey. I think it helped we were girls. The only other peeps brave enough to wear Titans jerseys were two 20 year-old 220 lb guys. I have a picture of the three of us. Besides, everyone loves Eddie George. A couple guys gave me high fives when they saw I was wearing #27.

When the Titans took the field, I thought I was going to burst. Yeah, yeah, I know, it was just a pre-season game, but it was my first. I can't believe I waited twelve and a half years!

This was an important game for Tennessee and the energy was electric. Coach Munchak has yet to decide who the starting quarterback is going be. It's between rookie Jake Locker and veteran Matt Hasselback. It turns out if I was going to wear an opposing teams jersey I picked the right one. I knew Hasselback had played for Seattle and was still well loved (a lot of people wore his Seahawks jersey), but I didn't know Locker was born and raised in Washington state and played for the Washington Huskies at UDub.

Century Link Stadium is amazing. It has an open roof design and so has a view of Seattle's skyline. I'm so glad we got to see an evening game because the sunset was breathtaking. The stadium is insanely loud. I had heard it's acoustics were designed to make it the loudest in the league, but I was not prepared for this. It affected the rhythm of my heart.

Our seats were way up high, which was cool because we were surrounded by all the rowdy diehards. These are not businessmen entertaining clients from out of town, oh no, you know these fans spend their entertainment budget, and perhaps a couple months rent, on season tickets, and they are going to suck every ounce of enjoyment out of it.

One thing that did surprise me was how strong the beer was. Canadians always gloat how American beer is so weak, but I couldn't finish my 'second-half' draft. I have never, *not* finished a beer in my whole beer-drinking career, but I just couldn't. I was wasted.

Seattle won, but who cares? It was just a pre-season game.

Afterwards, we went to some pub, shockingly the only place open on a Saturday night. I guess the downtown establishments have gotten wise about the post-game crowd. Needless to say, this place was hopping. When we walked in, some guy pointed to my Titans jersey and said, "You! Go hang out with the others in the back."

Apparently, there were a few of us Tennessee fans. Guess who the *others* were? Jake Locker's mom and brother-in-law! His mom is super cute. I posted a picture of us on Facebook.

Then Christine and I grabbed a seat and ordered a bunch of snacks and a couple more beers. We were starving. Not sure why I felt I needed more beer, though. There were two guys and a girl sitting at the table next to us. The guy on the far end was quite handsome. He kept glancing at me. I shocked myself. I smiled at him. He shocked me. He came and sat with us.

His name is Adam and is from Wisconsin originally, but now lives just north of Seattle. The Wisconsin accent really is the cutest. I could hear myself absorbing it - I have to stop doing that. He works in aviation or something... I can't really remember.

We flirted. I was actually doing not too bad until our food came and I started pigging out. It's hard to be sexy when you're gorging on hot wings. Poor Christine was left to chat with him, nibbling politely on crab dip. I could see her wanting to tag team me in, but I just couldn't stop stuffing my face.

On his way out, he gave me a hug and told me I had nice legs. Not sure how he could tell, me wearing my oversized jersey and all. They were off to a party, but he asked for my number. My cell didn't have service, so I gave him my email. The next morning, I checked and he had sent me a message. Hahaha. He was hoping to see me again. Who knows? Maybe someday.

We checked out, then walked all the way down to the water and spent the morning at Pike Place Market. I bought my mom a handmade purse and a fancy carved cheese knife for her birthday. Some lady asked if I was from Wisconsin. Too funny.

I love Seattle. It is fresh and clean and has a cool, funky vibe. It also has great coffee! It's like Vancouver's cool older cousin. I can't believe I've lived here for so long and never been there. I love this year.

Wild Rose Country

Part I: Ouellette Family Weekend

<u>August 16, 2012</u>

Deep, cleansing breath... Exhale. I'm at the cabin and it is mesmerizing.

It was a crazier trip than usual - wrong turns, sketchy accommodations, $30 cell phone call. I alternated between Michael Jackson and Garth Brooks. I thought I would do a lot more thinking, but no major epiphanies. Just promises to keep balanced while here.

Dr. Pez once said, "If you ever think you're enlightened, go spend a week with family."

Well, I'm here for two and I don't want to throw away all the work I've done the past seven months. It really is a gorgeous drive. I radiated and vibrated love and compassion a lot. Gave thanks for my new brakes, especially at the peak of the Coquihalla.

About half way here, I got a text from Celina - a sketch of the tattoo she wants to get.

Are you kidding me?!!!

Nope. She decided. We are getting tattoos! I almost peed my pants. I hope Tracy decides to as well, but no pressure.

I gave my dad his Father's Day gift last night - the chapter I dedicated to him. His expression... it was one I've never seen and will never forget. I was walking back from the outhouse and he popped out of the cabin for a moment. He just gave me a hug, said thank you and popped back in. He had tears in his eyes.

Sunday, August 19, 2012

9:30 PM: What a weekend! So much to write about, I'm not even sure where to start.

Alex is in the hospital.

When Tracy and the gang got here Friday night, he just came in and curled up on the couch. Not like him at all. All my nieces and nephews are super active, especially at the cabin, especially Alex. He had a tummy ache and the only time he got up was to go to the bathroom, which he shuffled to hunched over like an old man.

I teased him that this was a pretty extreme way to get out of giving me a hug. We play a little game where he pretends not to like getting hugs from me. I'm sure it's a game. All my nephews played it at that age.

He still wasn't better this morning, so Martin and Tracy took him to the St. Paul hospital. Then Martin called to say Tracy and Alex had to take an ambulance to Edmonton, to the Stollery. The Stollery is the children's hospital in Edmonton and just hearing the name always makes me sick. It's extremely respected and attracts specialists from around the world, but I still never wanted to have to visit one of my nieces or nephews there.

A *two-hour* ambulance ride. The poor little guy must've been scared, Tracy, too.

Turns out it's his appendix. He is in surgery right now, and we are just waiting to hear.

The rest of the weekend was crazy.

The Ouellette Family Weekend. Oh my gosh, the Ouellette family is by far the funniest and funnest family ever. My whole life, I thought the dad, Marcel, the craziest man alive, was my dad's cousin, but it turns out they were childhood friends. His wife, Sylvianne, is the sweetest, bubbliest lady.

In addition to inheriting their parents' sense of humor, their two kids, Shawn and Dee, my pseudo-cousins, are amazingly talented. They both sing and Shawn plays the guitar. They mostly do country music and raunchy campfire jingles, but they are my favorite. They sing *It's Your Love* better than Tim and Faith. I'm not even joking. It makes me cry, and since it was René and Celina's wedding song, I get to hear it every time we're all together.

It has been a long time since I got to hang around their family for a whole weekend and it was awesome. I laughed a lot. Seems to be a theme this summer. Music and laughter.

Dee is married to a super awesome guy, Bryan. Two things about Bryan: he looks like my ex-husband Matthew and he loves Pilsner beer. I don't hold either against him. *Just kidding.* Matthew is a handsome fellow and Pilsner, well, at least it has rabbits on the can.

Celina and I had a mind-blowing, heart-sealing conversation at the campfire last night. It was about my first divorce and how she has carried guilt for how she treated me all those years ago. I never knew she felt this. She was hard on me, there is no denying that, but I understood why. I guess I felt I deserved it.

She confided how out-of-control she felt; crying on the Beaumont Hill after seeing Matthew dancing at a hall party one night. She lost her big brother. She felt I had ripped him from her life and she had no say in the matter. Celina has never shown me this vulnerability.

She cooed, "You were so patient with me."

I don't remember this, but with tears in her eyes, she recalled one time sitting at the kitchen table just pouring abusive toxic shit out and me sitting at the other end just taking it in.

Finally, my Dad turned to her, "Enough, Celina."

I wanted to stop her, but I let her talk. She needed to get this out. I didn't sugarcoat it. It was hurtful. It was the lowest point of our relationship. She defended Matthew and thought I was a stupid idiot. Even said so numerous times. Jennifer begged me to stand up for myself, but how could I? I agreed with her.

I let her finish and then said, "Celina, there is nothing to forgive."
It's been 14 years. We've had hundreds, thousands of conversations, but this is the first time we've ever talked about this. She wasn't ready before. I wasn't ready before.

Then my beautiful little sister scanned my face, "You're so different now. So happy. So healthy. I never worry about you anymore."

I never knew she had.

"You used to have a heaviness about you that's gone. I never believed in auras before, but..." she took me all in, "yours is so light and clean."

She gets it. I am so part of this family for a reason. Tracy is reading a book about Chi running. She has always been an amazing athlete and it has worn on her body, but she is the last person I would think would be reading about energy healing. Still, it thrills me she would be open to this. The collective consciousness is rising.

I told everyone about the Emotion Code and they were all over it. The yellow over my eyes being cleared is hard for anyone to dispute. Except for René. Years of being a cop have turned him into a relentless cynic. He's the only person who the hand-growing trick hasn't worked for - the power of the mind. I need to learn how to EC others. I tried it on Sylvianne, but couldn't get clear. Probably shouldn't try it after drinking beer for three straight days.

Had my first Alberta *Inspired Idea*! I kneeboarded for the first time and like a lot of my *Inspired Ideas* this year, it turned out to be an opportunity for the Universe to get a good laugh.

René was pulling me behind his seadoo and Shawn was spotting. I was wearing my bikini. Not proper attire for water sports. At one point, I hit the wake hard and my body ended up perpendicular to the board. They were both killing themselves laughing. They didn't know what the hell I was doing, but I couldn't maneuver my way back on straight, because my bikini bottoms had slipped off my butt and was lingering around my knees. I had to bend my legs to keep them from being whisked away.

How traumatic would that have been for my nephews watching from the shore?

I also went on the tube for the first time in about 20 years. I've been sitting on the sidelines for years just watching all the fun... at the cabin and in life.

Now, it is just me and my mom and my dad and the pelicans chillaxing for the rest of the week. My cousin Greg's wedding is Friday, when the mayhem will begin again.

I hope Alex is doing okay.

10:03 PM: I just got a text from Tracy!

Alex is out of surgery. Pretty sick little boy. His appendix ruptured and an abscess had already formed. I'll know more tomorrow when we talk to the surgeon, but right now it looks like he'll be in the hospital for most of the week.

Ruptured? Don't people die from ruptured appendixes?! Oh my God, please let him be okay. Ruptured! What the fuck? My poor, sweet little Alex.

Part II: A Lesson in Love

August 20, 2012

Text from Tracy: *Talked to the doctor. He said because of the rupture and the bacteria that was in him he'll be in the hospital for 4-5 days. Has to stay on IV antibiotics for the duration. He had a really good night. Slept lots, had a couple popsicles. Was very happy the pain was gone. First thing he says, "Can I watch TV? I have to catch up on my sports."*

Thank you, God. Thank you, thank you.

11 AM: Josh is in Stony Plain. You've got to be fucking kidding me! He posted the cutest picture on Facebook with his grandmother. Greg's wedding is in Stony Plain on Friday.

Argh!!! I'm trying to let go, Universe. Can you help me out a bit?

August 21, 2012

Update: *Alex didn't have a very good night. His intestines aren't quite working right so there was a lot of abdominal pressure and stomach was rock hard. They had to give him a nasal gastric tube to drain what was in his stomach and intestines.*

What? I thought he was fine. I feel sick. We are driving in tomorrow.

I'm so grateful they let one parent stay with the child at the Stollery. Tracy hasn't left. I can't imagine how scary it would've been for Alex to go through that without his mom.

<u>August 22, 2012</u>

This is my last morning at the cabin. My parents have already left for Edmonton and I'm leaving in a few hours. I wanted a little time here by myself, to practice my yoga one last time on the deck overlooking the stunning lake and just reflect on how differently I feel than the last two summers I've spent here.

Sara and I had cuddle group, something we haven't done in years. Sadie and I cuddled, too, way different than a year ago. Holding them in my arms, I let my love for them radiate from my heart, but when I tried to allow theirs to flow in, there was still some resistance. I am yearning to receive their love. I know it is there.

Later: Okay, this is ridiculous. Josh is on some Alberta road trip! WTF? He posted panoramic rural pictures from around Vermillion, which is about 70 km away from Lac Santé. What the heck is he doing here? Looking for me? *JK.*

8 PM: The Stollery Children's Hospital: my new tithe. A humbling reminder Western medicine has its place. I have been so high and mighty about self-healing and Eastern philosophy I have forgotten this.

The Stollery is an entire wing of the University of Alberta Hospital, which is next to the campus of U of A - my alma mater. It's been a long time since I've been here, though, and I had trouble finding my way around the labyrinth. The truth is I could barely think or see straight. I asked the parking guy, "Where's The Sto--?" and just started to cry. The word couldn't escape from my quivering lips. That would make me being here, real. He must be used to the reaction though, because he just smiled compassionately and told me exactly where to go.

Storming through the hospital corridors, trying to find Alex's room, I was so cranky I wanted to snap at everyone. I was embittered - an emotion I haven't felt in awhile.

Fuck. I just wanted to find his room. Why is it so hard to find a fucking patient's room?

Alex hasn't smiled yet. So not him. He's always been like a grinning cartoon character... My Brownie Buddy.

I'm supposed to go home Monday, but I'm not leaving until he is safe and sound at home. I'm not leaving until I see him smile. I'm not leaving without that hug.

I am so grateful to be here instead of in Vancouver worried sick. I am so grateful I am here to witness Tracy and Martin's love and devotion to their kids on a whole new level.

I'm ashamed to say I've judged Tracy. I wasn't going to include this, but I promised to be honest. Besides, I owe her an apology.

It was Dr. Pez who first called me out on this. The first round of visits I had with him was the summer Lee ran away from home at fourteen to go live with his dad. In the six years since I had left, this was the only time I considered moving home. I flew him out to Vancouver for a visit, instead. I was worried sick about him. He's like me, super deep and sensitive - ideal ingredients for depression. I also ran away from home when I was a teen, and although I was living with Nicole and her loving family, it was a very low time in my life. One of my rock bottoms.

Days after Lee had run away, I was telling Dr. Pez how furious I was at Lee's dad for manipulating him and at Tracy for not listening. No matter what I felt about his father, Lee was 14 and it made perfect sense to me he would want to go live with him. *What teenage boy wouldn't?* Their shit was still affecting their child and it pissed me off.

Dr. Pez, "You're quite judgmental of parents."

"Me? Judgmental? I'm the most unjudgmental person I know."

Upon further investigation, it was revealed, I wasn't just judging Lee's parents, I was judging all parents. Actually, in all my years of teaching, this has been an ongoing issue for me, but witnessing Tracy and Martin in action, as parents in crisis, has been a humbling experience.

I don't know jack shit about what it means to be a parent.

Tracy has completely stopped everything in her life to be at Alex's side. She hasn't gone to work, and won't, until he is okay. It is obvious Martin wants to be there constantly, as well, but has taken on the role of ensuring Dylan and Erin don't get lost in the shuffle.

I don't know if I could be this selfless. I'm scared I will never know this level of love.

Dylan and Erin want to be there all the time. Lee has come to visit every chance he gets.

Family is beautiful and who am I to project my shit on theirs.

Part III: Let's Do The Time Warp Again...

August 23, 2012

Josh posted a pic of himself in a field near Vegreville hugging a gigantic Big Rock beer can. Two hay bales stacked on top of each other covered in a tarp. Advertising... Alberta-style.

I commented. He commented back. We're friends.

August 25, 2012

2:07 AM: *Chartrand Weddings - Seriously, we should charge admission.*

The Chartrand family is huge. There are nearly a hundred of us and we all *love* to dance. I'm lying in bed, scrolling through the pics on my camera... So much fun. I love my family so much... my family is so gorgeous. I'm so tipsy, but still so pumped. I love Flo Rida!

My God, my mom and aunties look amazing! I hope I look that good when I'm their age. It's so weird my mom looks like my dad's sisters. I guess it's some mysterious phenomenon when you're married to someone for 42 years... you start to look like your in-laws.

Note to self: before getting married again, check out in-laws. JUST KIDDING!

Celina and my Auntie Nicki are gorgeous - two generations of superstars! They are so much alike it is creepy, stereotypical babies of the family. It's funny because Tracy is a lot like my Auntie Cecile, the oldest. And me, well... I'm an amalgamation of the middle eight.

Tracy and Martin weren't there. They didn't want to leave Alex alone at the hospital.

Okay, time for sleepy, sleeps.

August 26, 2012

I never had any interest in attending reunions. I went to junior high with Greg, and him and Tracy also went to high school together before we moved to Beaumont. Greg still hangs out with a lot of the same gang, most of who were at the wedding last night. Tracy dated one of their best friends, Brett. I really liked Brett. He was super nice to me. He passed away a few years ago of cancer. William was there. I had the hugest crush on him when Tracy and Brett were dating. I may have blushed when he entered the hall.

The first boy I ever made out with was also there. We were in Grade 8. It was also the first time I got drunk.

Larissa was there, too. Larissa and I weren't exactly friends in elementary or junior high. She was the most popular girl in school; I was the least. She was also the ringleader of one of the most humiliating experiences of my life.

In Grade 5, her and three of her cronies cornered me in the hall at recess. Smiling from ear to ear, they said Bobby, my first crush, wanted to go out with me.

I was like, "Okay!"

Bobby and I dated for three months... only thing is he didn't know it. I should've known it was a hoax when he never spoke to me, but it was my first boyfriend and I was too shy to talk to him, too. I guess communication in relationships has been an issue for me from the start.

Anyways, when the girls found out I actually believed we were dating they laughed their asses off at me. I was mortified.

That was a lifetime ago, though, and it was really cool to see Larissa and catch-up. If there is one thing I've learned this year it is that my perception of my past is sometimes skewed.

What's hilarious is she tried to set me up with William! William actually talked to me, though, so I figured maybe she was on the up and up this time. I even allowed myself to flirt. He asked for my phone number and I gave it to him. I go back to Vancouver soon and will probably never see him again, but still, I'm proud of myself. Woo hoo! Two guys in two weeks.

6:24 PM: Tracy just texted a picture of Alex sitting the car! He's coming home!!! This is by far the most beautiful picture I have ever seen. There is even a hint of a mischievous smile at the corner of his mouth. When I think what coulda... No. I've been VVR'ing positive, radiant, healthy light to him all week, I'm not going to stop now. Just pure gratitude from here on out!

August 28, 2012

Celina and I got tattoos yesterday! Insane. We are bonded for life... not that we weren't already. We settled on butterflies. They are simple and darling and as Celina said, "What this year is all about." She has been so supportive. My God, she got a flippin' tattoo! I hope she never regrets it. Simple black outlines with little purple highlights on the wings.

Celina was extremely nervous, so went first. We got them on the top of our left feet, which has absolutely no cushion. The outlining is always the most painful, but as soon as the lady started, Celina seemed disappointed, "That's it? That's what I was worried about?"

Tattoos: one of the great metaphors for life.

Tracy decided against it and that is totally cool. I told her it is an open offer, even if she decides when she's 65.

My mom's birthday is tonight. Alex is home. I got my hug. Today is a perfect day.

August 30, 2012

Alberta. Kicked. My. Ass.

Driving home yesterday was interesting... Still thinking about you-know-who.

How can I live the Best Year of My Life and not be with my soul mate? I have been holding on to this vision of Josh. It is an illusion and I really want to let it go, but the bastard was touring around Alberta! I know I'm reading into this. I am. I know it.

If I'm going to be totally honest, I've still been holding onto having a romantic happy ending to my book. Wouldn't it make a great ending to 'the story' if we ended up together? Maybe this summer was the montage part of our romantic comedy. You know, where we are out having the time of our lives, but really not happy because we are not together.

Today, I walked from Jericho, past Locarno to the tip of Spanish Banks and back, repeating over and over again, "Letting go of the illusion, to make room for the reality."

Today is my last yoga session with Nick and I really don't want to go. I'm feeling so mushy and groggy - unbalanced mentally, physically, emotionally and spiritually.

August 31, 2012

I am so glad I went to my session with Nick. We did some detoxifying of my kidneys, along with some handstands. My left eye is really red, so

I didn't wear my contacts. I wore my glasses knowing I'd have to take them off and be 'blind'. Bizarre, because as soon as I got there Nick told me we would be doing the whole session with my eyes closed. Blind.

"When we shut our eyes, our brain can shut down and our heart can take over."

I wanted to be upside down as much as possible. Feeling the pulsating in my hands on the mat was stimulating to my core. I felt so strong again. He said my form is perfect. More than perfect. He teetered me back and forth and I easily rebalanced. It was profound. I could almost feel the blood flowing through my veins and the emotions being released. I can't believe how quickly I bounce back from Alberta trips now.

Nick did the Vipassana meditation retreat as well and had the same experience with nausea when observing the sensations around his throat. I always thought it was because of bulimia, but he thinks it's about speaking our truth. Interesting.

We talked about moving away and the anxiety you feel when you first start going back to visit. I didn't know it at the time, but when I left Alberta twelve years ago, I was running away. I said I was chasing my dream, but, actually, I was trying to escape. The problem is, the one thing I was trying to escape from, I was bringing with me - my past.

Even the thought of going back would make me anxious. The moment I would walk into my parents' house, I would instantly go back to that weaker version of myself. And grab a beer. Carlos would call me on it, which really pissed me off. It always did when he was right.

Nick went through the same thing the first few years. The beautiful thing is once you become truer to yourself, you don't waiver as much and bounce back quicker. That's what yoga is. Not living in a bubble of bliss, but being able to *go home* and stay balanced, even in Alberta.

I'm so proud of myself for not drinking yesterday. I wanted to go sit on a patio and just read, but my beautiful, healthy-self asked me not to, so I said, "For you kid, anything."

Summer Chief Challenge Hike #15

I am eating a succulent nectarine. Its sweetness is exhilarating every one of my taste buds. A chipmunk just ran over my chest.

Absorb... emit... radiate

I am attracting amazing men into my life. I have been for a while and now I am noticing and appreciating the ones who have been here for a long time. I took a moment at the cabin and glanced around the campfire at all the amazing husbands and boyfriends the women in my life are with. Why haven't I ever seen them before? Because they didn't fit my low-opinion of their gender and I like to be right.

For so long, the vast majority of relationships I witnessed were unhealthy, at the very least unhappy. This is what I chose to see, because it reflected and verified my bitterness. Now I seem to see healthy relationships wherever I look. Even the ones I thought were unhealthy seem to have been healed. Or I have.

My outer world is adjusting to reflect my inner world.

Later: Back to the real world! I am organizing the WIFTV Whistler Film Mentorship and just sent all the applications to the jury, which include my buddy Jason James, Trish Dolman from Screen Sirens, director Penelope Buitenhuis and writer/director Desiree Lim. I love the Vancouver film community. This is the inaugural year and we have ten rock-star applications.

43

Sexy September

<u>September 1, 2012</u>

I giggle as I write the title, but I'm serious. I am a nympho emerging from her nympha.

Now, all I need is someone to have sex with. No emotional or spiritual illusions. I am going to meet someone who is going to rock my body and rock my world.

5:30 PM: Well, that didn't last long. My Sexy September has turned into Surrender September. During my beach walk, feelings of anxiety and expectation rushed over me.

I asked myself, "How can I go with the flow?" The answer: Let go. Then I heard Corey Hart sing, "Never Surrrreeeeennnder!"

Surrender doesn't mean giving up, it means letting go.

ARGH!!! I'm never gonna get laid. I am going to die an old spinster.

Getting laid? As if. That's not what I really want. I am not looking for just a date or a playmate, I want my soul mate... my heart-mate.

This summer love affair was only the beginning.

6:30 PM: I have not done anything creative in months. I haven't even thought about *Making of a Faith Healer* or *Happiless* in weeks. I've been working on my book, but that's not creative, I'm just transcribing my journals. I'm going to color a mandala tonight. Watch a movie and color. I feel the need to CREATE! Even creating the Best Year of My Life has become logical, rational and predictable.

When I don't engage my left-brain enough, I overanalyze life; when I don't engage my right-brain, I over-dramatize it.

Unbalanced hemispheres = unbalanced life.

Inspired Idea! I am going to make tomorrow the most creatively out-of-the-box day of the year. Yikes! What does that even mean?

My instinct is to plan it. Plan all the 'go with the flow' things I will do, but you know what I'm going to do? Not plan. Not a thing. Wake up and then just... go. I can't believe the anxiety this is bringing up, which means it is exactly what I need to do.

"So Rachelle, what are you doing tomorrow?"

"I have absolutely no fucking idea."

Hilarious! I feel this exhilarating, no,... Shit. Fuck. Shit. Why did I say I would do this? My lists! My goals! Fuck. Fuck. FUCK!

Okay. Breathe.

I can feel myself planning and wanting to prepare my not planning and not preparing.

What should I wear? I DON'T KNOW!!!

What should I do for breakfast? Oh my God, this is too funny. I have honestly never lived a day blind to the next moment, let alone to the whole day. Holy crapola, I'm so scared.

What time should I go to bed? I'm relentless.

I'm turning in my laptop for my camera. No email. No Facebook. Living like a child. Totally living moment to moment. Dear God, I hope I don't end up in Abbotsford. No. If my spirit leads me to Abbotsford... I will go to Abbotsford. No shoulds, coulds, woulds.

I'm going to be a child and let the Universe lead me.

If I'm hungry, I'll eat. If I'm tired, I'll sleep. I will be Forest Gump. Maybe I'll spend the day in a handstand. Who knows?

Good night. See you on the flip side.

Surrender September

September 2, 2012

I woke up late and took my time, keeping present and open. The only place I wanted to go was Grounds... My whole life is a habit I need to break. I parked on a different street, though, and am going to read the Georgia Straight. No over thinking. Go with the flow. I have a fake purple flower clip in my hair that Kimmie gave me.

5:23 PM: Created my day through muscle testing - GPS style.

After Grounds, I went back home and had a glorious nap. Then I drove downtown and parked by the water under the Granville Street Bridge. Found a prime spot for free. *Sweet.* I started walking. At each corner, I muscle tested which direction I should go next - extreme anxiety every step of the way. My ego was going insane not knowing what was going on, having absolutely no say in what was going to happen next.

The process led me face-to-face to a woman asking for change in front of Starbucks on Helmcken and Howe. As I was giving her a loonie, someone handed her a muffin, but she said she needed eggs. She asked me for more money as I walked away. I muscle tested why I wanted to go back. Guilt. I kept walking.

I meditated at the water fountain in front of the Sheraton Wall Centre for a bit, and then carried on, wandering up and down random streets.

"Where the hell am I going?"

It is not the destination. It is the journey.

My ego didn't like that. It tried to crawl out of my skin and grab me by the throat.

I ended up at Blenz on Robson with a Taiwan Green Tea. Sat on the patio across from a lady in her forties working on her laptop holding a baby. I was meant to see her.

Strolled through Yaletown, down to the ocean. Got in my car and ended up at Locarno.

Laying there surrendering, I did the shadow process with my Control Freak. We sat in the wind, (he thought he could control the weather) and agreed I would let him control writing goals and career stuff, but it is time to surrender the rest.

Letting go of the illusion, to make room for the reality.

Now I am sitting on Benny's patio writing. My novel is my number one priority right now, and I am allowing Control Freak to achieve its goals, so it can be a constructive part of me.

I am surrendering. My small human brain cannot possibly fathom the great love my spirit knows. I am letting go of the brakes.

Just saw a squirrel almost get hit by a car. Time to go.

September 3, 2012

Struggling to surrender is my ego holding me back. I know I have no control. I know there is nothing for me to do. I know that I am already whole. I have the most amazing life and wouldn't change one thing about my past or present. Not even sure why I think about it so much.

My ego: her (yes, her) job is to keep me stuck under the illusion of moving forward.

Yesterday's experiment was fascinating. Not at all the day I thought I was going to create, but so many lessons nonetheless. First and foremost, my ego can't stand not knowing what is going to happen next, but the reality is, it never does. No matter how much it wants to.

Side question: Why do people always eat the cinnamon buns at Grounds with their mouth open? Disgusting. New shadow? Can 'Disgusting Eater' be a shadow? OMG, me when I was bulimic. I don't think there could be anything more disturbing than watching someone consume five thousand calories in one sitting... except, of course, them throwing it all up.

6 PM: I'm officially addicted to muscle testing. I even muscle tested if I should stop muscle testing. Why do I create things to make myself feel crazy? Besides, what if it is all a crock? No more. I am only doing it for health. I have no right to know everything. This is just feeding my Control Freak. The Universe is laughing its ass off at me.

Needing to know everything is based in fear, not love. Love grows and expands and trusts and is not defined by a yes or no. The beauty is in the *not* knowing, in the surrendering. I wrote a whole flipping movie based on this and it is still an issue for me. I'm quite pissed with myself.

I feel like doing something totally fucking crazy. I want to fuck someone! Seriously! I am having sex with someone this month and I don't care who it is. My God, I wish I were attracted to someone. I am going to meet someone so hot and I'm going to fuck his brains out.

I am busting out of jail, out of the monastery. I am not a nun. I am a sexy, beautiful, vibrant woman and if Josh doesn't want to be with me, fuck him. He is allowed to not want to be with me, but there is someone out there who does. I am moving on!

I haven't had sex in almost 3 years. Enough. Is. Enough. This pent-up energy is not healthy. I need to have a healthy release! This is what happens when you cage an animal!

September 4, 2012

Last night was so weird. I was feeling highly erratic and thought I was going to self-abuse, but I didn't. I just have all this energy inside of me and I don't know what to do with it.

I know what I need to do... Go inside. My soul is crying for a deeper connection. Whenever I get caught up with what is not in my life, it is a projection of something missing within. I know that some physical connection with someone *out there* will not make me feel whole. I am whole. I am complete.

What is the deeper meaning, the spiritual idea, of love and companionship? I don't know, but if there is one thing I've learned this year, the answers are all inside, so I'm going in.

It's a beautiful, wise place to be. I can't believe six months ago the idea of going inside scared the shit out of me.

September 5, 2012

I just read Monday's entry about having sex. Hilarious! As if. I talk such a big game.

I went for a two-hour walk last night and just surrendered the whole time. Over and over again, repeating, "I surrender. I surrender. I surrender."

By writing this book, and creating the Best Year of My Life, I have imposed this expectation I am meant to meet my soul mate this year. How can you have the best year of your life and not fall in love?

Letting go of this expectation of time is liberating. I have all the time in the world. My life is unfolding perfectly... and on time.

I had my first session back with Elliot yesterday.

As soon as he saw me, he deadpanned, "Your eyes are greener."

He is so deep. He's asking lots of questions about God and thought and consciousness. I explained the theory of the quantum field... he's only in Grade 9. I wish I had had someone back then when I had questions. Yep, he's definitely one of my soul mates. There is just so much flow with us. Except around other people. It's like 'our relationship' doesn't like to be observed.

I told him about my Sunday muscle testing expedition around downtown. He is probably the only person on the face of the earth I could tell. I've never seen him laugh so hard.

"Yeah, that is weird. It's totally something I would do."

September 6, 2012

Well, my fall just got a whole lot busier. Mary has had a house crisis and needs to take on a couple directing gigs over the next month or so. I am now *interim* president.

I will be chairing our first board meeting and speaking at Martini Madness. I also said I would join the festival committee which she was chairing. All of this is really great exposure and an amazing career opportunity, but mostly I'm grateful for the chance to support Mary.

September 7, 2012

Summer Chief Challenge Hike # 16
I'm getting old and set in my ways.
Then, I contemplated just getting old. An image flashed before my eyes of that old woman from *Something About Mary*. You know the one. Cameron Diaz's neighbor... yeah, her. I've tanned way too much this summer. I want to watch a comedy. I need to watch a comedy. I need a night of frivolous entertainment. Maybe I should rent *Something About Mary*.
Later: I'm watching a bit of news right now. Obama officially accepted his nomination. Canada has cut all diplomatic ties with Iran. Here comes the nightly murder report... CLICK.
Oh my God! *Something About Mary* is on. I am not even joking.

September 9, 2012
The most wonderful day of the year... First Football Sunday! The Titans are playing the Patriots. Too perfect. I flipping hate the Patriots. Go Titans!
Met some gals at the Tap & Barrel last night. It's a new waterfront patio in False Creek. The ladies were discussing the book, *50 Shades of Gray*. I'm so out of the loop. I can't believe it's about a younger girl! I assumed it was about a, um, cougar. All these older ladies are raging over it. I guess they are unsatisfied with their sex lives... maybe I should read it.
One of the ladies was going on and on how she wished she had bigger breasts. Do men sit around talking about how they wish they had bigger balls?
Whoa, wait. I'm at Grounds and the song playing just had the line 'shades of gray'. Weird. Maybe I should read the book.
5 PM: What an interesting day! After looking at my finances, I went through some major anxiety and realized (actually faced) the resistance I've been having to making money. I did the Timeline Meditation, which

I haven't done in ages. At first, I wasn't able to go back - unworthiness was rising intensely, but then I saw my Little Girl, who I haven't talked to in awhile. She said I wasn't appreciating her again and that not paying attention to my finances has made her feel unsafe.

I then went back in time, and dropped down in the big grey house, the house we first moved to in Beaumont. The kitchen counters were covered with bottles. I was having a high school liquid lunch party, the one that led me to getting suspended and then running away.

You don't deserve money because you don't value anything and will just ruin everything.

I stayed there a long time forgiving. Shining light seeped out of me, but with major resistance... and then something cracked and it all came flooding out. I am a 39-year-old woman. I am worthy of making lots of money. I will take care of it. Allowing money into my life is a metaphor for appreciating myself. You don't attract wealth and abundance into your life; you allow it.

Thank you, ego, for this crisis today. It was a catalyst for another leap.

I'm kind of nervous to rewrite *Making of a Faith Healer*. The first draft received such polarized feedback. I've also changed a lot since I started writing it. I have been healing myself through energy work for the past six months. *How do I write a movie that shows all faith healings as ridiculous and dangerous?*

Hmmmm... Maybe I should write a film that asks the real questions... *Why* do we believe what we believe? How do our relationships and experiences shape our beliefs? How do our beliefs shape our relationships and experiences?

Whoa, this is a huge shift. Of course... *Making of a Faith Healer*... page one rewrite.

Nuggets of gold.

The Titans lost to the Patriots... I flipping hate the Patriots.

September 14, 2012

Elliot keeps asking me about when I was teased as a kid. He's really challenging me on being 'weird'. He says I wasn't as weird as I think I was and I'm not weird now either. Elliot is the first person in my life to tell me how *not* weird I am. I think it's because we are so much alike and if I'm normal, that must mean he is, too.

I shrug, "We're not weird, we're unique."

He hates it when I say that. Elliot is in Grade 9 now and 'uniqueness' isn't appreciated anymore than weirdness is. I also think he *feels* weird and doesn't like it. Maybe Elliot is in my life to help me see my youth from a different perspective. Maybe I'm in his so he can be reassured he's not that weird. Or maybe it's time we both truly appreciated our weirdness.

We're also talking a lot about religion - why babies are baptized, how Jesus dying on the cross saved Christians... all the conversations I wanted to have when I was his age.

I swear I could write a book just about our sessions - math question, Catholicism question, math question, metaphysics question, math question, organic broccoli question...

<u>September 15, 2012</u>

<u>Summer Chief Challenge Hike #17</u>

On the way up, I brainstormed the storyline structure for *Making of a Faith Healer* I have been struggling with. Funny, it's more like the original idea from a couple of years ago.

On the way down, I saw three guys I found attractive. Three! Two of them just smiled at me and said hi, but the other was shirtless and I actually wanted to touch his chest. I'm healed!

Later: I have tried to make love and romantic relationships linear. 1 → 2 → 3. Love is not linear or timely. It just is. The relationship unfolds in all dimensions organically. No relationship is the same. Each has its own story. A life of its own!

A beautiful couple with a baby came into Grounds. The father looked so happy. I can't believe two years ago I was so cynical; a year ago, so scared; six months ago, so sexist.

Josh 'liked' one of those pervert pages on Facebook. Does he know people can see this? Does he care? It hit me like a stone in my gut. Judgment is always a shadow. Do I still have a pervert shadow? I saw this poster for a film playing at VIFF. Just a row of bikini clad rear-ends.

It really bothered me. It turns out the movie is directed by a woman. I have to see this movie.

September 16, 2012

This morning, as I was walking to Grounds through the back alley, I saw a girl on the walk of shame. She knew I knew. Heels and bar attire at 7 AM... I was gonna text Erik, but then noticed her blank look. I know that look.

There is nothing more meaningful than meaningless sex.

2:15 PM: I'm exploring a way to embrace my pervert. I want to embrace my pervert without objectifying it. I know I need to lighten up. I just don't know how.

Oh yeah, love this part of me. Love my pervert.

Speaking of pervert, I saw Josh today. I was walking to my car, which was parked on the side of his condo building. He was pulled over at the sidewalk. I knew it was him. He drove over to talk to me. It was nice. We're friends. No awkwardness. I was a bit shy, but okay.

I was meditating on a log at Locarno, 'Letting go of the illusion, making room for the reality", just breathing and releasing, breathing and surrendering. I opened my eyes and was overwhelmed by the gift that lay before me - the sun glistening low; the ocean shimmering its reflection; the silvery mountains in the distance... awe-mazing.

This is my home. This is where I feel safe. Maybe I'm a mermaid.

September 18, 2012

I'm having major resistance to planning my birthday party. Maybe because it will mean this year is over and I will be 40. Maybe it's because I haven't actually thought about *being* 40.

The truth is there is a part of me that is scared the party will be lame. What if no one comes? I feel like a teenager again. I thought about inviting tons of people to make sure some would show up, but that doesn't feel expansive or at all in line with my initial Inspired Idea.

The purpose is to appreciate my friends and family for all their support, and helping me make it to 40. A gathering of love and appreciation. This is really what a birthday party should be about. Not the music or the food or the booze (although those things will make it fun), but a celebration of appreciation.

Ha! That's what I'm going to call it. I'm gonna send the invites out this weekend.

September 21, 2012

Summer Chief Challenge Hike #18

Unworthiness keeps rearing its head. I thought I was feeling worthy.

Worthiness isn't something you feel... it is something you know.

Self-worth comes from doing what is worthy.

Bulimia: *The Rich White Girl Disease.* The transferring of guilt for wasting so much, to thinking I don't deserve anything. Writing this book is the most humbling thing I have ever done. Promising to be completely honest with you, has forced me to be completely honest with myself.

September 22, 2012

I'm gonna be on the jury for the Artistic Merit Award committee. WIFTV gives the award to a female director, screenwriter, editor or cinematographer who has a film in the Canadian Images Program at the Vancouver International Film Festival. What an honor.

Ana won the WIFTV Whistler Mentorship for *Sitting on the Edge of Marlene*! Her and Amber will both be there. Whistler times two, baby!

September 23, 2012

5:20 PM: I've been thinking about you-know-who again, wondering 'what if'... so off to the beach I went, *Letting go of the illusion, to make room for the reality.* The tears started to flow. Right there on a blanket at Locarno Beach. I wasn't crying out of sadness for *today*, I was letting that 14-year-old girl cry like she should have 25 years ago. I didn't care if anyone heard.

Later, I was in my bathroom and just started crying again. Bawling. Uncontrollably. This time for the girl, no, more like *with* the girl. We cried together.

She wanted to fall to the floor, but I held her up, "Don't be afraid. Take as long as you need. I'm here. I love you and I will never leave you."

What if I'm never ready?

"Even if it is just you and me forever. We are enough. We are more than enough."

I don't need a man. Not in a, snap-my-fingers, 'I don't need no man' way, but... just... I don't NEED a man. I finally realize why I haven't had sex since being single. I am starting again, a clean slate, a born-again virgin. Seriously, I get a second chance to write my story.

Self-worth comes from doing what is worthy.

Having sex with someone doesn't make me worthy, just like not having sex with someone doesn't make me unworthy.

Ho-ly shit! It's the end of September. I don't remember the exact date, but it would be almost exactly 25 years to the day I lost my virginity in the backseat of that car. 25 years! Wow. It took this long, but she's out and I love her.

I keep seeing her as my Unworthy shadow in my sanctuary, peeking out from behind a tree. She's been behind that tree for 25 years, but she came out today. She's been silent for 25 years... No, she hasn't. She's been crying out in many dysfunctional and self-destructive ways, but I've been ignoring her.

I have her picture! So weird. Tracy scanned and emailed it to me a year ago, because I wanted an awkward teenage picture for work. I've used it in other ways, too. I used it to try and forgive her. FORGIVE HER! Forgive her for what?

The picture is a retake. Retakes are done in October, so I had already lost my virginity. My pink shaker knit, teased hair, mondo pink earrings, green eyeliner... the zit on my forehead I obsessed about. She looks so young, trying to look so old.

I used to want to ask her why. Why did she drink so much that night? Why was she even in the backseat of that car in the first place? A part of me still does, but she's not the one to ask.

Why did 'I' choose to have this experience?

I believe our Higher Self chooses the experiences it needs in order to fulfill its highest purpose. If it wasn't for this amazing year, I don't think I would have an answer, but now I think I do. I think I chose that shameful, degrading experience, and all the others that followed, so I could know my worthiness at the deepest level.

I don't know it yet, but I will.

I support myself. I trust myself. Adios, brown journal, and thank you.

Functionista

They only have four colors of the journals I've been using from Banyan books. The last one is black. Not exactly the color I envisioned for my final quarter of this year.

In feng shui, black is the water element. Perfect. *Flow, baby, flow.* It's also the color of mystery, sophistication, power and protection, the complementary force, the unseen.

Wow. I guess there is more inner stuff I am meant to explore.

September 26, 2012

I loved myself to sleep last night. It's been awhile and I forgot how glorious it is.

Martini Madness is tonight! Each year, WIFTV puts on a big soirée to kick off the Vancouver International Film Festival and to honor women with films in the festival.

I have to write my speech now. Bizarre resistance rising. Public speaking has never been an issue for me, but this is the first time I'm doing it as WIFTV president.

VIFF is going to be busy, busy, busy, but fun, fun, fun!

September 27, 2012

Martini Madness was a huge success! The theme was Glitter. I had absolutely no idea what to wear. I ended up in a super short black skirt

Carlos bought me in Korea, a sleeveless shimmery top from Jen and painfully high heels. It was held at a nightclub on Granville Street, and I had to stand on a stage to say my speech, which made me feel half naked. Luckily, it was mostly women.

Why can't I just wear flip-flops wherever I go? Tank tops and shorts in the summer; yoga pants and sweater vests in the winter, life would be so much more comfortable.

Vancouver was voted 3rd worst dressed city in the world, because of folks like me. To all the fashionistas out there who've made it their mission to shame us functionistas into style submission, I say, "I'm sorry, obviously you don't know me, but I do actually need to be ready to do a Downward Facing Dog at any moment. I easily walk the beach, meet a friend for coffee, go to the library and hit the market all in one outing. Vancouver, at least Kits, is filled with active people and I'm one of them, thank you very much!"

September 28, 2012

7 AM at Grounds: Last night was the Opening Screening and Gala for the Vancouver International Film Festival. The film was Deepa Mehta's *Midnight's Children*. Cinematically speaking, it was beautiful, but structurally... there were issues. That's right, I just critiqued Salman Rushdie's writing. I think this was his first screenplay, an adaptation, and if there is one thing I am confident about, it is my structural sensibilities.

The gala was held at some warehouse-type place and had an India theme. The film, the music, the décor, the food... I miss India. I love the film community. People are so nice and open and happy for each other. I left with Christine without saying goodbye to anyone, though, not even Carolyn, who I went with. I didn't even realize it until I got home.

As we were leaving, Christine looked around at all the beautiful men and winked, "Do you have Josh Goggles on?" She is so funny. I haven't even mentioned him since July.

9 AM: Erik just offered me advice about dating. "You have to be willing to do work. It is hard work and it must be your focus."

"I'm just not attracted to anyone. Why am I not attracted to anyone?"

Erik made me promise to flirt with somebody at the party tonight, "Just look around the room, pick someone and flirt."

"Okay," giggle, giggle, "I promise."
I attract attractive people. I am surrounded by beautiful souls.

September 29, 2012

I got Adam Beach's phone number last night.

I really didn't want to go to the party, but didn't want to bail on Ros. It was the Canadian Images Party and it's by invite only. Ros' short film, *OMG*, is in the festival, but the director, Siobhan, was working, so Ros asked me. So nice of her, but three nights in a row is too much for me. Three nights in a row wearing heels is too much for my poor little toes.

The night was surreal. The party was at CinCin's, which is owned by Jack Evrensel, who also owns Blue Water Café, where I worked. The last time I was at CinCin's was for the Christmas party ten years ago.

I used to work these film festival soirées. I remember being jealous of the people. I wanted to be them so bad. Instead, I was left to pig out on leftover prawns from the chilled seafood towers behind the bar and drink the bottom of the bottles of wine. These parties always have free food and booze. I ate probably five pounds of prawns last night... I guess the only difference now is I'm pigging out in front of the bar.

I had propped myself there for the goodies, yes, but also so I could alternate slipping my tender tootsies out of my heels. *Seriously, would anyone even notice if I was wearing flip-flops?*

The night was going awesome. I was content with my prawns, beer and great conversations, when I realized I had only talked to women all night.

Erik's voice rang in my ears, "Just look around the room, pick someone and flirt."

Argh. Fine. I hate you, Erik.

I scanned the room. Adam Beach was standing in a group nearby. We caught each other's eyes. *Erik said it didn't matter who, so I might as well go for the movie star.*

I smiled. He smiled back. That first time I saw him was at the *Arctic Air* premiere in January, I was automatically interested. I wouldn't say attracted, although he is yummy, but definitely *interested*. He's charming and passionate and... I did mention yummy, right?

Later on, we were both at the bar with one person standing in between us.

I thought, *What the hell?* and introduced myself. He said he was admiring me. He said I was beautiful. He is quite the charmer. So what's the problem? His very stunning and equally charming girlfriend, Leah, for one. The other, well... Here I have a movie star telling me I'm beautiful and all I can think is, "Why doesn't Josh think so?"

Maybe I do have Josh Goggles on. How do I take them off?

Choosing the movie star in the room was also the safest choice. If he rejected me, it would be understandable. And, truth be told, I suspected Adam had a girlfriend, which made the flirting safe. It was friendly flirting. I really like her. She is fun and vivacious. The three of us ended up talking writing. They told me about a project they are working on. I wasn't really interested, but then Ros pulled me aside and said if I didn't take advantage of the opportunity she would, so I asked for his card. He didn't have one so wrote his number on receipt paper.

That's how I got Adam Beach's phone number. When I woke up and saw it, I laughed.

September 30, 2012

Final day of Surrender September. Whew... Now what?

October 2, 2012

Happy 8th Birthday, Sara!

Sara is such a fascinating little girl: one day singing a self-scribed song a cappella at her school talent show, the next carrying dead snakes out of the bush. Celina thinks she's going to be the next Lady Gaga. She once exhumed a femur bone on the beach at the cabin. Maybe she could make a bone dress.

Have I mentioned she's also the most fashion conscious little girl I know? I once mortified her at the cabin when I wore socks with my flip-flops. She still talks about it.

46

Chillin' the Fuck Out

October 3, 2012

9 AM at Grounds: Erik just gave me shit!

He was telling me about this incredibly beautiful woman he met at Wonderlust (a huge yoga retreat in Whistler). They became friends on Facebook and it turns out she's dating the captain of some NHL team. "*That's* how beautiful she is."

I pounced, "What the fuck does that mean?! What does her being beautiful have to do with anything? If she's just with him because he's the captain of the--".

"Whoa, you need to chill the fuck out!" It felt like a punch in the chest. "You have some serious hang-ups about beauty."

For the first time since the day Erik and I met, I was speechless.

He put his hand on my knee, looked me right in the eyes and said, "You are very attractive, Rachelle. There is nothing to be scared of. It's okay to be beautiful."

I wanted to protest, but instead I stared back at my friend, this man, and whispered, "You are so in my life for a reason. I'm listening to you." That was my gift in exchange.

He accepted, "That picture of you on Facebook in that dress (at Martini Madness) is hot. It's okay. You don't have to be scared of beauty."

I'm scared of being beautiful. I always thought I was scared of *not* being beautiful. I can't believe this is making me cry. I'm so scared of being conceited or egotistical and, up until now, have attracted people into my life to make me sure I wouldn't be.

The past flashes back. Matthew saying he didn't want to complement me because he didn't want it to go to my head. Carlos telling me, "Well *I* think you're beautiful, but I love you."

Why is not acknowledging physical beauty a good thing? We are encouraged to appreciate the beauty all around us, but if we do so for humans it is considered shallow.

Even writing about this is making me incredibly uncomfortable. Will you look at the back cover of this book or Google image me and laugh, "What is she talking about? She's not beautiful." My instinct right now is to list all the things wrong with my appearances before you look, so you know I am well aware of all my imperfections.

As a young girl, whether blowing out my birthday candles, throwing a coin into a fountain or gazing up at a shooting star, my wish was always the same, "Please let me grow up to be beautiful."

I see-sawed between this wish and self-sabotage for the next three decades. Yo-yo dieting as a teen, becoming chubbier and chubbier each time; playing the peacock to attract a husband, then going to the dowdy side once married - dying my hair dark, wearing sloppy clothes and ponytails for weeks on end; years of unhealthy eating and drinking, knowing it would adversely affect my appearance. I was bulimic for crying out loud! I chose a puffy face over puffy hips.

When I first lost weight at 19, I got a lot of attention and it felt good. I lost 30 lbs in 3 months, which on a 5'4' frame is significant. I wore those numbers like a badge of honor. But with pride, came panic. When my friends and I went out, I would have to go to the bathroom to check what I looked like at least every 30 minutes. The more I drank, the more I checked.

One night, during one of our deep talks, Jennifer said she thought I'd become conceited. Little did she know it was quite the opposite. I was obsessive compulsive. I thought if one hair was out of place or if I looked even slightly bloated, people wouldn't think I was beautiful anymore or worse, they would think I was gaining my weight back.

Rock-rock bottom was the spring before I started seeing Dr. Pez.

After a particularly intense self-loathing episode on the bathroom floor, I pulled myself up to the mirror, scissors in hand and pressed the blade into my right cheek... I don't know what stopped me. Maybe that young girl still hoping her beauty wish would someday come true.

I think this is why the pendulum swung when I started my spiritual work. I didn't want my appearances to ever be an issue in my life ever again. I wanted my inner beauty to come out, so I shunned the physical.

But is a butterfly scared of its beauty? Is a rose afraid of blossoming incase it will seem conceited? No. And why not? Because all the other flowers are just as beautiful. It's just some people prefer roses and some prefer tiger lilies.

I've become detached from my appearances, instead of truly accepting them. How do you embrace and appreciate your external beauty without getting trapped by it?

I'm scared. I am so fucking scared, but in the wise, caring, loving words of my coffee shop guru, "I need to chill the fuck out."

October 4, 2012

Elliot had a dream about me last night.

"We were standing in line at a grocery store and I was laughing. You looked at me serious and said, 'You're going to die.'"

He woke up so weirded out. Then today at school he found out one of the girls in his grade had stabbed another girl within an inch of dying. I thought this was barely a coincidence, but didn't say so. I read a lot into my dreams, too.

Then we were in the middle of solving radicals and I could see his wheels turning. Something was connecting. You can tell because of his smile. It is one of pure childlike bliss, and so obviously not about perfect squares.

He started clapping, the way he does when something really excites him, "Oh my God, oh my God, you're gonna freak! The girl who got stabbed, her name is Celina and the girl who stabbed her, her birthday is April 23rd."

I'll connect the dots for you. Celina's birthday is April 23rd.

Yes, I freaked. *What the hell is with me and this kid?*

Later: An old fling from my late teens invited me to be friends on Facebook. Now there's a mortifying story. Have you had enough of them? Maybe I'll spare you this one. It is interesting, though, how so many people from my past are re-appearing this year.

Canadian Films Suck

October 5, 2012

Well, I'm officially President of Women in Film and Television Vancouver. Who would've thought 2.5 years ago, re-entering the industry after years of being away, I would be president of this amazing organization? Not me, that's for sure.

Mary is getting amazing job offers and project opportunities and needs to step down. She was actually hoping to take a bit of a break from work, but her home, her sanctuary, has some interior problems. I think it is the Universe calling her to expand. Her career is bursting! I love it. She's amazing.

Your home is a metaphor. My friend was touching up scuffs on her walls with white paint. Once she started, she realized there were too many, so she got a glass of wine to help her enjoy the process.

What does my home represent? Simplicity. Roots. I'm looking out my window, but instead of seeing ground, I see abundance. I see grass and shrubs and trees and golden leaves, all the levels of an ecosystem. Partially in the ground, as I continue to grow my roots, and partially looking out at the infinite sky. I am a bamboo with bold bursting branches.

Now, I see a black cat wearing a red and white polka dot bow tie peeking in. Only in Vancouver.

October 7, 2012

I saw an amazing film as part of my jury duty at VIFF - Manon Briand's *Liverpool*. The best I've seen so far. Hard to classify the genre - a romantic-comedy-eco-thriller? It was so well done. It has inspired me as a storyteller. I need to watch more Québecois films.

I also went to see *Blood Relative*. It is a documentary also set in India - third movie I've seen at the festival set there. I love India. I miss India. This doc is about children with thalassemia and the doctor committed to helping them. The filmmaker is the super-talented Nimisha Mukerji, who is actually a friend of mine. Her and her partner Mark Ratzlaff (also insanely talented), won the MPPIA Award last year at Whistler... the one *Happiless* was a finalist in. That's actually how I met them. They were our competition!

The film is obviously heart wrenching, but also funny. Master storytelling. I was so inspired, I skipped the after-party and went writing until 10:30 PM. Being on this jury has re-motivated me to tell amazing inspiring films.

Later: I am so sick and tired of people saying Canadian films suck. Usually, it's people who have never seen one, but it really pisses me off when people in the Canadian film industry don't watch Canadian films. How can we expect others to support the industry if we don't?

I just watched Jason Buxton's *Blackbird*. This is the film I've always wanted to make about young offenders, but everything I come up with sounds like an after school special or *Dangerous Minds* with a... Hmmm... I just remembered. Matthew used to say I looked like Michelle Pfeiffer. I don't, but what a huge compliment.

Anyways, I can't believe it was the director's first feature. It was incredible. Incredible. I was so overwhelmed, I had to keep reminding myself, '*This is just a movie. This is just a movie.*' but it's not. This shit really happens. So many emotions. I was bawling throughout, but for reasons ranging from rage to hope. I want to be a bolder, braver writer.

Stephen Harper and the Conservatives, actually, anyone who thinks the place for kids is in jail, needs to see this film. I'm vibrating at a cellular level. I'm at a sushi restaurant half a block from the theatre guzzling a beer and journaling on a red paper napkin. Totally trying to chill out, because, fuck, now I have to go watch *Inch 'Allah*. Yeah, wish me luck.

October 8, 2012

On my way back to the theatre yesterday, after my 20-minute beer break, I saw Connor Jessup, the lead actor from *Blackbird*. I pretty much accosted him, telling him how amazing his performance was and thanking him for being part of such an important film. I gushed. I hope I didn't smell like beer.

Inch 'Allah, written and directed by Anaïs Barbeau-Lavalette, was amazing as well, but it was hard for me to get into it, as I was still numb from *Blackbird*. Numb, but wired. I went home, not knowing what to do with all the energy. I ended up having more beers and made nachos, not too many, because I wanted to have a piece of Thanksgiving pumpkin pie Sam gave me.

I had ice cream with it. I kept going back for a little bit more. I was eating unconsciously while researching *Blackbird* and the director Jason Buxton. After about 30 minutes, I realized I had eaten half a carton of ice cream and the insides of half the pie. I don't know what came over me, but I finished the ice cream and the pie and then threw up.

What the fuck?! I woke up extremely frustrated with myself, obviously. Pure self-destruction. I've been feeling the urge lately; not knowing what to do with this pent-up energy. Not vibrating very high. Not feeling grounded. Sugar is definitely a trigger for me. A drug.

I can't believe I'm 39 and still dealing with this shit. The weird thing is, before I started all this work this year, it had been almost a decade. *Blackbird* stirred up a lot of emotions and anxiety and I didn't know what to do with it. I was trying to numb it with beer and sugar, but that just gave it something in form I could purge. That's how it felt. Like I was purging negative energy.

Even now, as I'm writing this, I feel high and erratic, like I could go home and binge and purge and crash. My insides are racing... like I could take on the world, but have no idea how or what to do. This is how I felt all those years ago when that doctor told me I was bipolar.

Dr. Pez asked, "Who are you to save the world?"

Who am I not to try?!!

Breathe. Relax. Breathe.

That's what this is. Watching *Blackbird* brought up anger, frustration, sorrow, grief, guilt, regret... things I thought I had worked through and released, but I guess not completely.

Love is not linear. Life is not linear. Spiritual awakening is not linear. This is not a step backwards; this is a catalyst to leap forward.

I am committed to making this the boldest month, the bravest month. My ego is scared. It will do everything in its power to hold me back, to drag me back a decade, but I will push forward. I am grateful last night happened. I am. I am not self-destructive. I love myself.

<u>October 9, 2012</u>
What would make somebody unworthy?
When I was first considering leaving Carlos, I was talking to my friend about the thought of being divorced twice. "That just looks great on a resume, eh?"

He frowned, "What resume?"

I meant the figurative resume I walk around with. The one I created to increase my value. Physics teacher to prove I'm smart, traveling abroad to prove I'm worldly, blah, blah, blah.

What would make somebody unworthy? If they were damaged.

I've spent most of my adult life trying to figure out what's wrong with me mentally, emotionally, psychologically and physically. I've created labels: bulimic, alcoholic, depressive, diabetic... Creating illnesses because illnesses have causes. I wanted to know why I was the way I was. Why I was damaged. I became a person who had to figure things out in my head, so I wouldn't have to be present in my body - so I wouldn't have to feel.

On the surface, I have created a façade of 'I'm such a great catch', but inside feel worthless, assuming once someone sees my flaws they won't like me or find me attractive anymore. Carlos once said, "I know I married up." I still don't understand what he meant by that, but I do know the way he treated me was 100% what I felt I deserved. You attract into your life at the level of your self-worth. No, you *allow* into your life what you think you are worth.

I'm not going to do a spiritual bypass on this. There will be a time to do the countless 'I am valuable' affirmations, but first I need to go in and meet this damaged shadow, with no expectations of where she came from.

Shadow process for Damaged Girl: I spread out a blanket in front of the waterfall and lay down naked. I try not to judge where this is going.

A hairy monster, like from *Where the Wild Things Are*, runs towards me with his penis hanging out. At first, I think I have it wrong, that

257

I'm the damaged one (interesting), but I go with it. I assume the hairy monster wants sex, but I am wrong.

He looks up to the sky and in a deep booming voice shouts, "I am damaged!" A gust of wind rushes out of him.

I console, "No, you're not damaged. You're perfect."

He's furious. He yells at me, "I AM DAMAGED!!!"

I get it. He isn't using 'damaged' as an adjective... That's his name: Damaged. He is my Damaged Shadow and he is tired of me trying to fix him. He wants to be loved and accepted.

Present day flash: Lately, things have been breaking around me - another crack in my windshield; the hand mirror I just broke; my window blinds; my kitchen light. Things I have not fixed, but have settled with. I've been so concerned with fixing myself, my outer world, which is, of course, a projection of my inner world, has been falling apart all around me.

Damaged retorts, "Fix those things and leave me the hell alone."

Okay. How else can I love you?

"Look people in the eye. Don't be embarrassed of me; be proud of me."

Suddenly, I am. This is a really cool part of me. He is an obnoxious, kooky character and I love him. He's gonna be a blast to have around.

Trying to be perfect is BORING! Oh, shit, that dream of my dad calling me boring? This is what it was about. I am damaged. I am a human being and I am damaged. We all are.

October 10, 2012

I have a new chemistry student. Nigel is 14 going on 40. He is super cool and bizarrely fascinated with the way I look. I always catch him scanning, no, scrutinizing me. It's extremely awkward. Yesterday, while I was trying to teach him to balance hydrocarbon combustion reactions, I glanced up to find him fixated on my face.

Me: What?

Nigel: You have very interesting facial structure.

It wasn't a compliment or an insult, just an observation. I smiled. *Ah, teenage boys... so in my life for a reason.*

October 12, 2012

Celina and René have been married for 10 years. I am so incredibly happy for them. They are the most amazing couple. Seriously, they inspire me. I know in the past I've been guilty of holding each of them on very high pedestals, and have worked to not build an illusion around their marriage, but today I'm letting myself admire them.

People say marriage takes work, but I don't think it is that as much as a conscious effort to co-create a life together. I think Celina and René have a vision for their marriage and when something is not inline with it, they figure it out. Their family is their number one priority. They never call each other names and they still have date night.

Later: Just saw Sarah Polley's *Stories We Tell* - geez, another great Canadian doc directed by a woman.

We chose the winner for the Artistic Merit Award - Manon Briand for *Liverpool*. What an exciting time to be working in the Canadian film industry! It truly is exploding.

I had a chance to go to the Closing Awards and Gala, but am festivaled out. Besides, my feet told me if I put heels on again there would be a bloody mutiny. So instead, I'm sitting on Benny's patio having a beer reflecting on how much Canadian films rock... in my flip-flops.

48

Poop in the Pool

October 13, 2012

Avi sent the coverage his reader, Adam, wrote. I want to hug this guy, maybe even kiss. I definitely want him to write all my reviews. *'A champion for low-concept writers everywhere.'*

He commented on my honesty... the greatest complement ever and motivating as I re-write *Making of a Faith Healer*. This is like finally getting a good grade on an English paper!

My ego wants to read this document over and over and over again. My ego wants everyone to read it. I don't even care if they make the movie. I just want everyone to read Adam's coverage. I'm going to enjoy this for today, but I know there is a danger in-- No! I'm enjoying this. I am a talented writer and this feels good.

Whoa, I just realized that's the third Adam who's come into my life in recent months and the only Adams I know... weird. Adam - the first man to ever walk the Earth. Hahaha!

October 17, 2012

Woo Hoo, Wednesday! I woke up and the first thought to enter my mind was, "I love my life!" What a wonderful thing to wake up to. I've been having crazy ass dreams lately.

Last night: I was swimming with Josh in a pool with a bunch of people. It was my birthday and the gifts I got were swimming related - beach balls, flutter boards, water noodles.

There was also poop in the pool. Josh and I were swimming in the deep end trying to avoid it. There were also nachos between us, keeping us apart.

Dreammoods.com: *A swimming pool suggests you need to acknowledge and understand your feelings. It is time to dive in and deal with those emotions. You need to cleanse yourself and wash away past hurts. If you were swimming on the deep end, then it means that those emotions are deeply seeded and may be harder to confront.*

WTF! Is my psyche an endless abyss?

To see or come in contact with feces signifies aspects of yourself that are dirty and negative and which you believe to be undesirable and repulsive. You need to acknowledge and express these feelings, even though it may be shameful. Release the negativity in your life.

I think I know what the nachos between us mean.

October 19, 2012

What kind of person always thinks 'it's just not the right time'?

Shadow Process: Scaredy Cat is a worm, a little blue worm. It was created, because I hated being afraid of my mind, so did everything to escape it. At first, I tried to think of something else (I didn't like that answer), but Scaredy Cat got frustrated at me, so I listened.

What are your gifts? It has made me strive to be courageous and brave.

When I left Carlos, and was feeling like a coward, there were many people, including Dr. Pez, who said I didn't realize how much courage it took to do this. How brave I really was.

Bravery has become my mask - my light shadow, but I am also a Scaredy Cat. I am a Scaredy Cat who's scared shitless. Oh, maybe that is what the poop in the pool means.

What can I do? Flirt. List all the things I'm scared might happen.

Date. Face my fears, not by hiding Scaredy Cat, but using her as a little piece of intuition.

Trust. I do not have to be scared of the whole idea of a relationship. By trusting her, I can trust my intuition more completely.

I'm gonna hike the Chief tomorrow, even though it is supposed to be pouring and the rock will be slippery. I'm scared of getting hurt, but I'll just take one step at a time and if real danger arises, I will listen to my Scaredy Cat. And then later, I will flirt.

October 20, 2012

Summer Chief Challenge Hike # 19

It was barely raining. The hike turned out to be beautiful, one of the best. I slipped a couple of times, but I let Scaredy Cat be my ally. I let her be my internal guide - my worm guide, reminding me to be cautious along the way.

At the top, all alone, I lied back and meditated, "I don't *need* money." Then Needy Ned, a smooth talkin' fox of a figure, appeared and yelled, "Get me Indian!" I knew what he meant. I've been craving Indian food for a while. Perfect. I'm in Squamish. I'll go pick up a couple dishes from Sandhu in town. Cheap and delicious, just like India.

Later: Sandhu in Squamish is closed! Heaven and Earth on Broadway, closed! Our two favorite places... *ohhhh whoa...* that is the first time I have used the word 'our' (or us or we) when referring to Carlos and I in a very long time. It was time to find a new place.

I'm writing at the Dunbar Pub now. It's quite dark in here. I was going to flirt with this guy at the table next to me, but then his dad showed up. Turns out he's engaged. He is asking his dad to help out financially with the wedding. I'm trying not to eavesdrop, but the tables are close and the dad is talking really loud.

"I'll see what I can do, but isn't it usually the bride's family that pays?"

My poor parents: Three daughters, five weddings.

The son looks at me out of the corner of his eyes, he is visibly uncomfortable. It's a very awkward conversation, mostly because it sounds like his fiancée put him up to it. The way he talks about her is, um, interesting.

"I know she's hard to handle, but I can handle her."

October 21, 201

Inspired Idea! I bought a ticket to Edmonton to surprise my dad for his 65th birthday party next weekend! Only Celina and René know and I swore them to secrecy. Fun!

Inspired Ideas that come from a place of love and abundance are the ones to follow. It's been awhile, but I am trusting them again. I can already feel the weekend flying by, though, and I'm not even there yet. Stop. Breathe.

October 22, 2012

Had some Indian last night. It was tasty, but oily and I'm so glad I got that out of my system. When I went to bed, Needy Ned laughed at me saying he just wanted to prove that when you think you need something external to fill or feel, you will never be satisfied. *Interesting fella, that Needy Ned.* This is what he is here to remind me of. I don't *need* anything.

Tonight is my first meeting as President of Women and Film and Television Vancouver - talk about stepping into my vision. I'm excited to share my vision for the organization with the ladies, which is mostly around raising our profile and increasing membership, but to also invite them to create one for their committees and for themselves as board members.

I also convinced Christine to rejoin as interim Secretary. The plan is for her to run for vice in June when I officially run for president. We'll be the dynamic duo!

October 23, 2012

I feel like a complete shithead.

The meeting went great, but as soon as it ended, I bolted and left Christine alone at BC Film, not knowing anyone, to clean up. I was completely oblivious and insensitive. She phoned me later and called me on it. She gave me shit and rightfully so. I convinced Christine to rejoin the board. I sold it to her as us being a team and then I bolted on her.

Maybe I've forgotten what it means to be on a team. Maybe I never knew. Christine is the first friend I've made since Carlos and I broke up. She's the only person I've let in who wasn't already here. I am so grateful our friendship has evolved to a point where she could call me out, but I still feel like shit.

As part of my President's Report, I said I saw my role as a supportive one. While reflecting on my vision for the board this weekend, I knew I wanted all the ladies to feel supported and appreciated, but the first thing I do is make Christine feel unsupported and unappreciated.

I think since being so single and alone for so long, I haven't had to be considerate to anyone but myself. I've been focusing on appreciating myself, but forgotten everyone else. Now that I am opening my life, it is time to be aware and conscious of others, too. It was also a reminder that when you stand in your power, like Christine did, you provide an opportunity for the other person to grow. When you are afraid of conflict, of challenging someone when they have hurt you or let you down, you have cheated them. Thank you, Christine.

October 24, 2012

I hung out with Unworthy Girl last night. Finally, I understand her gift. She is humble. She allows me to be in awe of this awesome Universe. She said she felt neglected; that I cared more about the other shadows and meeting more of them, than spending time with her; that

I liked Damaged and Needy Ned, because they are cool and… hmmm… because they are guys.

I am unworthy as a humble human being. We all are.

October 25, 2012

There's this video of an 86-year old gymnast online. When I saw it, I thought, *'Hey, she's living my dream!'* I registered for gymnastics last night. The Best Year of My Life would be incomplete without my lifelong dream coming true.

If I start now, when I'm 86, I'll be like, *'Oh, I've been a gymnast for over 45 years. No biggie.'* I can just see myself cart-wheeling around the room, swinging from the uneven bars. I can't wait to be able to do flips. Back flips! Maybe I will join the adult Olympics.

Apparently, Derek starts every morning with the intention of making it the best day of his life. How is that even possible? What a humongous intention to set! How could you do this authentically? Would you get bored of the best? Obviously, I need to give it a try.

Each day, even Saturdays and Sundays, my morning ritual will be yoga, VVR and then asking, "How can I create the best day of my life?" This does feel way more expansive than the old 'live each day like it's your last.' How depressing. Beginnings are way more exciting. Live each day like it is your first!

Later: It's noon and I'm on the plane. Almost there! I can't believe I've been gone for 12 years and this is the first time I've come home as a surprise. This is too much fun!

Driving to the airport, *Titanium* came on the radio. I started singing and then crying. I can't believe there was a time, many times, when I was deeply, darkly depressed. I was overwhelmed with the memories of trying to kill myself. Thank God I failed.

Not only does it get better; it gets spectacular.

Yesterday, during my session with Nigel, I was leaning on my left elbow with my hand holding up my head. He smiled that mischievous grin, "What's that?" He pointed at the scar on my wrist. He's the first person to ask me about it since I put it there at the age of fourteen.

"It's not what you think. Stupid dare with a friend." Not sure where that came from.

It wasn't one of my suicide attempts. It was... unconscious self-mutilation... with a safety pin. Alone in my room, talking with friends on the phone about meaningless school events, I would stick my special beaded pin under my skin and rip it up in stitches, repeatedly. The half-inch wound would heal, then I would cut it open again. Eventually, it scarred.

I had never even heard of self-mutilation until I worked at Youth Futures. We had a girl once who couldn't come on the school trip, because she was cutting. When you are numb on the inside you will do anything to feel on the outside.

Last night, I held the picture of my 14-year old girl, looked at the scar on my wrist, then to my quad-colored heart tattoo just below. I loved her. I thanked her. She has taught me so much. Depression is there to tell you when you are on the wrong path.

Struggle - the opposite of 'go with the flow'.

Lately, I feel like I am resonating with the Universe at a new level and want to connect with every soul I meet. While I was walking to work on Monday, bliss washed over me for absolutely no reason at all. An old guy actually stopped me, "Well, you sure look happy."

I've been experiencing these moments of uncontrolled joy, pure ecstasy quite regularly. Like my smile is going to break my face. Elliot gets these when he is excited to tell me about his dreams. I even find myself clapping sometimes... just like he does. Maybe kids on the spectrum know more about connecting than we give them credit for.

Oh, I see land... fuck, the prairies are flat. I think I can see Matthew's family farm. I can't believe part of my morning ritual was once feeding the pigs and shoveling their poop.

49

Illusionary Arbitrary Boundaries

<u>October 29, 2012</u>

It's Monday morning and I'm at the Edmonton International Airport. My flight is delayed and I'm not sure why. I had to cancel my first two sessions. That sucks. It is cold and snowy, but this is Alberta for crying out loud!

I had an awesome trip, but am feeling sluggish. Three days of beer and beef will do that.

Celina picked me up at the airport on Friday. I was worried about seeing someone (it's only 10 minutes outside Beaumont), so snuck through the corridors with my hood up - all incognito. I felt like a spy. So much fun.

We drove to Camrose and surprised Sara and Sadie at school. When Sadie saw me she hugged me so tight and then told everyone shyly, "This is my Auntie."

When Sara saw me, she smiled and shrugged, "I knew you were gonna come."

That night I hung out with Celina and René and watched their wedding video. Celina claims it is the best movie ever made and I have to agree. Best part: Tracy and my 'Roast to the Bride'. It was a no holds barred payback speech. Even though Carlos and I were married, Matthew was invited and you can hear him off camera laughing the loudest.

One thing Matthew appreciated in me was my sense of humor. He always said I was funny for a girl. Which is a bizarre comment as his sisters are two of the funniest people I know. Actually, his whole family is hilarious. We laughed a lot, which was probably why they were so confused when I left.

Saturday, we drove to Tracy and Martin's. I had called Tracy earlier in the week to tell her I was coming. I wanted to let her in on the fun and am really awful at keeping secrets. She texted us all the way in the house to ensure it was a surprise, and it worked. My dad didn't have a clue. Nor did my mom or the kids. *Seriously, why haven't I done this sooner?* The whole family was together, like it should be. Oh and Alex is 100% back in action! I hugged him so hard.

The meal was amazing. My dad ended up paying for it with his first pension cheque. So cute. So glad I didn't miss it. The whole night was amazing. We stayed up late drinking and chatting - some really great conversations about parenting. How they all want their kids to be happy and just don't want to screw it up. No judging on my part. None.

On the plane: Imagine if I treated myself with total love and nourishment for a whole month, and worked through whatever comes to the surface without any coping mechanism. Imagine what would flourish. Holy crap, the thought scares me.

Turns out the reason my flight was delayed is because Hurricane Sandy is expected to hit the East Coast of Canada. It's interesting how when I saw this on the satellite TV, I actually said aloud, "Oh, no!" Yet when I thought it was just hitting the States, while I was concerned, it felt so far away and I was detached. *Illusionary arbitrary boundaries.*

It's not like I know anyone on the East Coast, except Melissa and Nichole. Is Montreal considered the East Coast? Oh shit, now I'm really worried.

Later: There was an earthquake off the coast of BC on Saturday - 7.7 on the Richter Scale. There were Tsunami warnings and Haida Gwaii was evacuated. Holy shit!

October 31, 2012

Happy 1st Pension Cheque Dad!

Monster Mash - Worst song ever. Can someone please write a new Halloween song?

Nigel told me I should've painted my face green and gone as the Grinch. The funny thing is, I do a killer Grinch impersonation that would give Jim Carrey a run for his money.

"I musht shtop Chrishtmash from coming!" Carlos would make me do it incessantly. He always said I was funny. Hmmm... just like Matthew.

Nigel also said I look like a cat. He's right. I do look like a cat, mostly because of my noony. A noony is what I named the deep valley between my nose and upper lip before I learned its scientific name - the philtrum. I also have green eyes that squint when I smile. When I laugh, they seal shut. One time, I was driving with Celina and she made me laugh so hard, I had to pull over. I used to call them sperm eyes, but cat is probably nicer. My laugh lines are so deep they look like whiskers, if cats had whiskers around their eyes.

When we were teenagers, instead of writing notes in class, Jennifer would draw cartoons about our weekend debauchery. Her representation of me was always a cat.

Come to think of it, Matthew didn't start saying I looked like Michelle Pfeiffer until after she played Catwoman in *Batman Returns*.

I had a dream last night I was approaching a church and a raccoon was following me. I wrestled with it over something. I think my water bottle.

Dreammoods.com: *Raccoon - deceit and thievery. Not being completely honest.*

Church - seeking spiritual enlightenment and guidance. Perhaps past mistakes have set you back. With proper support you will get back on track.

Obviously my Higher Self does not feel it has any more time to be subtle.

Later: Oh My God! Just checked my email. I was all set to join the NFL Fantasy Football League in August, but decided I didn't need another excuse to procrastinate. I still get emails, but haven't opened any of them since I set up my account. I usually delete them automatically, but for some reason today I opened it.

The name of my team: Rachelle's Raccoons! You have got to be fucking kidding me.

Later: I've decided to make November the Best Month of My Life.

I bought a blue journal covered in water drops special for the month. It is gonna rock. Living my vision every day, every moment. Being present. Every 15 minutes, I'm gonna stop and meditate on love for 17 seconds. Healthy in, healthy out. This month is gonna be... Hmmm... I never thought of November as a turning point... until now.

Okay, see you in 30 days Black Journal. I'm curious to see what will be written on the next page. Will I blow my own expectations?

Oh yeah, right, I have no expectations! Expectations ruin the fun. Instead, I will set daily intentions.

The Best Month of My Life

November 1, 2012

I will accomplish this by making each and every day the Best Day of My Life. In order to do this, I have to start and end each day from a place of health and wholeness. I made a sign, 'Today is the Best Day of My Life!' and taped it to my fridge.

Opening myself up to the limitless possibilities this month will bring. Imagining what it will feel like vibrating at the level of my vision for 30 days straight. Conscious that everything I put in my body, every thought I entertain will influence this.

I can only breathe in the now. I can only live in the now.

Last night, as I fell asleep, I realized, *I know everything I need to know.* A peace lay with me; a peace with who and where I am. Lying in bed, listening to myself breathe, intimately.

I am whole. I am love. Knowing my wholeness is the reward.

Intention for the Day: Have the most creative day of my life!

November 2, 2012

The right side of my body is numb, yet tingly. I'm reflexologing my ear all around the outside and inner top to unblock it and it is burning up.

I love my body and I want to show it how much I appreciate it.

Intention for the Day: Love and appreciate my body like never before.

November 3, 2012

I dreamt I was chased by monsters. Monsters! Seriously, how old am I?

Dreammoods.com: *To dream you are chased by a monster represents aspects of yourself that you find repulsive and ugly. You may possess some fears or some repressed emotions.*

Argh! Does this never end!!!

Later: I posted about my monster dream on Facebook and blah, blah, blah a 'friend' called me a liar in French. Even though the comment makes absolutely no sense in this context, it feels like a dagger in my chest.

Last week, when my mom drove me to the airport, I was saying how I felt guilty about having to cancel the two sessions because my flight was delayed. It brought me back to the days of calling in sick when I really wasn't. I didn't want BrainBoost to think I was lying.

I boasted, "Because I don't lie."

Holy shit! My chest is imploding from the pressure. I am tingly all over. I haven't seen this guy in a decade, but I feel like he is serious. That's why he said it in French. I feel like fighting back.

Authenticity and truth have become light shadows... perhaps even a mask. I tried to do the shadow process months ago for Liar, Liar, Pants on Fire, but wasn't able to fully love, accept and integrate her. Maybe now I'm ready.

Intention for the Day: Forgive myself... Once and for all.

Shadow Process for Lying Lizard: The most intense experience of all the others.

It slithered out. I looked into its reptilian eyes and said, "Talk to me. I'm listening." But it attacked me! Bit me right on the throat, where the lies emerge. It must've felt like I was judging it. I probably was. No, I definitely was.

Flash: as a kid again being told, "When you lie, the nails go deeper into baby Jesus' hands." Nothing makes a little boy or girl 'bad' like lying.

Aside from sociopaths, I believe people lie out of fear, usually fear of rejection or fear of losing something. To be fully authentic, I can't be afraid of standing in my power.

When I asked what it needed, it replied, "Be honest about being a liar and a lizard."

I had an image of Simon and Stanley, Carlos' Uromastyx lizard from a previous relationship. When we brought Simon home from Korea and picked up Stanley from Carlos' parents' place, Simon was fascinated by the little green creature. Stanley was scared shitless of the intrusive furry beast and didn't hide it, but this just made Simon more curious.

Maybe being completely honest won't turn people off, but draw them in.

Lying used to be like breathing for me. I could list all the things I've lied about, but that would take a book on its own. Lying has been such a huge part of my life and this is the one shadow I know is a source of great power and connection for me. I am opening myself up to the guidance and loving my Lying Lizard.

51

Crazy Cast of Shadows

November 4, 2012

Michele came for a coffee visit yesterday. We were talking about horoscopes and she asked if I was a Leo. "A lot of Leos look like cats." She is the second person this week to tell me I look like a cat.

While driving to pick up Christine to go to this birthday party of Craig's friend last night, I really focused on opening myself up to connecting and flirting. At the pub, I did have brief eye contact with one guy a few times, but was scared to smile. I was scared if I smiled at him, he would think I liked him. I can't believe how scared I still am to flirt. My Good Friend once told me, "You have this energy about you men find intoxicating." That has scared me for a long, long time. I don't want to be scared anymore.

What kind of person flirts? Desperate. I flirt all the time with women and men, too, but only when I know it won't lead anywhere. Like with Adam in Seattle and William at Greg's wedding... easy to put myself out there when I know I'm leaving town. I was also drunk both those times.

Okay, I'm going to be 100% honest. I have Josh Goggles on. I still think about him and I feel like if I was to flirt with someone else... well... I can't believe how monogamous I am in a relationship that doesn't even exist.

Intention for the Day: Love and appreciate myself for all the work I've done.

November 5, 2012

7:10 AM at Grounds: Today is the Best Monday of My Life. *Why?* Because I feel grounded and healthy and at peace. I never drank a drop last night; didn't even have the inkling. My body and soul are speaking to me and I am listening.

I woke up feeling icky at 4 AM. For some reason I asked, "What's the opposite of being authentic?" Then Fraud appeared. I was anxious and afraid, which was weird, because usually it is a fascinating process. Even with LL, I wasn't afraid until he bit me, but right from the start I knew Fraud was my most formidable shadow.

It had no gender, just a really big head with no mouth. It was blue. I could hold it like a baby, but was wary of its power. I wanted to spank it, but instead I hugged it tight.

Fraud was created while I was being scolded after being a bad girl at Mémère and Auntie Cecile's store. We were running around and being real brats and when we got home we were disciplined for it. In the middle of being spanked, I broke into laughter.

In that moment, something shifted deep inside me. A divide was formed; a decision was made. "From now on I will be a bad girl in secret." My fraudulent world was created.

Why are you appearing now? I am ready to be truly authentic, in all my lightness and all my dark. I can help others bring their shadows into the light. I could never have done this process with Fraud before. I needed to integrate and love my Lying Lizard first.

Its gifts: creating boundaries, learning to be alone, becoming a teacher, turning my life around, becoming healthy. So many things that began by me trying to look good or have a great résumé or even hide, led me on this path to a deeper love for myself. My secrets have made me compassionate and fascinated by what makes others do the things they do.

While living a façade, I was able to heal the scars on the surface of my relationships, while I healed myself behind closed doors, so that the relationships could heal for real.

I relived the event. I felt the spank. This time I cried.

Making Fraud an ally: I can be different parts of myself in different situations expressing different talents without wearing a mask. My Fraud is smart and will be able to see when others are being a fraud. I can have compassion for this person, because I know where it comes from.

My Fraud protected me from others judging the parts of me I didn't yet understand. My Fraud protected the insecure side of me who was scared of not being loved and accepted by others and more importantly, it protected me from my own judgmental side.

Fraud then called forth Fuck-up.

The truth about how I feel I will react if I do get it all - I will fuck it up.

Fuck-up was not as intense, skinny and goofy and funny, perfect in her imperfections. I don't want to always make the right choices. I am a human being who takes chances and lives life bravely. If you never make mistakes, you are living in a world too small.

Fuck-up rocks. She makes me laugh.

Every step of my life led up to this morning. I have never been more whole. I can finally ask all my shadows, Fraud being their Queen, how I can make them feel loved and appreciated and safe and they can trust I'm telling the truth.

Sometimes, as I write this book, I feel there is a really bad, on the nose, soundtrack playing in the background. The song on right now is Kelly Clarkson's *Everyone has a dark side.*

But it's true, everyone does. Projecting perfection on someone else is an illusion and steals their humanity. It is just masking our own insecurities. When Christine called me out for deserting her after the meeting a couple weeks ago, right away my fear was she wouldn't like me anymore. I felt I had fucked-up. The reason I went out Saturday night, if I'm going to be totally honest, was because I wanted to make sure she still liked me even though I made a mistake. Not that I think she thought I was perfect, but our friendship had never even had a ripple before.

Later: A lady and young girl are sitting next to me here at Grounds. The lady is asking the girl why she insists on dressing like a boy. Liona, a former student of mine, always dressed in army fatigues. She had been sexually abused and was hiding her femininity. I dress in baggy clothes, too. I have for a few years, even before that, too. When I thought Josh and I were going to go on a date all those months ago, I was going to dress in a short skirt and skimpy top. I'm so glad we didn't go. Could've been awkward. Would've been awkward.

If nothing else, the thoughts I have about Josh have called me to become whole. I used to blame my nervousness around him on the coffee on an empty stomach, then the awkward stage, but I think our friendship vibrated at a level higher than I was at. I was fragmented and being around him shook my creviced core.

Intention for the Day: Enjoy this wholeness awareness.

November 6, 2012

I'm reading the *Shadow Effect* by Deepak Chopra, Debbie Ford and Marianne Williamson. In Debbie Ford's section of the book she talks about how our shadow is responsible for our addictions and hypocritical actions, amongst many other baffling things we do. As I am doing all this work this year, it really is no wonder I have had a couple of 'sessions' where I drink, eat, go to sleep, wake up needing to throw up and then feel like shit - emotionally, physically and mentally - the next day. I've even had two full-on relapses.

Bulimia is an extremely violent form of self-abuse, but that's not what these sessions have been about. There is also a spiritual meaning behind binging and purging - some dark energy inside trying to get out, desperate to get out, and demanding the physical to release it.

When I decided to become bulimic at the age of 19 (yes, it was a decision. You have to be very dedicated to throw up every day), it was because I wanted to lose 30 lbs and I wanted to do so fast. After my initial success, I continued because I thought I had discovered the Holy Grail of dieters everywhere. *I could eat whatever I want and stay thin? Genius.*

When the negative side effects started to appear and I tried to quit, I was petrified of gaining weight. I remember waking up in the middle of the night with what I now know were panic attacks. My hands would immediately fly to my hips and belly, convinced they were expanding in my sleep.

When I told my friend Terri, my doctor, my family, Matthew and Jen, I really believed I could stop with their support and a healthy diet, but by this point it had become so much more.

Puking felt *good*.

Food, which I always loved, had just become the mechanism. When the need arose, I would eat whatever, wherever, just to have something solid in my stomach to throw up. Anxiety and excitement, which apparently the body reads the same, were the two biggest triggers. I think because you feel these emotions in the stomach, so consuming copious amounts of food, usually carbs, seemed to absorb them and then I could rid myself of them.

It might be surprising that excitement is something I would've wanted to get rid of, but you can't pick and choose the emotions you are open to feeling. If you want to numb yourself of one, you have to numb yourself of all. Every single emotion was uncomfortable to me. The only time I felt grounded was post-session, when I was physically drained and emotionally comatose. My mind wasn't too active either. I had muted my spirit long, long before.

It is no surprise I trapped so many emotions. Many from my first couple of decades, for sure, but from the age of 19 to 29, when I finally told Carlos, I don't think I processed one emotion in a healthy way. Even from the age of 29 to 39... drinking and lying to myself about my marriage and then hiding from the world... well, there's some from then, too.

When I got back from India, Carlos suggested we have a night on Ecstasy. I didn't want to, I was the healthiest and happiest I had ever been, but he said he wasn't feeling close to me and thought this would help. It had before, so I agreed. That night, we took Simon and Daphne out for a walk. I got very agitated, anxious... angry. My stomach started hurting intensely and I got severely bloated. My belly was rock hard. When we got back to the apartment, I barely made it to the washroom. I didn't throw up, though. This time all the negative energy came out the other end. That is how it felt, like toxic emotions were rushing out of my body.

Carlos and I had some interesting, brutally honest, conversations about our relationship that night. It is sad to say, but the Love Drug was what opened my eyes to know that what Carlos and I had was not love. It couldn't be... We still didn't love ourselves.

Later: Had a visit with Erik. Got updated on the US elections, which apparently are today. I am usually all up on them, but I guess I don't feel they really matter. I do hope Obama wins, though.

I still have this ridiculous relentless resistance around making money, specific dollar amounts even - $10,000, I'm open; $50,000, no problem, bring it on; more than that... BLOCK.

Intention for the Day: Release this resistance to money.

I've decided to add a daily reflection.

Reflection of the Day: What is my relationship with the present moment?

I wrote the question on an index card and put it in my pocket to remind myself to check-in throughout the day.

November 7, 2012

My reflection and intention yesterday led to an interesting revelation. I EFT'd around $400,000. I don't know why, but this is an amount that seems to be relevant - that I am meant to receive, but have some resistance to. During a round, seemingly out of the blue, I paused and asked, "What kind of person doesn't live up to their potential?" I struggled with this one for a while. Usually, I think 'loser', because that's a common example Derek uses, but it never really had a charge for me before.

I picked up a pen and with my left hand wrote: *If I get lots of money, I will... Lose it.*

Oh, two meanings of the word! I am a double loser.

Loser Shadow: At first, the figure looked like Carlos. Not surprising since at the end my favorite slur to sling at him was, "You're such a loser." Yeah, not my finest moments.

It was, but of course, a projectile of projection. I was actually calling myself a loser. I never thought he was living up to his potential and I blamed him for me not living up to mine. I felt I invested so much of myself and my money in him, and it was all for nothing. I had lost my money and myself and was pissed I had to start all over.

This shadow sitting in front of me was just a reflection of the loser in me.

I lovingly told the Faux-Carlos, "You don't have to hide behind a projection. You are safe to show yourself."

Then, just like in a *Looney Tunes* skit, he unzipped his skin from head to toe and disappeared, leaving the smallest little pea of a girl. I could barely see her.

I kneeled down and squinted, "When did I create you, you Little Loser?"

A few events flashed: Being put in special math class in Grade 6, being friends with girls specifically because I could hide in their shadow, all the way back to Heather in Grade 1. Heather was the most popular girl. She had gorgeous brown curls; I had a stringy blond mess. I saw the pattern. Always being and feeling not as good as *that* person. Good things (popularity, boyfriends, nice hair) happened to *that* girl, but not to me.

What gifts did you give me? Wanting to become smart in high school (although I still played ditsy around boys), idolizing others made me a dreamer, and boy, did I dream big, but instead of really trying, I would aim high and then self-sabotage, ending up the loser.

Why now? I am a wonderful woman who is ready to live up to her potential.

I had to lie there for a while before I could ask the next question...

How can you be my ally? I had to just allow and meditate and not think about it. I know the usual gifts - I've learned more from my losses than my wins, blah, blah, blah... then it came.

My Little Loser, who I thought was going to be fun loving and goofy, is actually the source of all my wisdom. She is literally the seed (or pea) of all the wisdom I've gained until now and by embracing her I will be able to gain so much more. I realized having only the desire to succeed, but not opening myself up to the potential of failure, has limited my learning.

What can I do to make you feel loved and accepted and safe? Play games. Find ways to be a kid. I start gymnastics tonight! Reflect on the *winner vs. loser* illusion. Celebrate losses!

Imagine if they made a theatrical production about my shadow world, what a crazy cast of characters that would be!

Regarding relationships: You can only lose when you give love, but don't get it back... this is an illusion. Love is all there is. It isn't something you give; it is something you share.

Oh yeah! Water is a covalent compound. *WTF does that mean?* I'm glad you asked.

In ionic compounds, for example sodium chloride, the metal atom (sodium) loses an electron for every electron the non-metal (chlorine) gains. These ions are then attracted to each other because they have opposite charges. In covalent compounds, for example water, the elements (hydrogen and oxygen) *share* electrons, but retain their wholeness. Not surprisingly, covalent bonds are much stronger than ionic bonds.

Christine told me about an interview with a young starlet who recommended always being in a relationship where the man loves you a little bit more. This makes me want to cry.

Intention for the Day: Be a kid.

Reflection of the Day: Sharing breath.

Cheater, Cheater, Pumpkin Eater

November 8, 2012

I started gymnastics last night and it was so awesome. Super nice people and, woo hoo, I wasn't the oldest! Surprisingly, the class is mostly guys and they are really good. Super athletic.

There is a man there who is very flirty and calls me Blondie. Why do I get so offended when people describe me as blonde? He asked me to go for a drink after.

Really? Does it look like I'm here to pick up men? I'm a serious gymnast!

There was another earthquake off the coast of British Columbia last night. West Coast geological upheaval; East Coast meteorological mayhem... Mother Earth shaking things up.

How can I shake things up?

Intention for the Day: Shake things up!

Reflection of the Day: Sharing unique compliments.

November 9, 2012

It was absolutely gorgeous out yesterday. I went for a walk during my break because it was too gorgeous not to. I walked all the way to Benny's and sat outside with a coffee. There were a few of us on the patio just talking about what a spectacular day it was. Vancouverites love to bond over the weather. Vancouver is stunning in the fall. It makes me wish I were a poet so I could adequately describe the range of colors of the falling leaves.

Death never looked so beautiful.

Intention for the Day: Let's do this!

Do what? I have no idea. But whatever it is, I'm doing it.

Reflection of the Day: Death can be beautiful.

Oh my God... It's Remembrance Day Long weekend. Let me clarify - natural, timely, *peaceful* death can be beautiful.

Summer Chief Challenge Hike #20: COMPLETE!

A final avalanche of epiphanies:

1. Spanking split - that time I started laughing while I was being spanked, when Fraud was created, another split occurred in that moment. My physical and mental worlds detached. It was the first time what was happening to my body was not the same thing as what was happening in my mind. My body was being hurt, but I was happy.

As I got older, the choices I made caused the divide to get bigger and bigger, eventually leading to an eating disorder, self-abusive sex and two intimacy-less marriages. Yoga, meditation and love have brought them back together.

Ironically, I started doing yoga because I was lazy and could do most of it without getting off the floor. I just followed the video, mindlessly moving my body. It wasn't until we lived in our tiny one-room residence in Korea, when I had to do it silently in the dark while Carlos was sleeping, that the connection began to fuse. I guess my soul knew the gifts it would eventually bring.

I need to talk to my parents about putting spanking in the book. I need them to know it is not about blame or judgment. It was a different time, but some people still spank. Maybe they wouldn't if they knew its potential effects. Besides, I love every single moment of my rich journey and this detachment has allowed me to discover a deeper, more profound connection with myself. A self-love I never thought possible.

2. In a time of *Fifty Shades of Grey*, who is going to want to read a book about a 39-year-old woman who is <u>not</u> getting laid?

3. Woman. This word still holds so much power for me. I forgot this year's original goal was to write a book about becoming a woman. How do I become a woman? I am a woman. I am a WO-man. I am a wo-MAN. I am a WOMAN... still practicing. I've got 43 days.

4. Reflection on death. Are mountains dead? No. They are part of the lithosphere, which is the skin of this living, breathing planet we

inhabit. Yes, dead skin is sloughed off; just like erosion and avalanches, but the rock is replenished from deep within... it just takes a lot longer.

5. When we say, "This is who I am" we shut the door to all we could be.

6. Mother Earth = Feminine Body. Disrespect of one = Disrespect of the other.

Not only men are guilty of this. If everything is a projection, we wouldn't accept it if we didn't agree. Some things Carlos would tease me about would hurt (my boxy hips and gummy smile), because I believed they were ugly, but other things (my round nose and gap between my lips) made me laugh, because I thought they were cute. I wonder, now that I love and appreciate my body so unconditionally, if I would take most things he said as compliments.

7. I am so loyal. Even to a mountain. I am the most monogamous person I know... Just in my case there is just one person in the relationship. I'm solo-gamous. I just made up a word!

Thank you, Stawamus Chief for 20 amazing hikes filled with countless epiphanies. See you in the spring!

Later: Driving home, I had one more epiphany. This one was about my relationships with Carlos and Matthew. I was gone long before they started. I usually feel guilty about setting us all up for failure, but I realize I was in their life for a reason, too.

Later: Josh has a new female friend on Facebook. Instant jealousy. Jealousy! *Seriously?* Why does this bother me? I'm so pissed off. I am going to be 40 years old in 43 days and it bothers me he has a friend. I feel like screaming! I'm so frustrated with myself. He isn't even my boyfriend and I feel like he's cheating... Ohhhh...

Shadow Process for Cheater: I thought Fraud was scary.

Cheater was deep in a cave. Shelob's Lair from *The Lord of the Rings* comes to mind. Chills ran down my spine. "Cheater is a part of me. I need not be afraid."

I called out. Birds and bats flew out in swarms. Then this tall, blue, cartoon bat woman emerged all stoic and serious.

"When did I create you?"

She swooped around me, "You know."

I did, but it is not my story to share. I wish I could, as it was one of the most surreal and shocking discoveries of my life, but it would hurt a lot of people, so I won't. I can say that I was young and the world I knew as 'affairs only happen on *Dynasty*' was shattered. This traumatized my entire idea of relationships to the core, matched only when that ex-uncle left my auntie for another woman after 35 years of what everyone thought, was marital bliss.

But now, for the deepest darkest secret of all... I've sat here for about twenty minutes contemplating this reveal. I could very well lose the respect of those I care most about, but when I decided to write this book, I promised myself I wasn't going to sugarcoat anything.

I am ready to be whole and I am ready for the backlash.

I cheated on my husband... with a married man. Yes, I've been the cheater. Yes, I've been the other woman.

I'm not going to say which husband, because he doesn't know and it wouldn't be fair for me to tell this part of my story at this point in his life. He's moved on. Besides, the painful truth is it had nothing to do with him. He did nothing wrong and he did everything wrong, but that's not why I cheated. I cheated because I chickened out. I chickened out on our marriage and I chickened out on myself.

It would also hurt the man whom I was involved with, who as far as I know, is still with his wife. They may even have a family. We never officially consummated the affair, but it was physical and it was emotional, the most hurtful kind. He loved his wife and was always open about that, but I'll tell all those wives out there who are afraid of their husbands cheating the secret: appreciate them. Pay attention to them. Compliment them. When they compliment you, receive it and say thank you.

To all the men out there who are afraid their wives may stray, here is the secret: appreciate them. Pay attention to them. Compliment them. When they compliment you, receive it and say thank you.

Affairs don't just happen. I'm not talking about drunken one-night stands - I have no experience with those. I'm talking about *affairs*. Affairs happen when you start talking to someone and they listen. When they appreciate you for something you want to be appreciated for. I remember the moment our friendship turned into something more: I told him something I would have normally only told my husband and he supported me like a partner should.

People cheat for other reasons, of course, to punish themselves, to break out of self-made prisons. Sometimes it is as simple as self-sabotage - not believing you are worthy of the relationship you are in or the person you are with.

I'm not defending affairs. I am deeply monogamous, which is why when I went outside the marriage, I knew it was time to go, cowardly as it may have been. Being the other woman only intensified the patheticism of the situation, but in a warped sense of self-abuse it was perfect, because it was safe. I knew he'd never leave his wife and I didn't want him to. It ended before my marriage did. I didn't leave my husband for this man, but I did leave because of him.

Why are you appearing now?

Cheater smirked, "You're not scared of your soul mate cheating on you; you're scared of cheating on him. It's not men you don't trust. You don't trust yourself. You will never be able to be in a loving, healthy, respectful relationship until you forgive yourself."

Well, maybe I don't deserve to be.

November 10, 2012

The Shadow Effect: The more acceptance and safe expression we find for our dark impulses, the less we will have to worry about being blindsided by them.

I have to go back and visit Cheater. Holding on to this guilt is not helping anyone and I know she will just wreak havoc in my life until I love and accept her... and I don't want to hurt anyone ever again. I created her from a place of shame, but I can integrate her in love.

She was still waiting for me in my sanctuary. I sat facing her.

Cheater, what possible gifts have you brought me?

"Commitment and loyalty to friends, family, places, dreams, jobs. Even with your husbands. You pursued one patiently for five years and stayed in an unhealthy relationship with the other for nine."

How can you be my ally?

"Never settle. Live a flavorful life of trying new things. Meeting new people actually makes you more committed to your beloved. Shake things up. 'Cheat' on the inanimate things you have been ridiculously loyal to."

How? Hike a new mountain! Shake up diet in healthy ways. I ate the same supper for four years! Tomato spinach soup... every night. All my weekly meals are the same. It takes me 20 minutes to grocery shop, because I buy the exact same things. I have been monogamous to a person I'm not even in a relationship with, feeling it disloyal to flirt.

I have been afraid of Cheater. I have created attachments (men, mountains, coffee shops), which have held me back from experiencing life. Cheating in a healthy way is expansive and invigorating. I have created a loyalty mask, which I am now ripping off, so Cheater can breathe.

I have attracted cheaters into my life. I have turned people into cheaters (I'm only taking responsibility for my part in this). This is huge. I am so aware and so grateful. Breathe.

This is invigorating, but terrifying work. I'm gonna need to go to some deep, dark places in the next couple weeks. I have camouflaged all these parts of myself I labeled undesirable. My soul has helped me get to where I am through my experiences and circumstances, so I am able to do this work. I have the dark, dank soil in which to grow my roots deep, deep, deep.

I need to forgive those involved in that discovery 27 years ago... and that man who left my auntie. Whoa, that might be a hard one.

Thank you, Chief, for helping me realize how crazy it is to be loyal to a mountain!

Thank you, Cheater, for reminding me there is more out there. Not in an ungrateful or unsatisfied or unfulfilled way, but in an unattached one. I love and admire her. She has huge blue wings and is unafraid to fly. She appreciates everything, but is not attached to nothing.

There is a gorgeous authentic Rachelle emerging. I love her and am fascinated by her.

I just realized I have always thought of my soul as separate, like a different component. I am my soul... I am my soul mate.

Intention for the Day: Forgive, forgive, forgive.

Reflection of the Day: I am a cheater.

Later: I just bought a toque at a funky store on Commercial. I think it was Peruvian. The owner was such a flirt. He's about 60 years old. He touched my hand as I was paying and I let him. It felt good. Maybe flirting isn't evil. Maybe it is time to get my flirt on.

Aphrodite & Artemis

<u>November 11, 2012 - Remembrance Day</u>

4 AM: I call forth my Flirt shadow.

She looks like me at 14, but edgier, "Actually, I prefer 'Slut. Bloody Slut'."

Bloody Slut pulls out a screen and projects a scene from the morning after I lost my virginity: I'm sitting on my bed wearing his hockey jacket, giddy he gave it to me. I think it's a fair trade, knowing how precious a guy's team jacket is to him.

Monday morning he asks for it back. No fair. At least he could.

She takes me back further - to the boys I had experimented with prior to the backseat - the neighbor in the back alley, the 100 boys I met the summer of Expo 86, Bobby at Heather's birthday pool party in Grade 6 and the look on her sister's face when she caught us holding hands under water. Being called a flirt over and over again. I connected flirt with slut.

Sensing women were very, very sexual scared me and I labeled it wrong. Bad. I never talked about this curiosity, because I didn't want to be labeled bad. It all came out when I drank. Even the very first time I made out with that boy in Grade 8. *Flirt. Slut.*

I was so curious, but way too young to be experimenting with this powerful feeling.

What are your gifts, Bloody Slut? Three years of celibacy! I'm clean. Wait. Why do I think having sex would make me dirty?

Why now? There is a massive sexual power in me trying to emerge. I want to be a woman. No more girl. Woman.

9 AM: I'm at Calhoun's. It is weird, because I actually do feel like I'm cheating on Grounds. Already it is different. The muffin is sweet and fattening, the coffee isn't as strong and no one's here, I mean, not even the staff. A guy just came in and stood at the till for 2 minutes before calling into the kitchen for some service. Nothing. He shrugged and left.

I'm going to get 4 hours of solid writing done today and then back to Grounds tomorrow. Sometimes cheating makes you appreciate what you already have.

Intention for the Day: *Be* my woman.

Reflection of the Day: I *am* a healthy, wealthy woman.

11 AM: A moment of silence. I don't believe in war, but I can say a prayer for those who did and for those who still do.

5:30 PM: I was meditating on being a woman and mused, "What can I do to feel more like a women?" Flirt and... fuck.

At the word 'Fuck', I was bolted by pent-up sexual energy. I masturbated. Hard. I was *not* making love to myself. I was full-on fucking. I was angry. It was surreal. I was scared. I thought I was losing my mind. At one point, it felt like I was possessed, like I was undergoing an exorcism and all my past partners were leaving my body through my vagina.

I am a woman! Why so much fear of this sexual power? I didn't know whether to cry or scream or destroy something.

True fear: No one will be able to handle me. I would scare a man right now. I am scaring myself. I don't know how to make Bloody Slut feel loved and appreciated. I've judged her for so long. I wish I could play football right now. ARGHHHHHH!!!

November 12, 2012

I'm at Grounds... Home, sweet, home.

I'm worried I'm taking this shadow work to the extreme, but I also feel like they are coming out because they trust me and I don't want to shun them anymore.

Seriously, why do people have to make such disgusting noises when they eat the cinnamon buns here? Oh... right, I keep forgetting, I'm disgusting.

Disgusting Pig Shadow: Me, super skinny with a bloated face, wearing my favorite baggy blue jeans and white lace sweater from my first year of university.

When I asked how and when I created her, I immediately went to blaming my mom's dieting, but called myself on it. Not everything is about my mom. No, this was something earlier... the obese spinster... Holy crap. That's it. *When you are fat no one will love you.*

Flash forward: Matthew and I in the hot tub when we first started dating. We were talking about my weight. *Why were we talking about my weight in a hot tub?* This was at one of the low points of my bulimia. He didn't know yet, though. He said he didn't care about my weight. I didn't believe him. I was relentless with the questions - ice pick in his eye relentless.

"No, seriously, at what weight would you break up with me?"

Frustrated, he finally blurted, "As long as you don't become like Delouise."

Delouise was a huge girl with a huge personality.

Okay. Thank you. Now I know. There is a point when you won't want me anymore and it does depend on my weight. I knew it.

Living on the farm. Big fat sows out in the pens pigging out on oats; me in the house pigging out on oatmeal. More water. More water. *Easier to puke it up, my dear.*

Carlos and I doing E after India. It was a skinny time for me and in the bliss of the Love Drug, he felt comfortable confiding to me that before I left, he secretly wanted me to lose weight.

I knew it. So, fuck you. I'll gain it all back with a couple bonus pounds just to piss you off.

When I hated my body, I attracted people into my life who were judgmental. No. That's a cop out. *I* made my weight an issue. Their judgment was always a projection of how I felt.

Why now, Disgusting Pig? Something is trying to emerge. It'll get out, but not by puking.

What are your gifts? Conscious eating. If you've ever seen pigs eat, they're oblivious to anything else that's going on. Unconscious eaters... No! They are 100% focused on that one task. They are conscious eaters! I can do that. I can be a disgusting pig... at a slower speed, of course.

What else can I do? Consume life.

Later: I stow all my girl pictures in my hope chest and place my Aphrodite statue on top; her ceramic breast and buttock exposed. There is a reason she was always my favorite goddess. I bought her in Greece when I was 25, but am only now comfortable with our connection.

I stand in front of my full-length mirror wrapped in my silk sari from India, my breast and buttock exposed. I am a Goddess of love, beauty and sexuality.

But there is someone else trying to emerge... Athena? No. Artemis. *The huntress.*

I drop my sari and practice yoga to try and Zen me down, but something primal surges and I assume the poses AS the animals - Cobra, Downward Dog, Active Cat - purrrrRROAR. I prowl around naked, swaying my hips side to side.

The wild. I need to get into the wild.

UBC Endowment Lands. Fifteen square kilometers of trails, the closest thing to wilderness. I park at Locarno, don my hiking boots and Peruvian toque, bolt across the street and up the steep path leading to the trails. It is pouring rain, so I am alone.

My blood is pumping. My heart is racing.

I'm wielding my power. My power is unyielding.

I am a warrior. I am a huntress.

Slow and calculated, I moan my way through the trees. I am the oak; I am the leaves.

Grunt. I am a predator. I am on the prowl. What am I prowling for? My eyes are open. I am alert. No prey will go unnoticed.

I race through the woods. I *howl.*

Am I crazy? No. I am the beast.

Someone comes around the bend... I don't care. I am incognito.

Gollum... My precious...

One Ring to rule them all, One ring to find them;
One ring to bring them all and in the darkness bind them.

My Precious Pictures. YES!! My company name.

More people...

On the way back to my car, I decide to whip by my dream house and get a closer look. The address: oh yeah, 4666 - I knew I liked this place... The number of the beast.

Thank God I am not in a relationship. This energy is not meant for a relationship. This is pure masculine energy. I need to channel this into my career. I cannot fear my power. I cannot fear losing control. Sometimes I am Aphrodite; sometimes I am Artemis.

Later at home: I feel like destroying something.

Out of the blue last week, Elliot asked me, "Don't you just want to smash something?"

I laughed, "Uh, no, not really."

"Like you wouldn't want to kick through this door right now?"

"Why in the world would I want to kick a door?"

"To feel it break."

I smirked, "I'm a creator, not a destroyer."

He hates it when I come out with sweeping generalizations, so has been challenging me ever since. "Like, you wouldn't want to watch a car drive off a cliff and explode?"

I shrugged, "I'm a creator, not a destroyer." I love to get his goat.

But now I understand. I need to destroy something!

Later: Obviously my wilderness adventure did nothing to expend the energy pulsating through my body, because I've been jazzed for hours. I'm watching Monday Night Football and can't sit still. I'm bouncing off the walls here and wishing I could be in the game.

Two Minutes Later: Holy shit! The scariest most fucked up thing just happened.

I was walking back from the washroom and felt a pop in my right arm. I looked and in the exact place they insert the needle when I donate blood... a popped blood vessel. No, it's more than a vessel, it's a vein! I popped a fucking vein.

A centimeter of my vein in the bend of my arm is protruding out. Holy Fuck!!!!

November 14, 2012

I'm not writing today. The thought of my laptop sends electrically charged needles up and down my right arm. I have gymnastics tonight. Not sure if I should go.

Intention for the Day: Love the right side of my body.

Reflection of the Day: I love the right side of my body.

Later: Gymnastics was awesome. I'm trying really hard not to analyze and just be present. I actually have to remind myself I'm there to have fun. This is a childhood dream I am finally living, a gift to my Little Girl. I want to allow her to enjoy it, but... there are just so many metaphors for life. Like all the fears I'm facing, for example, the huge pit of sponges. I can't get myself to spring board into it. I can stand at the edge and do a little dive, but if I run up to the springboard or try to trampoline my way in, I hit an invisible wall.

My favorite apparatus is the uneven bars. I pretty much just hang there, though. The instructor is trying to get me to swing a bit, so I can build some momentum, but my hands won't leave the bar enough to make space to swing. I love them, though, for the potential of what I know I will be able to achieve. One day, I am going to swing around those suckers like a perpetual pendulum.

So funny the right side of my body doesn't hurt during gymnastics.

November 15, 2012

Intention of the Day: Live every moment as the Best Moment of My Life!

Reflection: What is my relationship to this moment?

Laughing Yoga: Hahahaha... just start laughing and keep going until it takes over. I tried it this morning and it influenced my whole day.

Nigel noticed and asked what was wrong with me, as it wasn't a Grounds-for-Coffee-high-on-caffeine-day. I told him about my morning laughing session.

"You should try it."

"You should see a psychiatrist."

Then I showed him my popped vein, which totally grossed him out.

"No, seriously, you should see a psychiatrist."

Oh, if he only knew.

I also showed Elliot my arm and told him about wanting to destroy something. He wasn't at all grossed out; in fact, I think I made his year.

Spiritually, the right side of the body represents the masculine. My excursion in the wilderness makes so much more sense. No wonder I popped a vein. I couldn't handle all that masculine energy coursing through my body. It had to get out somewhere and where I donate blood was the perfect spot.

Halfway through the Best Month of My Life!

George

<u>November 17, 2012</u>

Ended up drinking five beers alone last night... Addiction is rooted in loneliness.

I know the difference between drinking because I like beer and drinking because I am using beer and it is when I reach for the 3rd beer. That's when I'm drinking because I'm lonely.

Timeline Process: When did this lonely feeling first appear?

It brought me back to the night when I was about ten, and had to stay in the Glendon Hospital overnight. It was a big Chartrand camping weekend at Minnie Lake and I got really sick with canker sores down my throat that needed to be zapped. I'm not even sure why Glendon (population: negligible) has a hospital. I swear I was the only one there, just me and my Archie comics - by far the loneliest, scariest night of my life.

I've created situations to distance myself from my family, mentally, emotionally and physically in order to be lonely. I needed to do this, not only to become independent, but also to leave and come to Vancouver, where I could start this spiritual journey.

As for romantic relationships, the belief guys only want one thing... a delusion that gave me an excuse not to connect with anyone on an intimate level.

Dr. Pez and I talked a lot about loneliness our second round. It was a confusing time for me, because all I wanted to be was alone, but yet I was feeling lonely. I knew this had nothing to do with having people around me. I had just gotten out of a marriage where I felt extremely lonely. I knew this wasn't about Carlos either. I felt the same way with Matthew and even around my family and friends. I have always felt really alone in the world.

"Loneliness is an illusion. You are not alone."

I thought what he meant was that I was just not connecting with those around me. I thought he meant I wasn't around the right people. This led me on my search to find my soul mate... and we all know how that turned out.

Shadow Process: Lonely Loser - a little girl with blonde pigtails licking a lollipop.

Wetting the bed. Plastic sheets. Airing my sleeping bag over the clothesline at the lake for everyone to see.

Who's going to want to marry someone who wets the bed?

Hating sleepovers. Didn't sleep a wink. Mom picking me up in the morning commenting on the dark circles under my eyes. I still have dark circles. Not being comfortable looking Josh in the eyes. My God, I didn't even look at Carlos when we were saying our vows. Never liked him looking me right in the eyes. I thought this was about him... poor Carlos. My greatest teacher.

My soul is calling out. Be with Lonely Loser - she has something to say. Loneliness is a call, a cry, to connect with myself. This past year, I have begun developing a connection to myself and my relationships are flourishing as a result.

The deeper connection I have with myself, the deeper connection I have with others. The deeper connection I have with others, the deeper connection I have with myself.

Intention for the Day: Connect.

Reflection of the Day: With ease & with grace....

Later: Carl Jung quote, "I'd rather be whole than be good."

This whole month is about wholeness. My soul is projecting all the shadows ready to be integrated and they sure are taking the opportunity to be heard!

Shadow Process on Jealousy: two teenage girls came out. Jealous Jane (she lets me see in others something in myself crying to emerge) followed by Conceited Connie (she teaches me to appreciate myself). These two girls are actually friends with each other, and now with me, too.

Next up: Sneaky Thief.

I was shocked when Uncle Art first appeared.... then I cried. It's been a long time since I thought about him. My Uncle Art was, um, the Black Sheep of my dad's family. Obviously, I felt a special bond with him. When I was 17 yrs old he died of a drug overdose. I didn't even go see him in the hospital. It happened just days before Labour Day weekend and I *had* to go camping with my friends at Lac Santé.

About twenty of us stayed in the public campsite on the other side of where our cabin is now. I was sitting in the passenger seat of a friend's pickup, wasted out of my mind in the middle of the day, when Lee's grandma tapped on the window. Tracy's first husband's family also had a lake lot there and my parents had called her to find me.

I looked up into her kind, yet disappointed eyes. She whispered, "Rachelle. Your uncle passed away."

The only picture I remember of Uncle Art is of him sitting at a picnic table smoking a cigarette. He was so handsome. All the Chartrand men are, but Uncle Art looked like a French Canadian James Dean. I always liked that picture until I realized the tall brick structure in the background was a correctional lookout tower. The photo had been taken when he was at the Edmonton Remand Centre for stealing or dealing drugs or something.

Uncle Art often sat with the nieces and nephews at weddings. Some may think that weird, but I don't think he felt he fit in with the other siblings. I loved it, because he would sneak me rum and cokes. He never made me feel awkward. I always thought he liked me. I thought I was like him. He called me George.

My Uncle Art Shadow: Good. Bad. Rich. Poor. Success. Fail. Holy. Shit.

I shoveled shit with him. This was the longest session ever. Endless shit to shovel. We were swimming in shit. All these dreams of feces I've been having lately... this is it. Wading in shit, so many lies, self-sabotaging by choosing to get caught, unhealthy relationship after unhealthy relationship.

Farming pig shit. Getting stuck in it with my oversized rubber boots. Stepping out of the boots because the suction around my bulimic legs was too strong.

The sows laughing at me, "Welcome to Hollywood, Sweetheart!"

This manure is going to be fertilizer for my soul. Mushrooms grow in shit and they are some of the most medicinal organisms in nature.

That was all extremely uncomfortable for me to write. I hate poop stories. I hate poop jokes. I hate poop in movies. Everybody loved *Bridesmaids* so much; the poop scene ruined it for me.

When I decided to write this book, I never thought in a million years the word 'poop' would be in it, let alone 'shit', except when preceded by 'Holy'.

Deep aversion... maybe this was why.

My biggest shame comes from being a thief - sometimes sneaky, sometimes not.

Forgive me Sneaky Thief. You can show me that when I want something it is a sign I'm missing something and whatever is missing is what I'm not giving.

My soul created these experiences for me to learn deep compassion. The soft spot I've had for young offenders, for Uncle Art... and now for my own past.

Additional wisdom? Not everyone appears as they seem. What does that mean? I need to let it settle in for a bit.

November 19, 2012

Met Scott and Mike for drinks yesterday. I love male energy!

I showed Christine my burst vein and told her about my right-side-masculine-realization.

"Yeah, that's too much. You're out of balance." She said the right side represents giving, the left side receiving. Sexually, men are the givers and women are the receivers. The egg receives the sperm. The vagina receives the penis. Even relationship-wise, it's the man that pursues and the woman that accepts. Yikes, except with me... I have not been receiving. I've been pushing, go-getting, giving, putting all this energy out, but still feel the block whenever it comes to receiving.

She suggested using my left side more, like standing on my left foot. I've been using my right side for almost everything. I barely use my left hand even to type. I barely touch people with my left hand. Even hugs. I always lead with my right and feel more like I am giving a hug than receiving one.

Intention for the Day: Balance my yin.

Reflection of the Day: Receive. Receive. Receive.

November 21, 2012

Balancing my yin. Receiving. I have actually received a lot this year: new ideas, philosophies, friendships, deeper connections with people... the touch of Yoga Nick during our sessions. I've received love, abundance, opportunities, success and Inspired Ideas.

I don't mean I've been given lots, the Universe is constantly trying to give, I mean I've *received* lots. And I am choosing to receive more. I choose to receive all the love and abundance the Universe has to offer.

Tide going in, tide going out. Breath coming in, breath going out.

The sun. It is fueled through the fusion of two hydrogen nuclei to make one helium and then emits all the glorious radiation that supports life on Earth.

The more I give, the more I receive. The more I receive, the more I give.

Receiving is part of the flow and when others give, including the Universe, I must receive it or I will block the flow. The blocks are illusions of course, because we are all one. I am dissolving these blocks.

Sometimes the greatest gift we can give is to receive the gift someone is giving.

Intention for the day: Balance my yin. (This needs at least another day)

Reflection of the day: GiveReceiveGiveReceive...

Later: I spent more time meditating on 'yin'.

When we were in Korea, Carlos made a short film called *Yin*. It is a beautiful, surreal love story about a Korean man who is lonely and depressed until he finds a mysterious woman, Yin (played by me), passed out on his front step. The woman changes his life.

Carlos said it was a love letter to me.

I never *received* that letter.

November 22, 2012

Gymnastics was so much fun last night. I got some air on the uneven bars! My baby soft hands don't last long, though. I wish I had my calloused rock climbing paws back.

I really have to mix it up. I like to go off alone (shocking, I know), but I learn so much more with the other gymnasts around. Besides, this is supposed to be social! I always feel myself drifting alone to one of the activities and having to pull myself back to the group.

Realization: I have been letting 'what ifs?' hold me back. I'm driving forward. I'm *diving* into the unknown. I'm scared. Good scared.

Intention for the Day: Dive into the unknown.

Reflection of the Day: Where is the unknown?

November 23, 2012

I was going to write how I'm feeling doubts and frustrations around what I'm doing and my finances and then I wrote the date. Holy Crap! I am turning 40 years old in one month! I am mustering all my strength, gathering all my tools, focusing on all the abundance around me, all the love and support being offered, and doing a complete 180! I only have one month left in my first 40 years of this human experience.

I do not want to have one regret about one penny I spent. I have an incredible weekend of writing, meetings and prep for the Whistler Film Festival. I have so many great things to focus on and I will not be pulled down.

Intention for the Day: Trust.

Reflection of the Day: How are all the ways I'm wealthy?

Later: I was just in the washroom at Grounds wondering when this Poor Shadow was created. I thought back to when my dad had that company for a couple years. I think I trapped his stress and fear. Then I thought about that picture of my mom and dad that Christmas when it was first obvious the money was flowing in again. I hate that fucking picture. Mom in her full-length fur coat and dad with his diamond ring, even now it makes me want to gag. There is something big here. Huge. It was obnoxious and fake. Mom looks like she'd been eaten by gargantuan minx and Dad just looks lost.

The thing is, I don't ever remember my mom actually wearing that coat out. We didn't live in a world where that coat would be even remotely appropriate - curling rinks in the winter, campsites in the summer.

That picture also marks the beginning of the really hard times for me and my mom, so maybe on some level, I thought money was the cause of our issues. She seemed angry. I know this wasn't who she really was, but it is the illusion I burned into my subconscious.

Money makes you fake and angry.

Even now, I assume most rich people are probably unfulfilled and stressed with keeping up. *Who am I kidding?* This is how I judge all rich people.

November 24, 2012

Last night, while I was trying to fall asleep, I imagined I was on a raft on the ocean just riding the waves, just going with the flow.

I did the timeline around my frustrations with making money, or more accurately, not making money. The process brought me back to these super-rich friends of my parents. We stayed at their beautiful home while they were out of town. They had a pool off their living room and a bidet in the master bathroom. Only people I've ever known to own a bidet.

It was my first mansion. I loved it, but we were staying there as wannabes. Before that, I had always dreamt of being rich, but that weekend made me think it wasn't possible. We were only visitors, outsiders, squatters; sampling luxury while the *real* owners were away on vacation.

I was supposed to have that glimpse of luxury, but first I needed to do 30 years of spiritual and life work, so when I do own my dream home, I won't be afraid of losing it. I won't be worried my external world is a house of cards to my internal wrecking ball.

My dream home will fit me like a glove. My sanctuary. Maybe I will even have a bidet!

Flash forward: I had a vision about my dream day in 3-D, multi-angle, multi-experiential for the first time. Making love to my soul mate in our bed under a white duvet, the wind blowing in the open patio door; opening the fridge and looking at all the vibrant organic vegetables and creating a masterpiece meal; sitting on our balcony overlooking the ocean...

Before it was always like it was projected on a screen, this time I was in it... with a man I don't yet know.

Intention for the Day: Go with the flow.

Reflection of the Day: I am a raft on the ocean of life. Riding waves, going with the flow.

56

Leader from the Outskirts

WIFTV is in some trouble. We've had a couple board members step down and the Education Chair has had to cut back for family reasons. I am so honored, humbled and grateful I am the president and entrusted with this leadership role. This will be a huge learning experience for me. I admit I am stressed, but I believe in myself and now more than ever, we need a vision.

Intention for the Day: Be a leader.

Reflection of the Day: Where there is no vision, the people perish.

Well, my mojo must be flowing. I'm at Grounds and a guy just flirted with me.

He looked exactly like a 30 yr-old Jon Bon Jovi. Not Bon Jovi *at* 30 i.e. shaggy streaked hair, but Bon Jovi now if he was 30 years old. Super yummy. Did I ever mention I used to think Bon Jovi was my soul mate? And that I touched his arm? At a concert... security got involved.

Anyways, 'Jon' picked up his guitar (yes, he even had a guitar), looked right at me and smiled. He glanced back at me a couple times as he was leaving, and then just as he passed the window, he held up his hands and made a heart with them. It made me smile. He was with a girl, but I'm trying to give him the benefit of the doubt. She could've been his sister.

I am wondering, though, how many times he's done that, the hand-heart trick. It was so quick on the draw; it coulda easily come out a spade.

299

Later: I went to my first Christmas Craft Fair in about 15 years today. Clare rented a table and I am so proud of her. She makes plaques and racks and stuff out of old, rustic antique wood from her grandparent's house in Beaumont.

Her company name is 'The Board Broad'. Too funny. I bought a plaque engraved 'PEACE', because that's how Clare makes me feel - at peace.

When I got home, there was a message on my phone that I won a door prize. Cool. I wonder what it is... I hope it's the electric guitar.

November 27, 2012

My left eye is bloodshot and the area under my eyes is dry like elephant skin. My body is begging for love and support, too.

Intention for the Day: Love and support myself.

Reflection of the Day: Love. Love. LOVE.

November 28, 2012

I got paid and my cheque was more than I expected. It turns out last month there was a mistake and this month worked it out, but there was a moment I thought, 'What if I pretended I didn't notice? I'm sure it's right. Maybe this is making up for the fact my past few paychecks seem smaller. I could cover my weekend at Whistler. Perfect timing. Blah, blah, blah...'

Last night, I was reading the *Shadow Effect* and Marianne Williamson was writing about atonement. Giving up our sins to God. This is not *sin* in the Biblical-sense; it is sin meaning 'off the mark'. To me, God is the Universe, so it struck me as beautiful and loving and time to let go.

I prayed. There were two major things I needed to ask forgiveness for.

"God, please forgive me for all the times I have stolen."

I visualized as many times as I could, mustering compassion for that girl and then letting go of it to God. God accepted it all. Somewhere in my heart, I heard, "You're forgiven... Tell your work about the mistake."

This wasn't penance or him saying, "I'll only forgive you if..." Just, "You are forgiven. Period. Do the right thing. Period."

This is about more than acting with authenticity and integrity. It is about love and abundance. What would a loving, abundant person do? I knew the answer.

The other: my affair.

"Dear God, please forgive me. Forgive me for not keeping my relationship sacred and creating fear and heartache in the name of love. I now know it was not love. It couldn't be."

I was so lost and angry and bitter back then. I actually started the prayer last night, but fell asleep, dreamt of talking to God, woke up and continued praying.

"I will never cheat on my beloved. I will hold my relationship sacred in the heart, mind and body. Mine and theirs."

This is not an oath. It is a truth.

A glorious whisper, "You are forgiven."

Reflection of the Day: I am forgiven.

Intention for the Day: Accept this forgiveness.

Whis-la!

<u>December 2, 2012</u>

What an amazing weekend. What an amazing month!

I'm so exhausted, but I have a huge week ahead. I am torn about what to write about Whistler... It's a completely different kind of festival, with a 'gone away for the weekend' vibe and I kinda wanna keep it that way.

What happens in Whistler should stay in Whistler.

There were a few weird and a few cool experiences, though.

Cool: Got to hang out with the Finalé folks. The owner/president, Don Thompson, and his vice president, Andrew Jha, double handedly make industry events fun. Andrew was one of the first people to talk to me at my first mixer a couple years ago.

Weird: Andrew used to work with Cynthia, the girlfriend of the guy who wanted me to be his hooker in high school. Oh, how my life has changed.

Cool: Andrew served me up my first oyster in 20 years. It was de-lish!

Cool: Hung out at the hotel pub with Ana, Amber, John Dippong and a bunch of other industry peeps. Ana told everyone how awesome she thinks it is that I dance naked in front of a mirror. I wasn't even shy about it. I told everyone they should do it. Christine and I danced our butts off.

Weird: Ran into an old acquaintance, Damian, who was working for the festival. He bragged about dating a girl in her 20's. I bought him a drink and tried not to judge. Damian was friends with the guy who tossed me off the bed all those years ago. Oh, how my life has changed.

Cool: Ana and Amber were having their mentorship meeting with Mary Anne Waterhouse in the filmmaker's lounge, and I couldn't take my eyes off the woman. Her young son was there. She was having this professional consultation, while running her fingers through his hair. It was mesmerizing. I will always remember this image. You *can* have both.

Weird: Went to the Heenan Blaikie party at Araxi's. Araxi's is the first restaurant Jack Evrensel (CinCin's, Blue Water) opened. It is named after his wife, who I always found lovely and sophisticated when I worked at Blue Water. You would have to be with a name like Araxi.

Cool: Drank free wine, ate copious amounts of prawns, talked John Dippong's ear off... the usual.

Cool: *Beauty Mark*, the winning short last year directed by Mark and produced by Nimisha, was part of a special screening at Maxx Fish, a pub, so I went to support them. My buddies, Don and Andrew, were there. The film is about a child beauty pageant contestant who goes to extreme dark measures to get out of going to any more competitions - she cuts her face with a pair of scissors.

Weird: Went to the CineCoup party. I told Mark how I had almost done what the little girl in his film did. I almost slit my face once. I can't believe I told him that.

Cool: Went to the Variety's '10 Screenwriters To Watch' panel. I am so going to be on that panel in a couple years. Reid Carolin, the writer of *Magic Mike* was there... hahaha... I wanted to thank him for helping me get in touch with my inner pervert, but couldn't find him after.

By Sunday morning, Carolyn and I were both done, so came home early. Didn't even go to the awards brunch.

See ya next year, Whistler... you exhaust me.

Cruisin' and Coastin'

December 3, 2012

My place is a pigsty, but I need to decompress from the weekend.
Too tired to write. Too tired to clean. Too tired to unpack.
I turn 40 in twenty days. I'm too tired to turn 40.

December 4, 2012

I woke up at 4 AM, feeling all out of sorts. I asked, "What?!!" but couldn't relax enough to hear an answer. I tried meditating, EC'ing, listening to my breath, Yoga Nidra, but nothing helped. I lay there for a bit longer and then the guidance hit.

So, at 5 AM I got up and cleaned. Unpacked my suitcase, washed the dishes and cleaned my bathroom. At 6:30 AM, I went back to bed and slept until 8:30 AM. I woke up feeling like a million bucks.

When I got home Sunday, two of my plants were dead, but they are revived and so am I.

Feng shui, baby, feng-fricking-shui.

Later: On the last GCC, there was a lady talking about how furious she gets when she reads about animals being abused. Enraged, actually. I feel the same. I don't read the newspaper, anyways, but I have to turn the radio off if any such story is brought up. I don't want a picture in my mind and I hate that feeling of rage. The other day, two men at Grounds were talking about these abused sled dogs... I actually told them to stop talking about it.

Derek gently introduced the idea that we are all abusers... *Ugh,* right in the gut.

I am not an abuser. I am tender and caring and would never hit anyone or knowingly hurt a creature.... except maybe a Wolf spider. It's been bothering me all week.

The process: This was one shadow I had no interest in meeting. To be honest, when I called for Abuser to come forward, I was shocked something actually emerged. It was dark and scaly. It was created when I was bullied, but no one would believe me. We didn't visit long; we didn't have to. We both knew her true manifestation - I am my bully. I am my abuser.

I chose to be bullied, so I could hate. *Why?* Because by experiencing the rage and loneliness rooted in a lie of separation, I could learn the truth that we are all connected. I forgave my bullies, but began to abuse myself. I made this choice, so I would experience duality. I needed to experience this awful illusion of self-hatred, so I could know the beautiful reality of self-love.

What does she need to feel loved and to become my ally? The answer is not quite clear, but this revelation is enough to start.

December 5, 2012

I had the most beautiful time falling asleep last night. Just lying there, grateful for breathing, listening and loving my breath. I wept silent tears of joy, love and gratitude.

I awoke and it came to me. It was exactly three years ago I walked out of the place in Squamish. Walked out, and had my heart pulled out, or so I thought. I cried myself to sleep that night, too, but those were toxic tears.

I am so grateful for this year of healing.

Healing enough to know there was nothing to heal.

What an incredible year of adventure and insight. I am cruising my way to the end of this year and coasting into the next. There is nothing more to do, nothing more to say. My life is complete. I am whole. I always have been.

I woke up and had an *Un*inspired Idea to Facebook message Josh. Just to say hi, see how he's doing. I laughed. I won't. I am happy and healthy and don't need to do anything to make myself feel insecure. I don't need to self-abuse anymore.

Last night, as I lay there, each time I started to judge the outside, I loved the inside. Writing this book has caused some stress the last couple of weeks. I don't feel enough has happened. I'm scared the book won't be interesting enough. I am accepting and appreciating how incredible this year has been. I don't need any more plot points.

I read an interesting quote yesterday: *There are no guarantees in this life, so when we hold back we do so at the risk of never fully blossoming.... like a flower planted in North Dakota putting off blooming because it would prefer to do so in Illinois.*

I am blooming and blossoming in the here and now. I am a butterfly emerging from the last crusts of its chrysalis.

Later: I did a back flip tonight! I actually did a back flip off a mat and landed on my feet! My Little Girl squealed with delight. My lifelong dream came true!

<u>December 6, 2012</u>

Elliot is obsessed with my age. Seriously, every single day, he tells me how many more days it is until I turn 40. I usually counter it with my 'time is an illusion' mantra. He still hates it when I say that.

A Facebook friend posted: *If your sex life were a movie, what would be the title?*

My reply: *40-Year-Old 'Born Again' Virgin.*

Maybe that should be the title of my book!

December 7, 2012

7:15 AM at Grounds: I had the most bizarre dream last night where I was wielding this little black blade while giggling.

Dreammoods.com: *To see a blade in your dream suggests you are making some difficult and important decisions. You need to be able to make clear distinctions between your choices.*

This doesn't seem right to me. I feel like it represents a dangerous penis. The fact I was swinging it playfully means my fear of men has been a lie - a phallic fallacy.

Whoa... I just realized the meaning of the word *en-courage*. In Courage.

I've been scared of men for as long as I can remember, but this is not about 'Having Courage' in order to be with a man, it is about being 'In Courage' with myself.

This is not about going into battle... it is about being at peace.

Later: "Do They Know It's Christmas?" is playing. That song always makes me cry.

"The Chanukah Song" played a few minutes ago. That song always makes me laugh.

My Good Friend once said the thing he liked best about me was that I was always ready to laugh. I like that I am always ready to laugh, and cry, again. So different than a year ago.

Later: Okay, this is very BIZARRE. I just went and picked up my door prize from the community centre where Clare's craft fair was held. I was hoping for the electric guitar, but instead she handed me a little box wrapped in Christmas paper. Inside - a thick black and silver hand crafted chain bracelet with a *little black blade* as the charm! I'm freaking out.

December 8, 2012

While I was curling my hair this morning, I reflected on Christmas, and religion versus spirituality. If someone asked me what I am, I would answer, *"I'm just me. Actually, I am everyone. Actually, I am God."*

At that moment... my reflection... a glimmering flash enveloped me. My aura shimmered! It was for an infinitesimal second, but it was there.

I AM God. *Whoa...*

Intention of the Day: Be God.

Reflection of the Day: I am God.

Later: I just flirted with two guys at Grounds; unfortunately they were there at the same time. It felt good, though. One guy was just smiles, the other complemented me on my pink '80s shirt. I seem to be seeing more attractive guys lately. Could my mojo be beginning to flow-jo?

December 9, 2012

Carlos sent out party invites from him and his girlfriend - a 'Birthday-Christmas-Lots to Celebrate' party. It came attached with a picture of Simon, Daphne and another puppy in a baby carriage. *Wow.* Don't know what to say about that... I'm really trying to give him the benefit of the doubt on this one. I invited him to mine, after all.

During my VVR today, I really worked on forgiveness, especially around Carlos. Yeah, there's still some judgment there. I radiated forgiveness - forgiving Carlos, forgiving myself and realizing of course, there is nothing to forgive.

A vision of him and his pregnant girlfriend appeared. Smiling and laughing... a crack, like something in my energy heart-field broke open, and I was set free.

We are all one. I love him. I love his girlfriend. I love his baby. I am love.

Your heart doesn't break. It is the most powerful thing in the world. The love that flows out of it would blind us if we could see it.

Thank you for sending that picture, Carlos. I didn't realize I was still carrying this resentment.

You can't heal what you don't feel.

December 10, 2012

Elliot has been relentlessly pressuring me again for specific examples of how I was weird as a kid, one by one dismantling them. I am starting to think maybe I wasn't so weird after all.

Is it possible to change my story 30 years later? That's it. It's just a story. In the past few months my perspective of my story and to my story has changed drastically.

I thought about Carlos. *How could I retell our story?* I'm not going to go over the whole relationship; I've worked too hard to let it go, but what about the end? Could I change my perspective of that, now that I have a different perspective? Yes. Yes, I can.

That last year, Carlos wanted to make things work. In our final spring, he came to me. I was on the couch researching something on the Internet and he knelt before me. He placed my laptop aside and held my hands in his. I was super uncomfortable as he stared at me with a vulnerability he had never shown me. One I for sure, had never shown him.

He asked, "Are we over?"

I shrugged coldly, "I don't know."

He glanced away for a moment and then came back with tears in his eyes, "Well, I won't be the one to leave. I can't. I love you too much."

He made a promise to win me back, but with every effort he made, basking in all my bitterness, I would huff to myself, "Too little, too late."

That summer, days before he was to leave for a two-month shoot in Edmonton, he came to me again. I was painting my toenails out on our balcony. He sat across from me and asked if he could finish the job. I can't remember if I let him. I doubt it. I didn't realize it at the time, but I was enjoying making him suffer.

"I need to know if I'll be coming home to my wife or a roommate."

I shrugged coldly, "I don't know."

Finally, in November he surrendered, "I can't live like this. Living with *this* you."

He had done the best he could. It was a lot. It was all he had. I never saw that.

59

Voici Ma Voix

<u>December 11, 2012</u>

What can I accomplish in 12 days? The goals I had for this year: to find my soul mate and work full-time as a writer, I did not achieve... Yet.

How would I feel if I was with my soul mate? Sexy, fun, uninhabited, free and confident.

How would I feel if I was a full-time writer? Abundant, peaceful, creative, proud.

Even though the external may not have manifested, those internal qualities did. Wow. All of those attributes I now feel.

I had the weirdest dream last night. I know, I always say that, but this one was... *heavy*, but I'm not sure why. I was a teenager and went off with Tanner from Tanner's field and my mom was extremely worried. Tanner's Field was a piece of farmland on the outskirts of Beaumont where we held the bush parties. The thing is, there was no kid named Tanner. I think Tanner was the farmer's last name. Not sure why my mom was there.

Later: During yoga, I had the same heavy feeling that my dream meant something; like I'm still not dealing with something.

I lay down in Savasana - Corpse Pose.

I breathe. Gently on the inhale, "What is it?" Listening on the exhale. Silence.

Breathe in, "Who are you?" Breathe out. Nothing.

"Please come out. You can trust me."

Victim. Guys only want one thing.

A montage of torturous moments comes rushing forth. Every single time I was touched.

Breathe in... breathe out.

In the dark, in the pool, in the bush, on the couch, on the beach, on the raft at the water park, in the backseat, in the front seat, in many backseats, in many front seats...

The most agonizing: in the back alley at the age of 13. The boy down the street kissed me and I was smitten. He put his hand down my pants, and even though I was on my period, I let him. I couldn't speak. I was scared to say 'no', even though I knew it would be more embarrassing once he felt my pad in my panties. I couldn't say no. I had no voice.

Then to the dugout... Whenever I go back to that moment, I am standing at the entrance and he calls me to look over. The shock at what he exposed. I always stare back out to the baseball diamond, over to the bushes. Speechless.

Not this time.

This time I let myself, my young girl, get angry.

I hear her voice, "Put it AWAAAAAYYYYY!"

Then I let her run out of the dugout...

This time I am waiting for her. My young girl comes running out of that dugout and into my arms. I hug her tight. I've missed her so much.

I own my body. I own my voice. I can say no. For so long, the only time I would let someone touch me was if I was drunk, i.e. numb. I've avoided letting anyone touch me for three years, scared to even drink around single men. Scared to kiss.

Fear of flirting: Where will it lead? What will he expect? What will I let him do to me?'

Why now? It's amazing what you hear when you are willing to heal.

Sooooooo... Hummmmm...

I can listen to her. She will tell me when it's not safe.

Anything else? You have been touched by someone who loves you.

Carlos loved you. Matthew loved you.

I see my story different now.

12-12-12

Nigel blurts, "You're turning forty and still work at BrainBoost?" Ouch.

I'm not judging my circumstances; I'm observing them objectively. I became a teacher to work with youth, because I had some issues to work out and some lessons to learn.

St. FX - being accepted, teaching physics, having fun in high school sober.

ESL abroad - traveling, meeting new people, running away to realize you just bring your crap with you, allowing yoga and meditation into my life.

Youth Futures - facing my mistakes, judging myself, inspiring others, being inspired by youth, learning that I am not my past.

BrainBoost - creating new relationships, new experiences, with teenage boys. Learning how sensitive they are. Deep. Connected. I am ready to bring men into my life. There are amazingly beautiful men out there and I want to meet them.

No more boys, no more guys... *Men.*

Something still scares me about being with a man. No. This fear is not about being with a man, it is about being a woman. To fully be a woman, I need to let go of my attachment to my youth. I'm ready to dive in and let this part of my journey be what it is. I'm ready to learn.

Thank you, Nigel.

December 13, 2012

What can happen in 10 days? I'm excited to find out. I am so proud of myself that I never gave up on making this the Best Year of My Life, even when I had no idea what that meant. Not the year I thought it would be, but, oh, so much more.

Gymnastics was just okay. I felt off. I was up at 5:30 AM and was very tired. My flips were not landing fully and... Hahaha... when did I ever think I would say that?

Okay, I will go to my last session next Wednesday and ROCK IT!

60

Connect-J-Cut

<u>December 14, 2012</u>

I am an idiot. I am a stupid idiot. I am a Stupid Fucking Idiot!

That's the shadow I'm working on. Loving it. I am opening my heart and my mind.

Last night was the WIFTV Holiday Meet & Greet. So many amazing women.

I'm not sure how we got on the subject of hiking, but one lady said she doesn't hike. She doesn't do any activity where she may end up an invalid. *Hiking? Invalid? Really?*

"What if I slipped and fell?" She's 52, don't you know, and the body doesn't heal itself as fast when you get older, don't you know.

Why do people believe the body is designed to fail us?

I won my second door prize in under three weeks! A gift certificate to a chocolate buffet. Arwen won one to the hotel spa and asked if I wanted to trade.

"A chocolate buffet would make a great date."

I snooped, "Who are you going to take?"

"I don't know yet."

Intrigued by her vagueness, I pried further about the potential candidates.

She smirked coyly, "I date."

Filled with admiration, "I want to date."

"Then you have to tell the Universe."

She made me declare, "Universe, I want a hot date."

312

CHRYSALIS

"Yeah, you didn't say it like you believed it." She walked away with the appetizer for love prize, leaving me with the one for a pedicure.

Later: There was a shooting at a kindergarten in Connecticut. I don't know the details, but really, do they matter? I found out on Facebook. It is times like this I really hate Facebook. People are horrified and angry, I get it, but posting hateful, HATEFUL, comments will not in any way bring those sweet children back or prevent another tragedy. In fact, it is that level of consciousness - fear and rage, that created the conditions for this atrocity in the first place.

Trust me, I realize how controversial this way of thinking is, and I don't vocalize it in public. I just stay off Facebook.

I left the coffee shop and came right home.

Something in me has shifted. In the past few years, when something horrific happened in the world, I would run and hide. I would block the information out: shut off the news, not look at a newspaper and avoid talking to anyone. I didn't want to feel anger or sadness. I had felt too much before. I knew the danger of empathy. I was afraid I would sink once again into the quicksand of despair and never get out.

It's true. I liked my little bubble of ignorant bliss, but today is different.

Sam has the heat jacked up, so I open my window. I lay on my bed in Savasana. The cool breeze floating in is hugged in a shroud of warmth.

I think about those children. I allow myself to feel the sadness. I imagine their faces and I want to stop, but I don't. I am strong and I have something to offer this tragedy. Love.

I imagine my heart radiating pure golden light filled with love and compassion. It expands to fill my glorious basement suite. Because it is so small, this immense, intense love has nowhere to go but out my open window. Thank you, Sam, for not caring about your heating bill.

Leaving my home, it diffuses out in all directions. At first, I think I should try to just focus it down to Connecticut, but then realize this tragedy has affected everyone and so should my love. I also realize I have no idea where Connecticut is.

I lay here emitting more and more love and light, knowing there is no end to how much of this healing energy I can generate. I am a divine power plant.

Eventually, my heart energy bathes the event. I am connected to the victims, the children and their families, but also to the perpetrator. It is not my job to ask why... it is my job to spread love. The only cure for something that sprouted from fear is love.

I fall asleep bathed in, and bathing others in, love.

LOVE. I meditate on love all day. I am going to the beach to love. Tonight I will write from love and watch *Love Actually*.

Many may call this frivolous, but in tragedies we have a choice: lower to the level of the fear that caused the event or rise to the level of love where it could never exist.

I choose love.

My Abuser Shadow... We are all abusers. We just usually abuse ourselves since it is socially acceptable to hate ourselves. What if the reason some people hurt children is because they are trying to rid themselves of their inner child they hate?

I'm not saying this is sane, but that's the thing with mental illness, you don't know when you are ill. When your leg is broken, you know it. When your arm is broken, you know it. Even when your heart is broken, you know it. But when your mind is broken, you don't know it. How can you? The thing that 'knows' is the thing that is broken.

I know. I was there. I've been insane.

Mental illness is so dangerous, because the stigma attached forces people to shove it in the shadows. I've seen parents rationalize their child's shocking behavior, not because they are bad parents, but because they want to spare them from being labeled.

When you are the one who has the inkling that things are off, you shove it deep in the dark out of shame, which is the lowest vibration of all. You then act from that place, and nothing good comes out of action from the level of shame.

I know some believe mental illness is used as an excuse or a cop-out, but if you are abusing others or yourself, by definition you are insane. You are disconnected from the reality that all there is, is love. You are living in a world of separation, which is an illusion, an insane illusion. I am so grateful for those who help the mentally ill.

Thank you, Dr. Pez.

Compassion is always the answer.

A year ago, an event like this would've sunk me into a state of hopelessness. It doesn't trigger me now. I own and recognize my anger, my sadness and my fear.

My heart is still breaking, but I don't feel helpless. My heart is breaking open. I am a powerful instrument of love.

God bless all those affected by this horrible tragedy.

December 15, 2012

Went for an amazing walk at the beach. I was surprised by how much love and kindness I was feeling considering the tragedy, wondering if I was blocking the reality of the atrocity out and just living in my blissful bubble again, but the truth is I am feeling more connected.

When we are not directly connected to a tragedy, or even if we are, we can still mourn, but ultimately we are called to love. It is easy to get angry. It is easy to be scared. It is easy to hate the perpetrator.

We all have a role to play in the tragedy. *What is my role?* I can absorb some of the pain; shower it with love and compassion. I can live in this field of love and help raise the collective consciousness. I can raise the vibration to love and compassion.

I don't expect everyone to have the same perspective as me, but you do have a choice. You can either be part of the problem, part of the solution, or better yet, part of the vision.

No matter what though, love and compassion are always the answer.

December 16, 2012

I turn 40 next Sunday. No. I *get to* turn 40 next Sunday.

Battle of the Sexes. Who came up with this term? It's awful.

This separation is an illusion. I'm as connected and one with men as I am with women. To think that some men only want one thing is ridiculous. Nobody only wants one thing. Well, that's not true. We all want to be happy. A man who sleeps around, feels something. A woman who sleeps around, feels something. No one is one-dimensional. I have objectified men by thinking this way. It was a way to project and protect. I've been protecting myself from a false threat. This is huge. Huge!

I am one with women. I am one with men. I am one with all.

Later: Hahaha... Proof of real inner change is when you react to situations differently. Josh 'liked' another pervert page. This time it made me laugh. Healthy perversion!

December 17, 2012

I'm a stupid, fucking idiot. I drank four days in a row, three of them alone. Last night after two beers, I was geared to have a Sunday Night Solo Dance Party, but didn't. I was in bed by ten, but had trouble falling asleep. Anxiety. I shut off my alarm and promised I would lie there and listen all night, until it spoke to me.

What's going on? Is it turning 40 in a week? My party? Talk to me. I'm listening.

Stupid fucking idiot.

Images from my stupid fucking past came rushing forth: me setting myself up in every relationship to be hurt, not ever having a boyfriend in school, the fear of being made a fool of, drinking alone, drinking and driving (is there anything more idiotic?).

Gifts? I am also a genius... and very, very wise.

Why do I drink? My ego keeping me stuck under the illusion of moving forward. Inspired Ideas and genius revelations emerge when I'm drinking, but they do not come from the alcohol, for some reason I just allow them to come out in an inebriated state.

I meditated for an hour and a half and cried the whole time.

Later: I'm exhausted. I'm on a break and need to nap. Desperately. There is this anxiety and tightness in my chest. Drinking four days in a row and I feel like shit. This weekend was exactly the same as one year ago. All this work and I still feel like a loser on Monday morning.

Have I learned nothing? Has this whole year been a waste? Or worse, just another illusion? Okay. Enough. Either this work is real or it isn't, but I'm figuring it out. Now. Once and for all.

I sit cross-legged in my sanctuary up against my log with my waterfall rushing behind. The cool mist condenses on my cheek and falls in chilled droplets.

Connecticut. Warm tears follow.

Connect - I - cut.

My Lonely Loser emerges. It looks like a troll
straight up in the air - a child's toy. Its hair shoot₁
its body with it. Towering over me now, it shouts,
an abuser!"

An abuser masking as a loser. My Loser is really
When did I create you? Abused little girl feeling ₁
the abuser.

Food, alcohol, bulimia, relationships, marriages, divorce₁
cutting, sleeping pills, ripping at my face on the bathroom floo₁

You don't abuse alcohol (drugs, food...), you abuse yourself ₁
alcohol (drugs, food...).

This is the big one. Splitting from my abused girl was the fracture
that caused the rest of the fissures. All my other shadows started with her.
She is the one who cries out for me to have a deeper, healthier connection
with myself. She has taught me so much about self-love. She may be the
mother of my shadows, but the abused little girl is still crying and I am
listening.

What have your gifts been all along? This massive chasm caused my
soul to cry out for reunification. My ruptured heart demanded to be
healed. Through this incredible journey, I have learned deep compassion,
deep connection.

What can I do to love you and make you feel heard and valued? I will
know in the moment. Every opportunity to love you, I will take it.

How can you become my ally? Promise to never self-abuse again. Use
the desire to do so as a sign I am off track and not being conscious - a
call to go deeper.

Then I will know a love so profound and powerful, nothing or no
one will be able to break me apart.

What God has joined together let no man put asunder...

December 18, 2012

Christmas Board Meeting last night and I didn't have a drink. Came
home and loved myself to sleep. I woke up at 4:30 AM and just loved
and listened. Lying there whispering to myself, "I love you. I love you."
Sweetly with compassion and understanding. I love you.

Still couldn't sleep, so did a session of Yoga Nidra.

o think of a different sankulpa, one that wasn't about anyone
ng external, but when the guiding voice suggested, 'Your true
esire.' The same one came to mind.

m in a loving, nurturing, fulfilling relationship with my soul mate.

fterwards, as I finally fell asleep, I thought, "The truth is I have
ated the best year of my life not *even though* I haven't found my
ul mate, but because I haven't. This year I have developed a loving,
nurturing, fulfilling relationship with myself. I have no lack. The truth
is I can live a whole abundant life all on my own."

Then I had the most bizarre dream. Sometimes I felt a bit awake,
slipping in and out of consciousness. I was masturbating, looking at
my body naked, and then I was having sex with a man, then back to
masturbating, roaring. I literally felt the sexual energy that has been
building up for months, years, bursting through me and out of me.

I was scared at first, because at times it felt like anger, rage, but I
trusted. I knew I was dreaming. I knew it meant something. It wasn't
anger; it was passion. This energy, this stagnant energy, was emerging no
matter what and so I allowed it to do so in this safe place. It feels good
to consider my subconscious world a safe place.

Back to roaring, masturbating, having sex, fucking hard,
masturbating harder. I never orgasmed physically, but I did spiritually.
And it was cataclysmic. I am a woman.

In one day, I met my beautiful, brave abused little girl and promised
to never abuse her ever again. That night I met this vibrant, sexual,
primal woman, who I can't wait to explore the world with. Coincidence?
There ain't no such thing.

61

So Annoying

December 19, 2012

7 AM: It's snowing! I'm sitting at Grounds staring out the window, hoping this will make me feel Christmassy. I haven't so far and am not sure why. It's just a light dusting, but this is Vancouver and the whole city's probably gonna shut down.

8:40 AM: Grounds is packed. A major bus stop is right out the door, which is also on a slight incline. The buses can't get enough momentum to overcome it and turn the corner so there are four of them lined up. The roads aren't even icy! The last stop on the route is UBC, so Grounds is filled with panicking students afraid they are going to miss their final exams.

I am so annoyed. My right arm is on fire again and I can barely get any writing done.

We had our last GCC of the year yesterday and Derek actually talked about his own struggles. He was very generous and vulnerable, but I didn't get to ask my question and again was frustrated.

What kind of person doesn't get their question answered? Ignored. Invisible. Annoying.

What do I make my right side pain mean about me? Nothing. It's just annoying.

Why am I so cranky? These UBC students are fucking annoying me. Do they not think the University knows it's snowing?

Noon: They cancelled my last gymnastics class! Are you serious? It could stop snowing any minute and then melt in about twenty. They are

319

going to reimburse me the cost of one session, but I wanted to flip into the sponge pit before I turned forty! So annoying.

On my way home, I followed a lady driving a BMW. She was literally going 10 km/hr and swerving all over the road. So annoying.

When I got home, I saw another posting of Josh's on Facebook. So annoying.

I changed my settings, so I can't see his posts. Why didn't I think of this earlier? Probably, because I needed to see them... so they could trigger something in me I needed to face. There was a truckload of them this year, all of which were integral to this incredible journey. I truly believe he is one of my soul mates. I am eternally grateful for the role he played, but I'm ready to learn from someone new. I still believe we would make excellent friends, though.

Maybe he is my male friend soul mate and I just haven't met my *Soul Mate* soul mate yet... hahaha, not even going there.

I just read the above rant.... how many times I wrote 'so annoying'. I was really on a roll. I was half-joking, but the realization is setting in: I'm annoying.

The thought of being annoying is really annoying. *Just kidding...* kind of.

Shadow Process on Annoying: She was tall and skinny and annoyingly beautiful. She guided me through our home in Argyll. I wanted to rush, but she made me go slow and then I realized she was trying to be annoying. I laughed.

Gifts? My fear of asking questions or for help, because I didn't want to be annoying, forced me to learn to do it myself. I became a great listener and hyperaware of people's body language. I'm also an awesome researcher.

Why now? It's time to ask for what I want and need. Even if people think I'm annoying.

December 20, 2012

Oh. My. God. If I didn't know it before, I just got undisputable proof Elliot is one of my soul mates. It's three days until my birthday and so, of course, the interrogation was in full session. I was a little more sensitive today, so switched the subject to his birthday. He asked me if I knew what I was doing the day he was born. I laughed.

"How am I supposed to remember what I was doing on a random day 14 years ago?"

He pleaded, "Just try. February 1st, 1998."

My wheels turned back... my eyes widened, "What day of the week was it?"

"Sunday."

Shivers rose up and down my spine, goose bumps covered my body. I could barely speak. He smiled that gleeful smile, his eyes illuminated. He knew I knew.

I whispered, "I know exactly what I was doing the day you were born."

He clapped his hands, "What?"

"It was one of the hardest, most pivotal, life-changing days of my life, but I can't tell you about it. It's personal."

He was not impressed.

"And emotional." I knew that would stop him... at least for a few minutes.

February 1st, 1998: The day I left Matthew.

The reason I remember is because it was at the beginning of that January, after a tense Christmas (everyone knew something was going on) and tragic beginning to the new year (Noah passed away January 2nd), that Matthew had had enough of my selfish behavior.

"I can't live like this anymore. Either stay or go, but make a decision."

I started looking for an apartment in the city. It didn't take long for me to find one... available February 1st.

Now, if the first of the month had landed on a weekday, it would be a different story. I would have moved out the following weekend, but the fact it landed on a Sunday... that was 100% the day. I also know it was the Sunday, because I woke up the next morning to get ready for work super flustered and disorganized and the shower wasn't working. I had to wash my hair in the sink and was almost late for work. The details you remember.

Needless to say, this was *not* one of the best days of my life. My mom, dad, Celina and René came to the farm to help move my stuff, and awkward does not begin to describe the vibe. Heavy is more like it. The weight of disappointment, judgment and sadness was smothering. My guilt had not yet set in, so my trying to make light of it just made it worse.

Elliot pried a bit, "Does what happened that day have anything to do with us meeting? With you moving to Vancouver?"

I fought back the tears, "Yeah. Yeah, it does."

There were many reasons Matthew and I split, but the big one I could never admit at the time was that I wanted more. Sure, I wanted to be in the movies, but it was also my soul crying out to embark on a spiritual journey that would know no bounds and to live a vision I couldn't yet imagine. It was the first step of me setting out on this path, leaving my past behind, becoming authentic and to this time with Elliot... my soul mate.

"Do you know what you were doing at 10:54 PM? That's what time I was born."

Yeah, crying myself to sleep. The guilt had finally set in.

God, I want to tell him this story. I want him to have this proof we are connected.

Actually, I don't think he needs it.

Bling, Bling, That's My Thang

<u>December 21, 2012</u>

Well, this is it... I'm at YVR!

So long Vancouver peeps... next time you see me, I's gonna be a butterfly!

I'm actually struggling. I'm feeling negative, but forcing myself to be positive. All week, I've been trying to do things to feel Christmassy - movies, music, rum and eggnog. Nothing worked. I know, I know, Christmas isn't out there; it's in here.

Realization: Rum and eggnog doesn't make me feel festive, it makes me feel fat.

I am in my final stage of emerging and this last little breakthrough is beautiful. Butterflies have their ups and downs, but I'll worry about that later. I am going to love and peace and joy my way out of my chrysalis.

No struggle or strain, with ease and with grace.

You know what I'm going to do? Listen to my heartbeat as I meditate on the plane.

My dream last night was Lee, Dylan, Alex, Erin, Sara and Sadie in a canoe, rowing on a calm lake. I jumped in and grabbed an oar. They were all dressed up, so I assumed they were on their way to my party and I was gonna lead the way.

They were actually going somewhere else, but didn't want to hurt my feelings. I laughed and told them to always be honest with me and with themselves.

Dreammoods.com: *To see a canoe in your dream represents serenity, simplicity, and independence. It is also a reflection of your emotional balance. You are moving ahead via your own power and determination... the lake may provide you with solace, security, and peace of mind. To see or use oars in your dream signify control over your emotions. You are able to navigate through life based on the lessons and skills you have learned.*

Beautiful - for me and for my inspiring nieces and nephews.

Remember! As I shop these next two days what my party and Christmas are really about: Celebrations of Appreciation.

Later: My mom and I had the best day together. She picked me up at the airport and basically drove me around shopping for my Christmas presents and birthday party. I hope she knows how much I appreciated it.

The only thing I like about Christmas shopping is the coffee break. I treated my mom to a skinny latte and we had an amazing chat. If someone would have told me when I was sixteen, that one day my mom would be one of my best friends, I would have laughed or cried or worse. I think my mom would say the same.

She told me about Arizona and all the great people there. (Oh, that's where they are this winter instead of Mexico. We are all thrilled.) As she sipped her latte, I asked if her and dad were exchanging gifts. She said the only thing she wants, he doesn't like to buy: jewelry. I never understood my mom's thing with bling.

For the first time, I asked, "Mom, why do you like jewelry so much?"

Her eyes glistened as she caressed her rings, "I don't know, I just do."

I got it. Jewelry makes her feel pretty, special, feminine. The picture of her in that ridiculous fur coat popped into my mind and then disintegrated.

My mom deserves jewelry. Lots and lots of jewelry.

Driving back to Beaumont, I was expressing my gratitude for this year, my spiritual growth, how I've fallen in love with myself... Sensing I was getting a tad esoteric, I caught myself and quickly blurted a comment about how weird I am... some habits never die.

With effortless acceptance, not even taking her eyes off the road, my mom smiled, "You're not weird. You're just Rachelle."

I couldn't take my eyes off her. *You and me, Mom, we are healed.*

December 22, 2012

My family is so awesome. I am so grounded and connected. I think the reason I can appreciate how awesome my family is, is because I am so grounded and connected.

I just met with my friend James, who taught physics with me at St. FX. He wanted to come to the party, but really he wouldn't know anyone and we wouldn't get any good visit time in. Instead, we met at Boston Pizza and shared a pitcher of Rickard's Red. Just like old times.

It was such a gift to sit and listen to this beautiful man talk about how much he loves his children and wife, his whole life. He also showed me a vulnerable side, telling me about something he wasn't proud of. Of course, my mind went to 'affair', but I should have known better. It was work related, and not my story to tell, but it was a reminder not to put people on a pedestal. Everyone has frustrations and struggles. He said he learned a lot about himself.

Oh, my dear friend, that's what struggle is for.

My party is pretty much all set. I think it is going to be fun. My parents have been incredible. I really didn't think about how much work this would be for them when I had this genius, Inspired Idea. They've been driving me around for two days solid. Food, party supplies, booze (I bought way too much booze) and there is more prep work tomorrow.

A weird thing happened though. I checked my email at 8:07 PM. I was only on it a moment, but in that time I received a Facebook notice that my Good Friend had invited me to be friends. To say I was shocked is an understatement.

My initial reaction was, *WTF?* Then... *Hmmmm...* Then... *No way, not even going there....* and finally, *You know what? New beginnings.*

By the time I got on Facebook the request was cancelled. Bizarre, but for the best.

Going to bed now. Nighty night.

Chapter 40: A Celebration of Appreciation

<u>December 23, 2012</u>

I. Am. 40.

I am a butterfly.

Every single moment of this glorious day, I will be present.

I will be grateful. I will be graceful. I will be love.

My birth date: December 23rd, two days before Christmas and eight before New Year's Eve. I've always either resented having my birthday lost in the holiday shuffle, or convinced myself I didn't care. (Indifference - is there really such a thing?)

What an honor to be born on this glorious day.

Early morning yoga: Overlooking the snow-covered park, the fiery sky, hmmm... *Alberta sure does sunrises right.*

Breathing through every pose, every flow, I reflected, "How do I feel?" I knew the answer... in every cell of my being.

Later, my mom asked, "So, do you feel different?"

"Yes, I feel like a woman."

My dad laughed, "What were you before?"

"You'll have to read my book." Then realizing that will NEVER happen, I simply answered, "A girl-woman. Now, I'm a *woman*-woman."

So, this year ends with my initial intent indeed being fulfilled: I have become a woman.

Going out, brought me right back home. What an incredible year.

I realize why I needed to have black as the color of my last journal.

Black: Yin. The feminine. The receiver. There is power in passive.

My parents gave me the most beautiful silver necklace with a diamond-encrusted heart. I love it. It makes me feel pretty, special and feminine.

2:14 AM: How do you describe the best night of your life?

The (not-just-for-seniors) Senior Centre was perfect. My family took turns working the bar. I felt bad at first, but they said it was the cool place to hang. Not surprising, knowing my family and friends. Lee was especially rad, because he was meticulous with his pouring. Erin enlisted Sara and Sadie to work the coat check. She spent the whole day making tickets. It was all her idea, which was great, because I had never thought about it. Erin is going to be an entrepreneur. She gets an idea in her head and she just goes for it. I hope the confidence she has now will never diminish. I will make it my mission to make sure it doesn't. She inspires me.

The trio set up a little table and laid out all the hangers on the floor. They had limited tickets, so were adamant with the guests that if you were married you had to share a hanger. Soo cute. They even made tips!

Dylan and Alex wore suits and ties. So handsome. When they walked in all dressed up, I thought my heart was going to burst. I am so lucky to have such incredible nieces and nephews who love me, or at least love a party. No. Who love me.

People started arriving right on time, but staggered enough that I could give every single guest a hug and thank them for being in my life. I was worried I would get all caught up in the emotion and excitement - that this part of the night would be a blur, but my goal of being present with each guest was easy. I borrowed a black mini-dress of Tracy's and each time I hugged someone I needed to make sure the back didn't rise up too high. This kept me in my body, and in the moment. In all about eighty of my closest, dearest loved ones came so I could celebrate my appreciation of them and for them.

I received their love, too.

Carlos came. Late. (Hahaha, just had to stick that in.) I was sitting at a table talking to Ken and my cousin, Allan, when my mom slipped in and said, "Carlos is here."

I did tell a few people ahead of time he might come, my immediate family, Jen, Nicole... just to give a little heads up.

He stood in the entrance with his girlfriend, and I don't think I have ever been so excited to see him. I ran up and gave him a huge hug and thanked him for coming. He introduced Lindsay. She is nothing like me. She has dark hair, big beautiful eyes, and exudes a calming confidence. She is an award-winning director of experimental documentaries. I don't even know what those are.

Carlos looked around the room at all the familiar faces, his former family. I can't imagine how hard that must've been. One by one, the closest members came up and said hi, even though I know they were shocked as hell he was there. A couple of my guy friends pulled me aside to profess their complete awe. The funny thing is, they don't even know our story, the old one or the new one, they just couldn't imagine a guy showing up at his ex-wife's 40th.

"I invited him."

They laughed, "Rachelle, you are one amazing person."

But I think Carlos is the amazing one for coming, not to mention Lindsay! She left a Christmas party to drive all the way out to Beaumont in the middle of an Alberta winter night to come to the father of her unborn child's ex-wife's 40th birthday party. I'm not sure I would do that, but I'm grateful she did.

They came respectfully late and stayed about an hour and a half. Classy. As we were saying good-bye, I mused, *'Eleven years ago I was preparing for our wedding. Who would've thought that at my fortieth birthday party, I'd be talking to you and your very confident, very talented, very beautiful, very pregnant girlfriend?'*

I looked Carlos in the eyes. *You and me, my friend, we are healed.*

Then glancing at Lindsay, *I hope you know how beautiful he thinks you are.*

Carlos rubs her belly. She lets him. Yeah, she knows.

Most of my extended family left by midnight. I had barely seen my friends all night, so my mom and dad said we could stay a bit later. Celina and René stayed to keep them company. They wouldn't even let me clean up.

"Go be with your friends."

The whole gang was there: Jennifer, Chris, Nicole, Terri, Kimmie, Shannon... my friend Rob, who I haven't seen in about a decade. It was so much fun.

Jennifer and Nicole gave me a Pandora bracelet... with a butterfly charm.

Now, I am lying in bed and can't sleep... My heart is literally bursting with love.

A year ago, I cried myself to sleep. Tonight I will, too, but for completely different reasons.

Oh, and I checked my email before coming to bed... Adam from Seattle emailed me! Weird. He doesn't even know it's my birthday.

64

An Epic Epilogue

<u>December 31, 2012</u>

7:15 AM at Grounds: I'm home. I don't mean I'm home in Vancouver. I mean, yes, I am in Vancouver, but what I mean is, I'm home in my heart.

That was the most magical Christmas, filled with love and laughter and I received it all.

Tracy and Martin gave me the most special birthday gift: A flight home whenever I want.

Celina and René gave me a Blu-ray player. Celina apologized for the impersonal gift, but said she wanted to buy it for me, because she knows my DVD player has been broken for months and I haven't been able to watch movies. I said that's what makes it so personal. She also gave me a necklace with a Chinese pendant. It means protection. Perfect.

At first, I felt bad, because everyone was giving me gifts way bigger than we usually exchange - just because I made such a big deal out of turning 40 doesn't mean everyone else had to. But then I decided to just receive. Receive and say thank you.

On Christmas Eve, God and I took our stroll around Four Seasons Park. Beaumont sure looks different now. Lighter. Brighter. Healthier. Or maybe it's just me.

Christmas Day, my mom and dad hosted Christmas at Tracy and Martin's house and it was so much fun. We had a shuffleboard tournament and Martin and I were partners. We haven't been on the same team in a long, long time. And we rocked it!

We played WII and charades, and I was present the whole time.

We talked about my book. Janelle wants to read it, but is scared. She still hasn't gotten over the trauma of watching *10:01*. Her boyfriend, Tyson, offered to read it for her first, but I'm not sure I want anyone in my family to read it. Maybe I will do a family-friendly edition.

Tyson asked if he could be in it. I told him it officially ended on my birthday, but, *hint, hint*, if he wanted to do something book-worthy in the next week or so, he might make it into the epilogue. Janelle blushed.

Most importantly, I had such a good visit with the kids. All the healing I've done this year was rewarded with many intimate moments with Lee, Dylan, Alex, Erin, Sara and Sadie.

One of my favorites was when I was sitting in the backseat of the van with Sara and Sadie driving who knows where. They each simultaneously grabbed one of my hands and started playing with my fingers, dancing them between theirs. I was present, connected... there was nowhere else on Earth I wanted to be. I relaxed and received their love. It felt warm.

Everyone seems so happy - so different from last year. Or maybe it's just me.

The last few days were spent relaxing in Camrose. We took our annual walk around Mirror Lake. Was that only a year ago? I went into the public washroom. This time when I looked in the mirror, I smiled, "My eyes are greener. I love you."

12:30 PM: Celina just texted: *Tyson wants to know how ur gonna get him in ur book.*

I replied: *Hmmmm.... Well, tell him he's got 11 ½ hours to make it into the epilogue :)*

Done! About 4 hours ago :) :) !!!!!

Yay!!!! *Tell him and Janelle congrats and thank you for the last happy cry of 2012!*

8:58 PM (11:58 EST): Thank you 2012, for all the amazing awesomeness you brought. Okay 2013, you have some big shoes to fill, but I believe in you.

I've decided what my 2013 New Year's pact will be:

I promise to fulfill my purpose, live according to my highest vision and follow my bliss.

All right, Universe, gimme what you got.

And that my friends, is all she wrote...

THE END

About the Author

Rachelle Chartrand is an award-winning screenwriter and past-president of Women in Film & Television Vancouver. She received a Bachelor of Education with a major in Physics and a minor in Math from the University of Alberta. Her eclectic teaching experience includes working with ESL students abroad, as well as at-risk youth, young offenders and autistic children at home. Rachelle lives in Vancouver, British Columbia where she continues to emerge.

CPSIA information can be obtained at www.ICGtesting.com
Printed in the USA
LVOW11s1654011014

406605LV00004B/11/P